INTROVERT DOODLES

BY MAUREEN "MARZI" WILSON

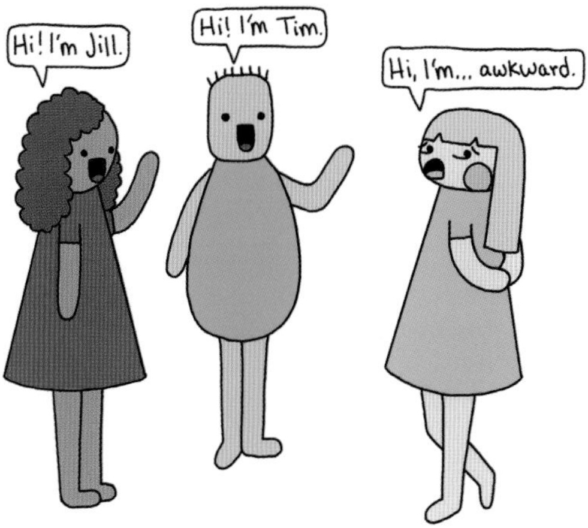
Hi! I'm Jill.
Hi! I'm Tim.
Hi, I'm... awkward.

AN ILLUSTRATED LOOK AT INTROVERT LIFE IN AN EXTROVERT WORLD

Adams Media
New York London Toronto Sydney New Delhi

Adams Media
An Imprint of Simon & Schuster, Inc.
57 Littlefield Street
Avon, Massachusetts 02322

For information about special discounts for bulk purchases, please contact Simon & Schuster Special Sales at 1-866-506-1949 or business@simonandschuster.com.

The Simon & Schuster Speakers Bureau can bring authors to your live event. For more information or to book an event contact the Simon & Schuster Speakers Bureau at 1-866-248-3049 or visit our website at www.simonspeakers.com.

Interior images © Maureen Wilson

Manufactured in China

10 9 8 7 6 5 4 3 2

ISBN 978-1-5072-0001-8

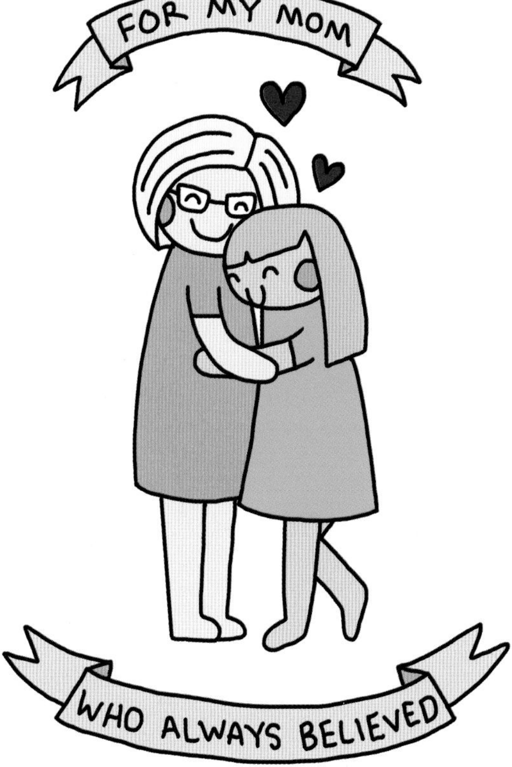
FOR MY MOM
WHO ALWAYS BELIEVED

One year ago, I drew two friends laughing on a bench. Sitting on the opposite side of that bench was a sad little girl, thinking, "Why am I so backward?" That doodle summed up how I'd felt my entire life. Why didn't I have a big group of friends? Why didn't I enjoy parties? Why did I spend so much time by myself? Why was I so **BACKWARD?**

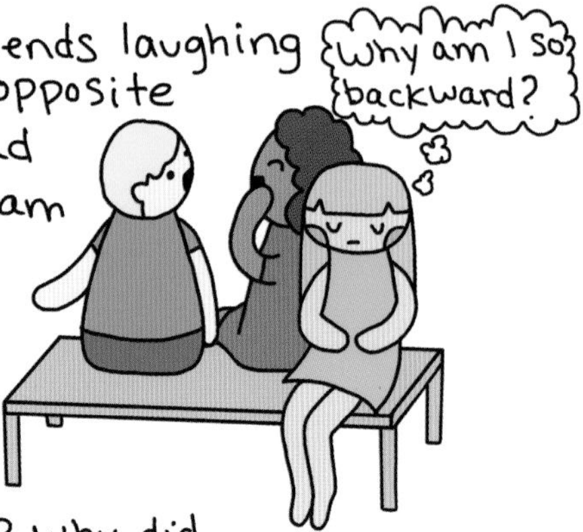
Why am I so backward?

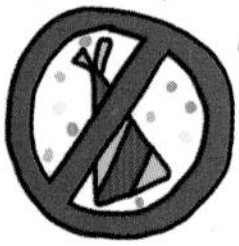

A week later, I came across an online article about different personality types. It was the first time I'd thought about the temperaments of introverts and extroverts. It was as though someone had flipped on a light switch: I wasn't backward; I was an **INTROVERT!**

I read everything I could about introverts, and discovered that I had many strengths I'd been overlooking, such as creativity, deep thinking, and being a good listener.

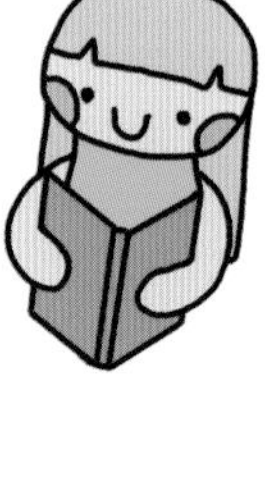

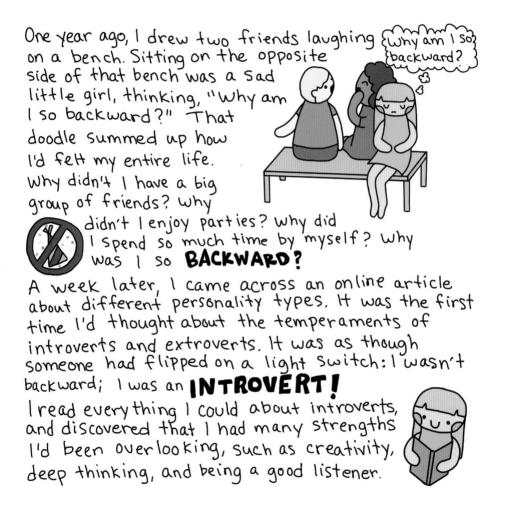

At first I drew these doodles as a way to better understand myself. But these little drawings sparked an online community of introverts, sharing experiences and ideas. It's been empowering to realize that, although we often spend time alone, we aren't alone after all.

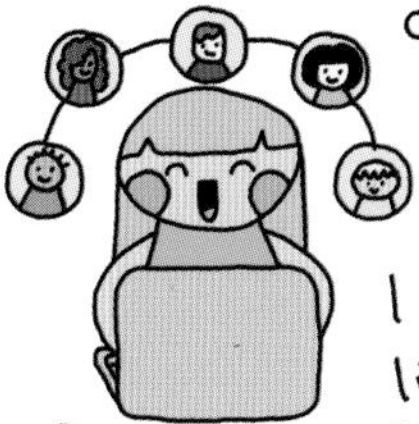

I happen to be an introvert who's a little shy and awkward, with a touch of anxiety. You might not share those traits, so a few of my comics may not apply to you. But if you're an introvert, I think you'll relate to most of them!

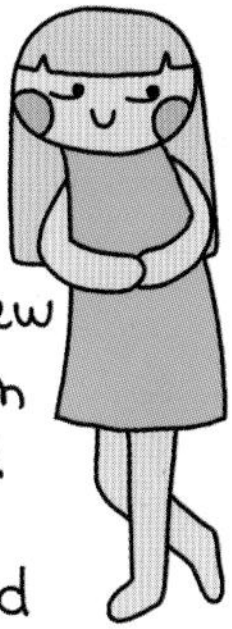

Or, perhaps you're an extrovert, and an introverted family member or friend gave you this book. This may be their way of opening up to you. These doodles are often silly, but some are icebreakers for serious heart-to-heart talks.

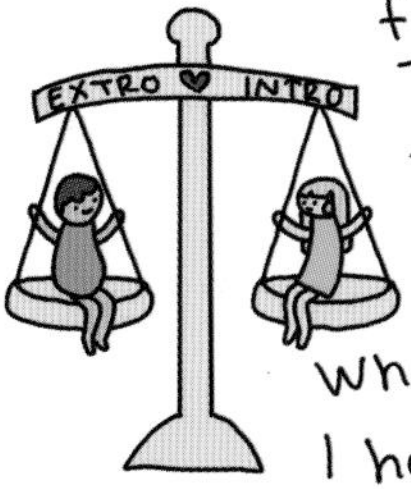
EXTRO ♥ INTRO

Whatever your reason for picking up this book, I hope you'll have the same realization I did:

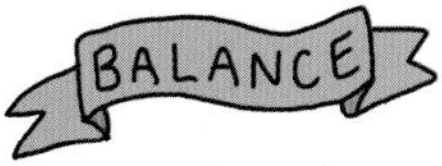
BALANCE

INTROVERTS ARE AWESOME!

So show some ♥ to an introvert today... even if it happens to be YOU!

xoxo,
Marzi

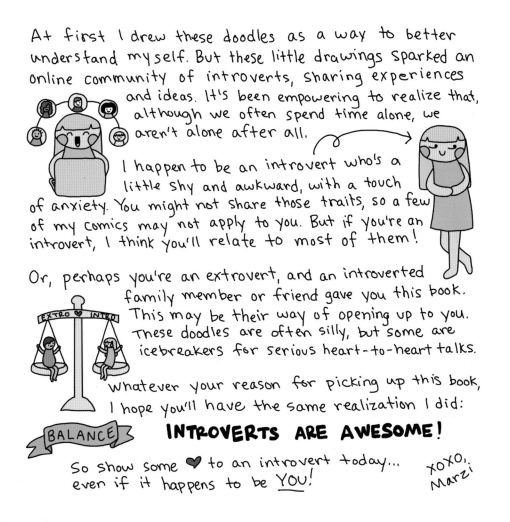

INTROVERT ANATOMY

HAIR often covers face

BRAIN is more active than most, great imagination

EYES see all but reveal nothing

CHEEKS are prone to blushing

MOUTH is typically shut

EARS have selective hearing. Able to tune out idiots, but also to hear words that haven't been spoken.

THUMBS are highly dexterous for texting

LEGS are surprisingly speedy when a quick exit is required

FEET should be in comfy slippers whenever possible

WHY I'D RATHER BE A CAT

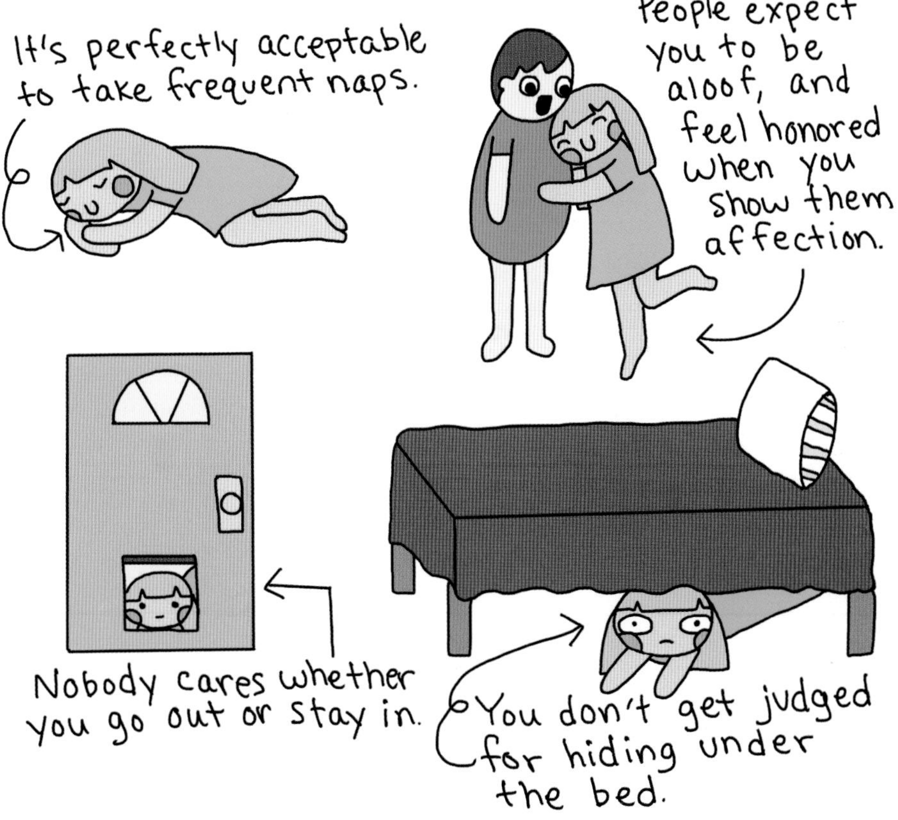
It's perfectly acceptable to take frequent naps.
People expect you to be aloof, and feel honored when you show them affection.
Nobody cares whether you go out or stay in.
You don't get judged for hiding under the bed.

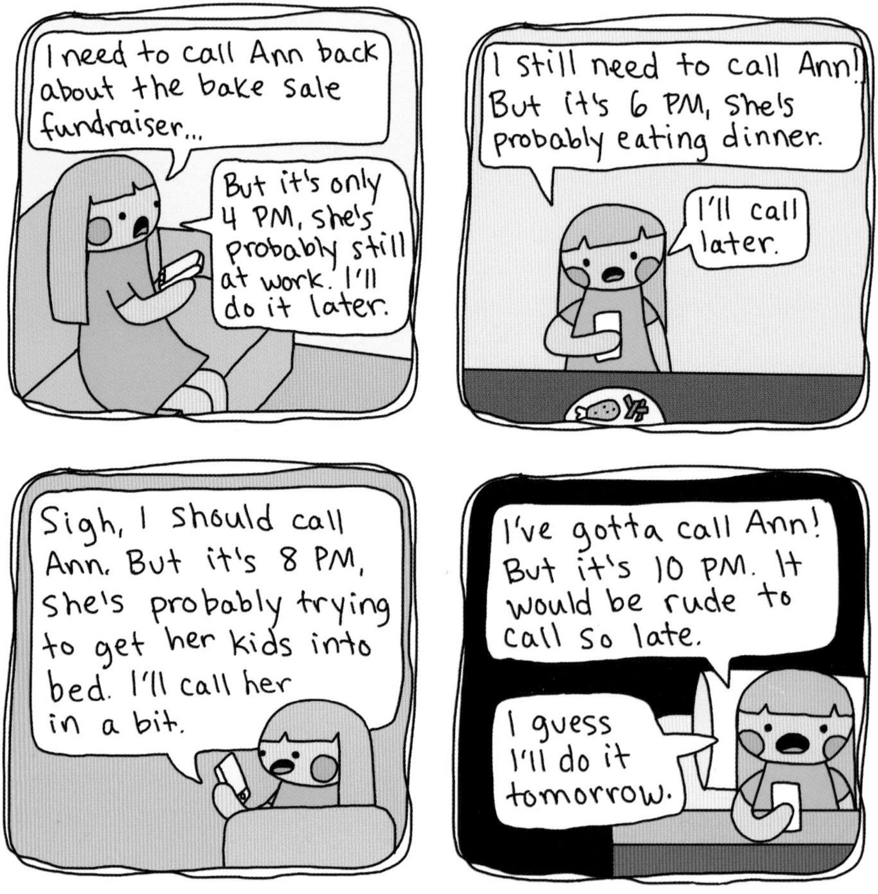
I need to call Ann back about the bake sale fundraiser...
But it's only 4 PM, she's probably still at work. I'll do it later.
I still need to call Ann! But it's 6 PM, she's probably eating dinner.
I'll call later.
Sigh, I should call Ann. But it's 8 PM, she's probably trying to get her kids into bed. I'll call her in a bit.
I've gotta call Ann! But it's 10 PM. It would be rude to call so late.
I guess I'll do it tomorrow.

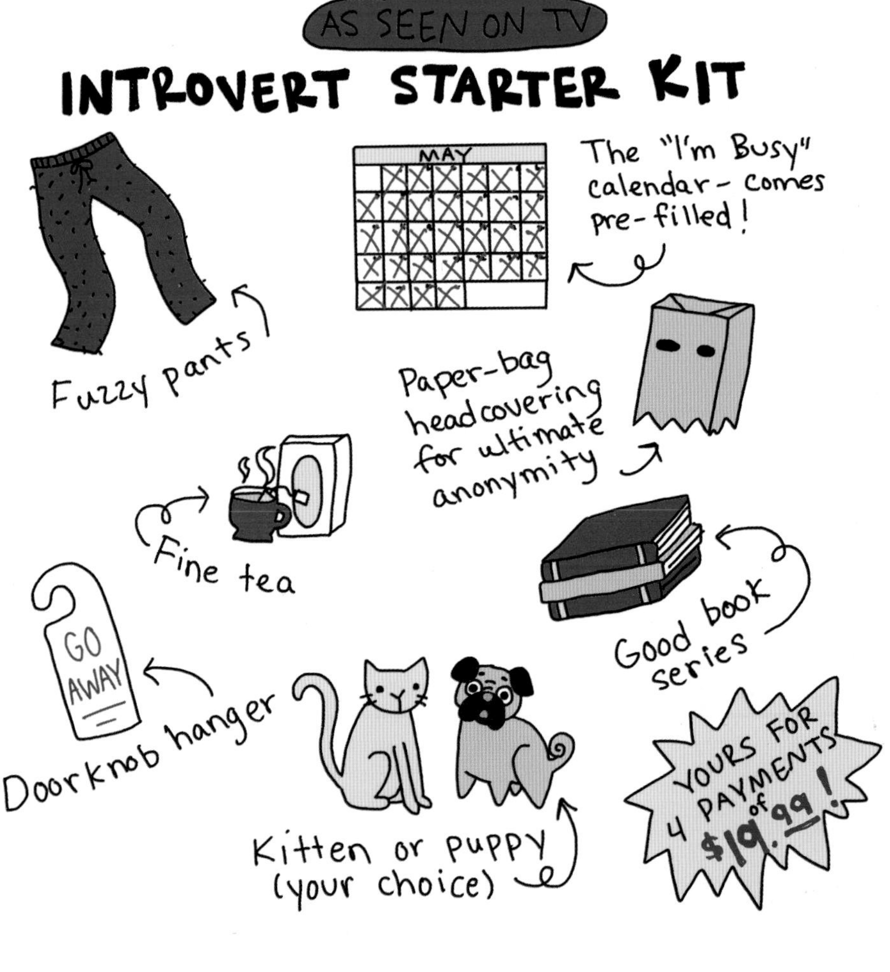
AS SEEN ON TV
INTROVERT STARTER KIT
MAY
The "I'm Busy" calendar - comes pre-filled!
Fuzzy pants
Paper-bag headcovering for ultimate anonymity
Fine tea
Good book series
GO AWAY
Doorknob hanger
Kitten or puppy (your choice)
YOURS FOR 4 PAYMENTS of $19.99!

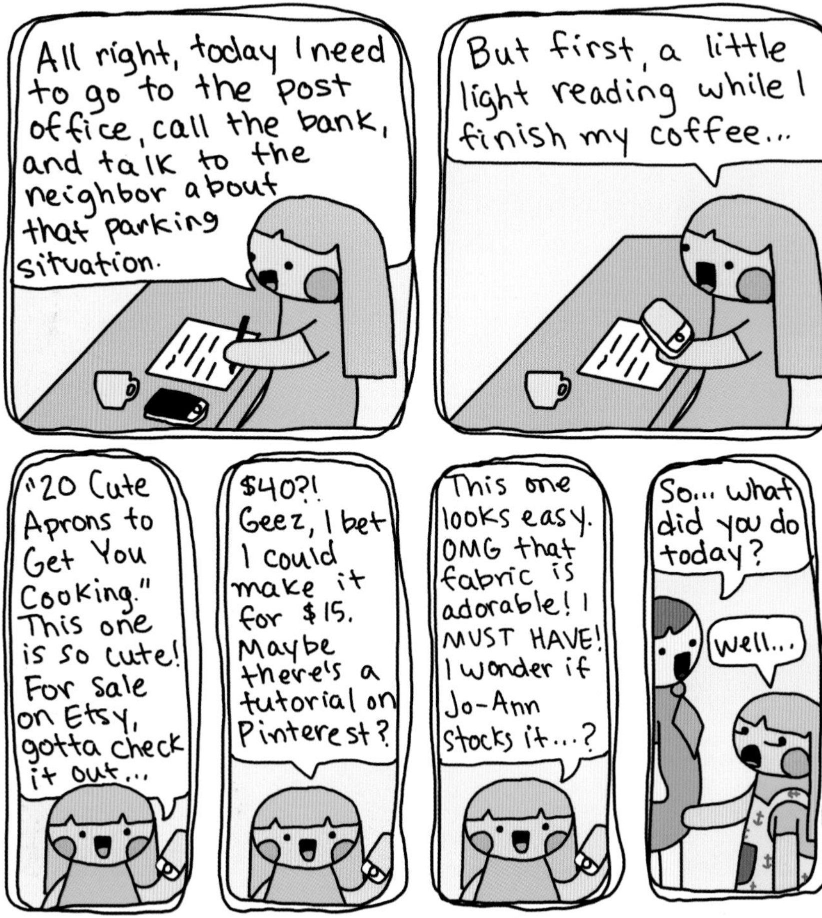

All right, today I need to go to the post office, call the bank, and talk to the neighbor about that parking situation.
But first, a little light reading while I finish my coffee...
"20 Cute Aprons to Get You Cooking." This one is so cute! For sale on Etsy, gotta check it out...
$40?! Geez, I bet I could make it for $15. Maybe there's a tutorial on Pinterest?
This one looks easy. OMG that fabric is adorable! I MUST HAVE! I wonder if Jo-Ann stocks it...?
So... what did you do today?
Well...

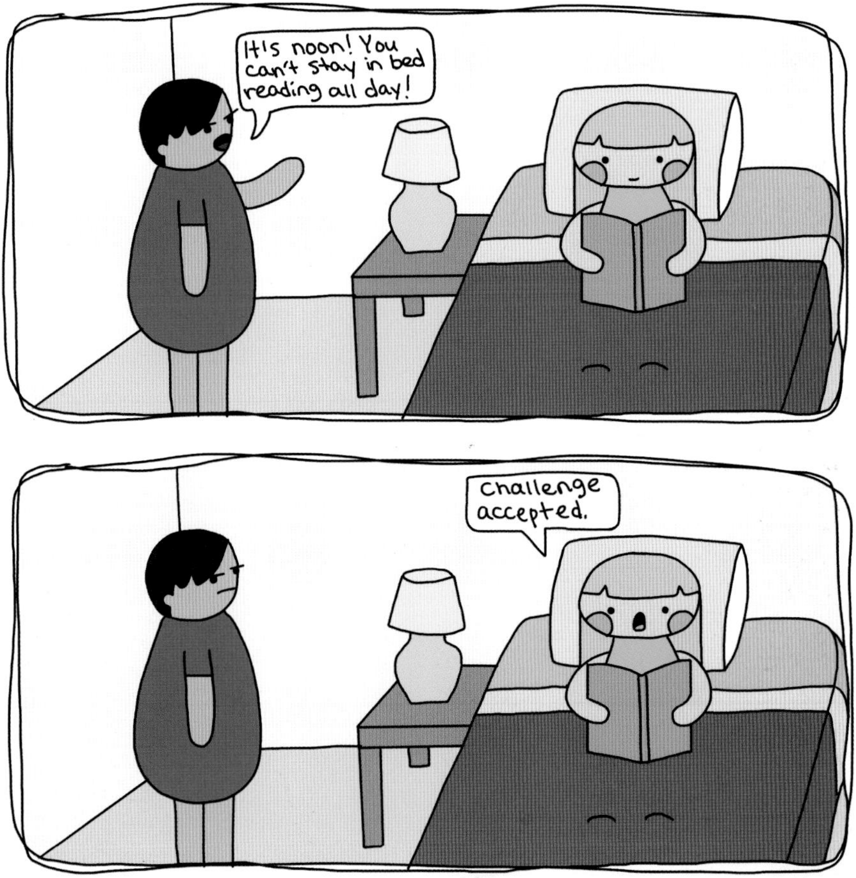
It's noon! You can't stay in bed reading all day!
Challenge accepted.

WHEN AN INTROVERT DIES

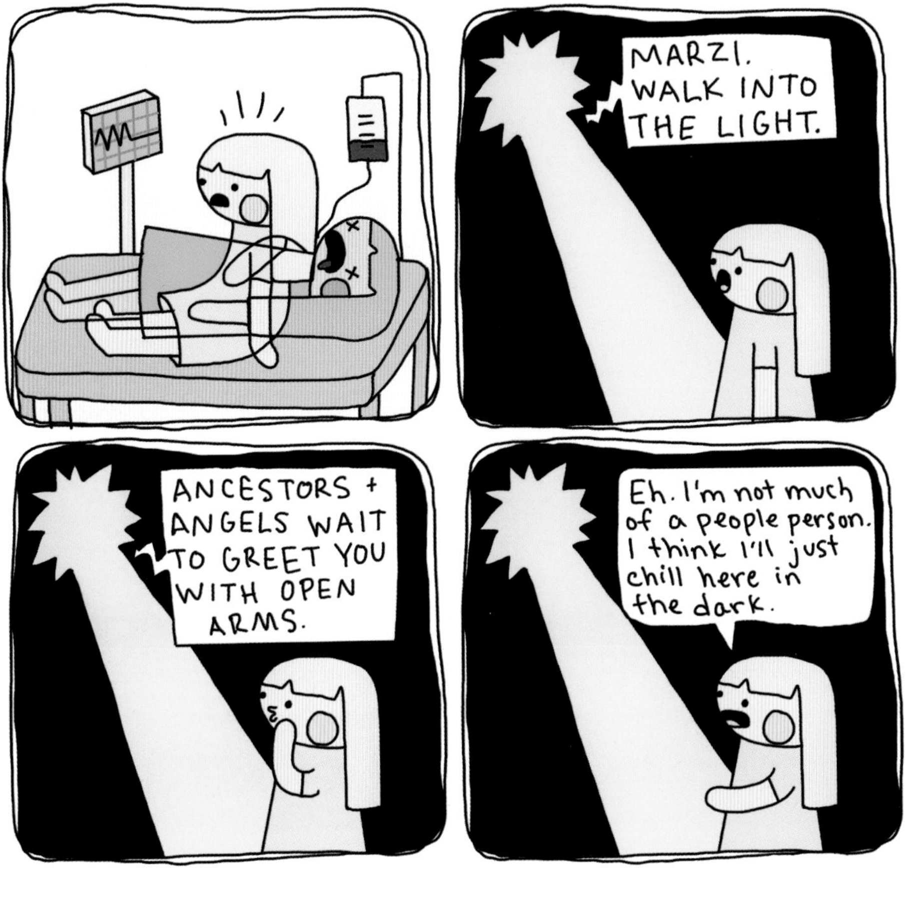
MARZI. WALK INTO THE LIGHT.
ANCESTORS + ANGELS WAIT TO GREET YOU WITH OPEN ARMS.
Eh. I'm not much of a people person. I think I'll just chill here in the dark.

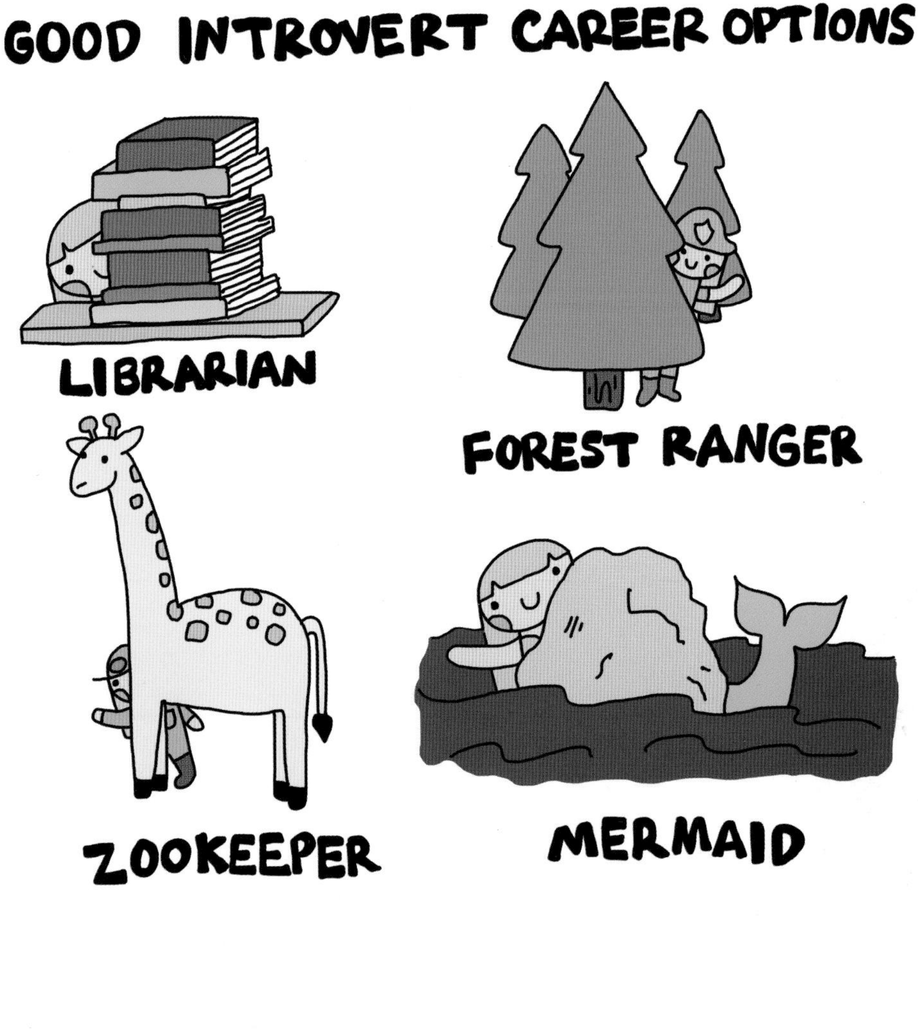
GOOD INTROVERT CAREER OPTIONS
LIBRARIAN
FOREST RANGER
ZOOKEEPER
MERMAID

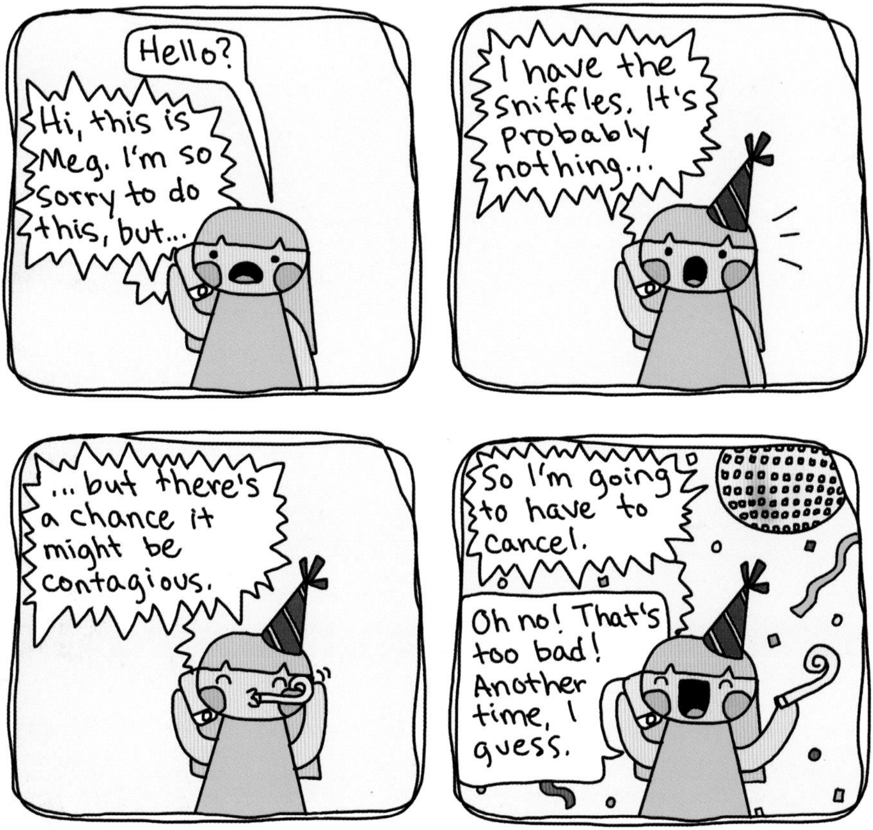
Hello?
Hi, this is Meg. I'm so sorry to do this, but...
I have the sniffles. It's probably nothing...
...but there's a chance it might be contagious.
So I'm going to have to cancel.
Oh no! That's too bad! Another time, I guess.

INTROVERT FASHION GUIDE

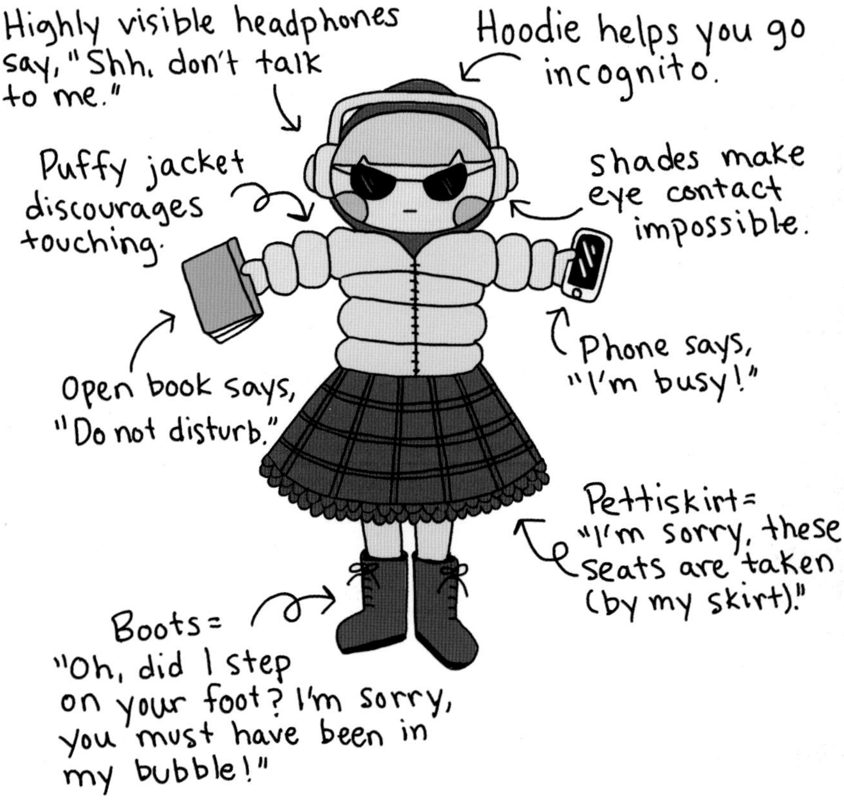
Highly visible headphones say, "Shh, don't talk to me."
Hoodie helps you go incognito.
Puffy jacket discourages touching.
Shades make eye contact impossible.
Phone says, "I'm busy!"
Open book says, "Do not disturb."
Pettiskirt= "I'm sorry, these seats are taken (by my skirt)."
Boots= "Oh, did I step on your foot? I'm sorry, you must have been in my bubble!"

HOW TO ESCAPE A DINNER PARTY

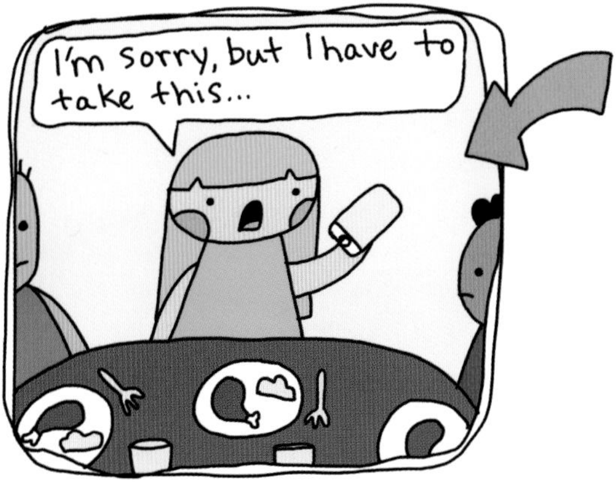
I'm sorry, but I have to take this...

Set a ringtone alarm on your phone and pretend it's an urgent call.

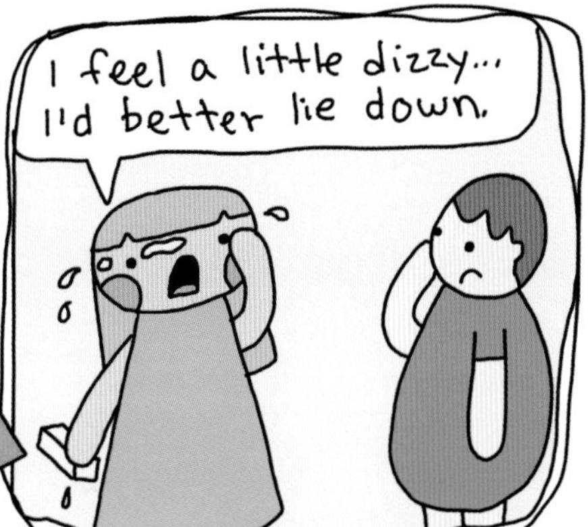
I feel a little dizzy... I'd better lie down.

Fake a sudden illness. (Smear butter on your face for a realistic, sweaty sheen.)

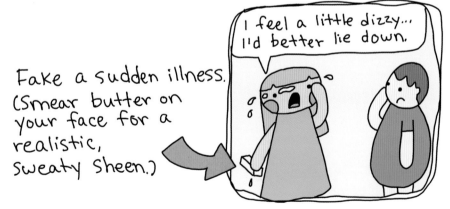

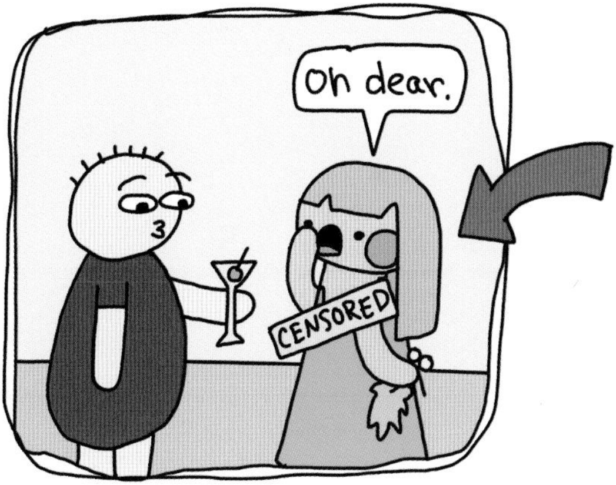
Oh dear.
CENSORED

Have a wardrobe malfunction.

Explain that you must leave early for everyone's safety, as you're a werewolf.

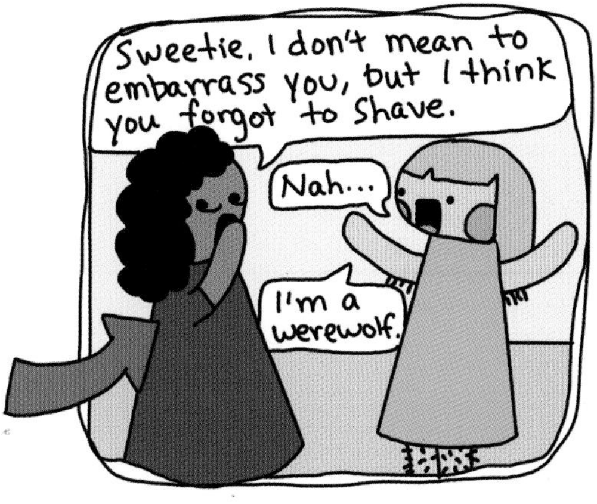
Sweetie, I don't mean to embarrass you, but I think you forgot to shave.
Nah...
I'm a werewolf.

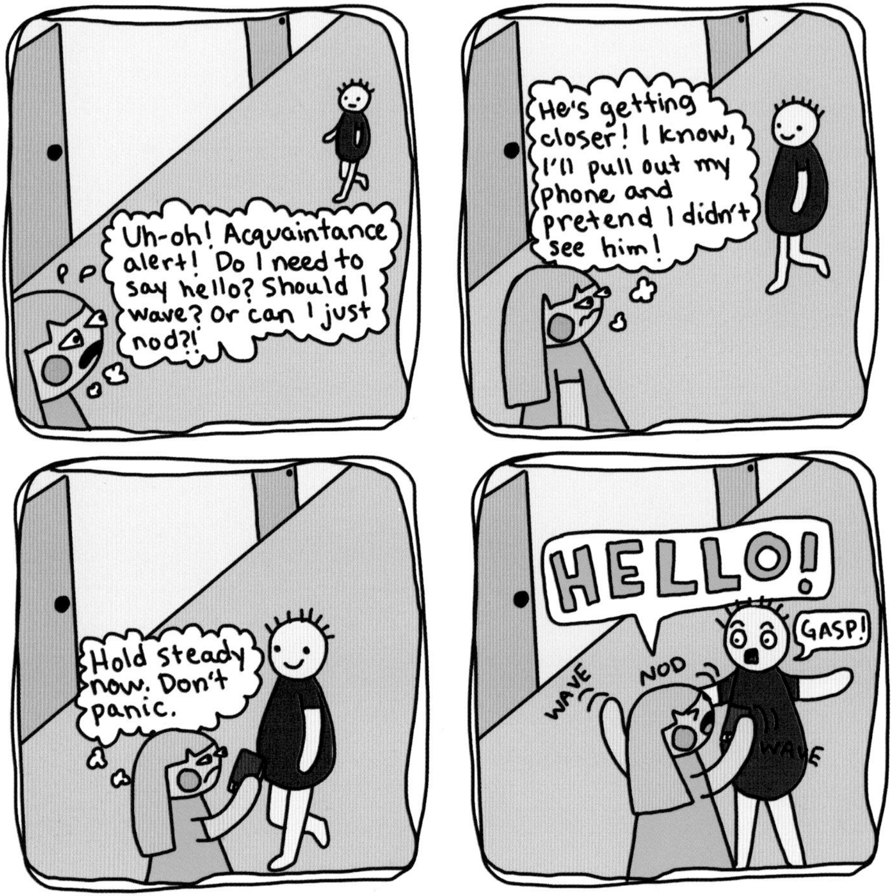

Uh-oh! Acquaintance alert! Do I need to say hello? Should I wave? Or can I just nod?!
He's getting closer! I know, I'll pull out my phone and pretend I didn't see him!
Hold steady now. Don't panic.
HELLO!
GASP!
WAVE
NOD
WAVE

CONVERSING WITH AN INTROVERT
-REFERENCE CHART-

Don't say it, man!	Slightly better...	Carry on.
Let's go out!	I'm going out. Can I bring you anything?	Let's get takeout.
Did you see that new movie? I hear it's based on a book.	Did you read that book? I hear they made a movie about it.	I see you're reading a book. This conversation can wait til later.
Why are you so quiet?	I like how you listen when I talk.	. . . [sitting together quietly]
Wanna hit the club tonight?	Wanna go to book club tonight?	Want me to make you a club sandwich tonight?

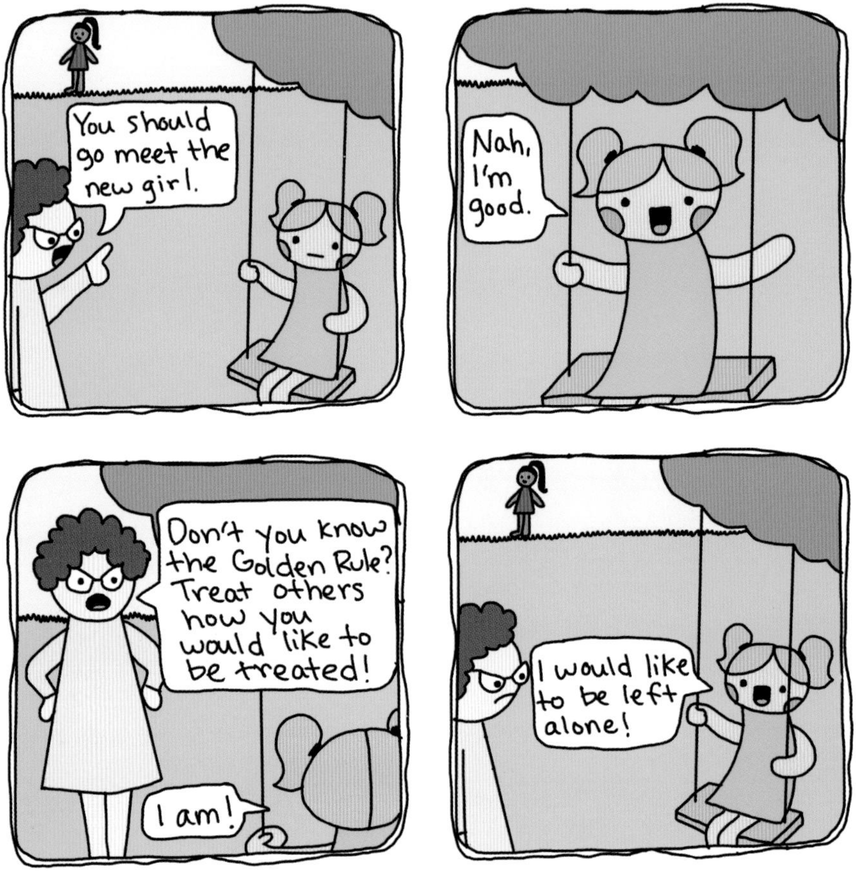
You should go meet the new girl.
Nah, I'm good.
Don't you know the Golden Rule? Treat others how you would like to be treated!
I am!
I would like to be left alone!

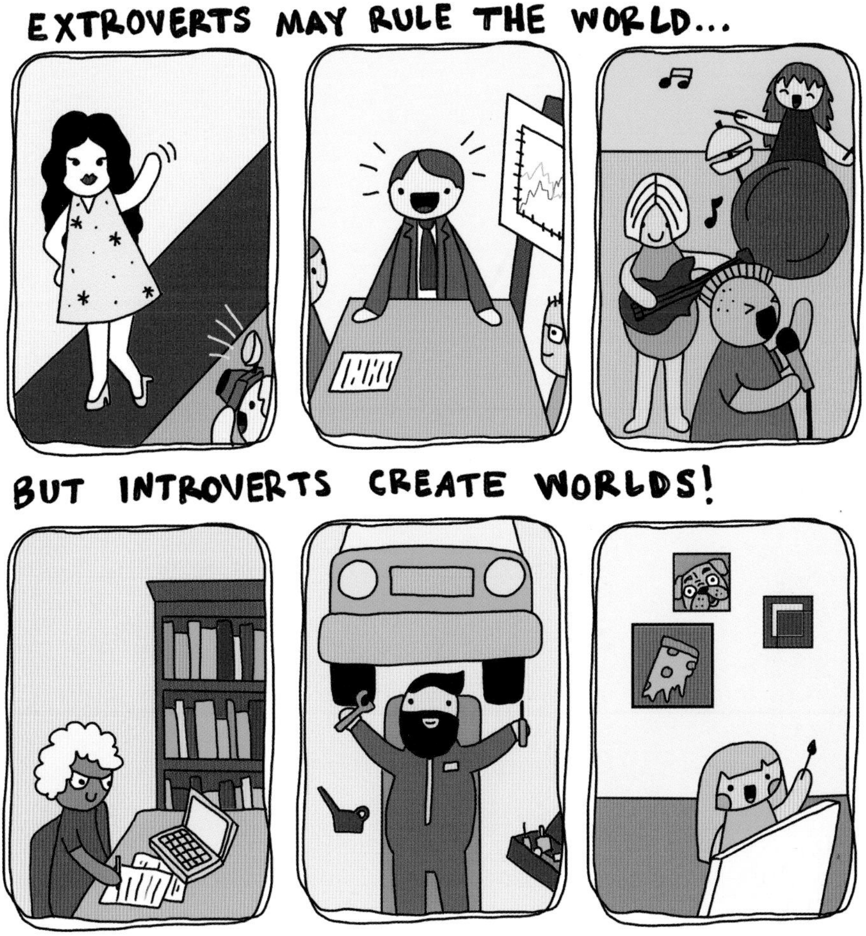
EXTROVERTS MAY RULE THE WORLD...
BUT INTROVERTS CREATE WORLDS!

ORDERING TAKEOUT

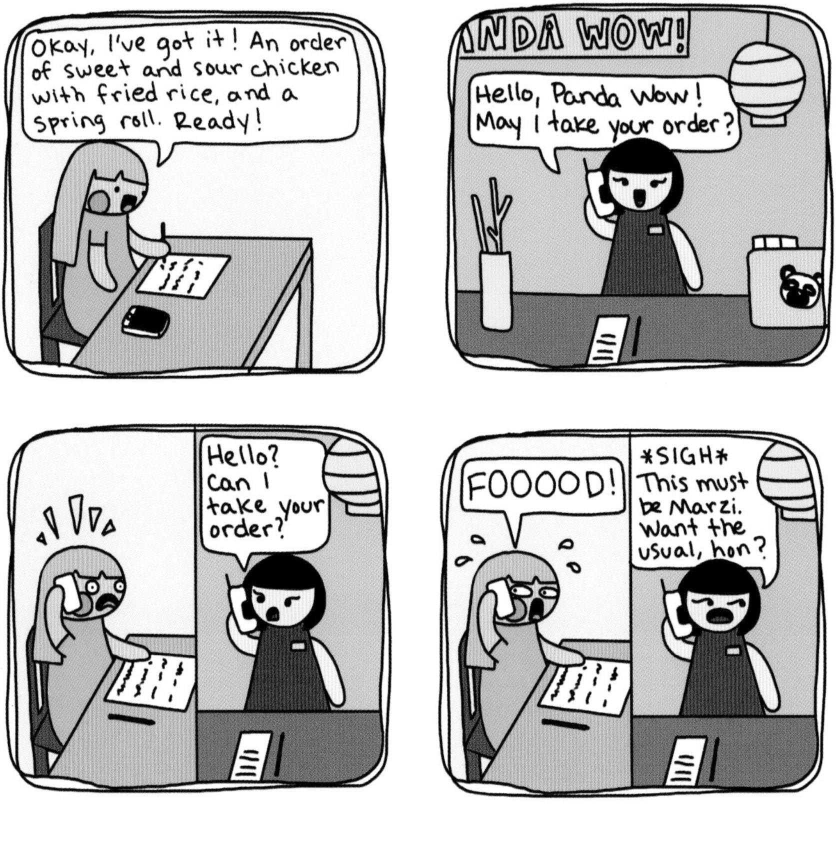

Okay, I've got it! An order of sweet and sour chicken with fried rice, and a spring roll. Ready!
NDA WOW!
Hello, Panda Wow! May I take your order?
Hello? Can I take your order?
FOOOOD!
SIGH This must be Marzi. Want the usual, hon?

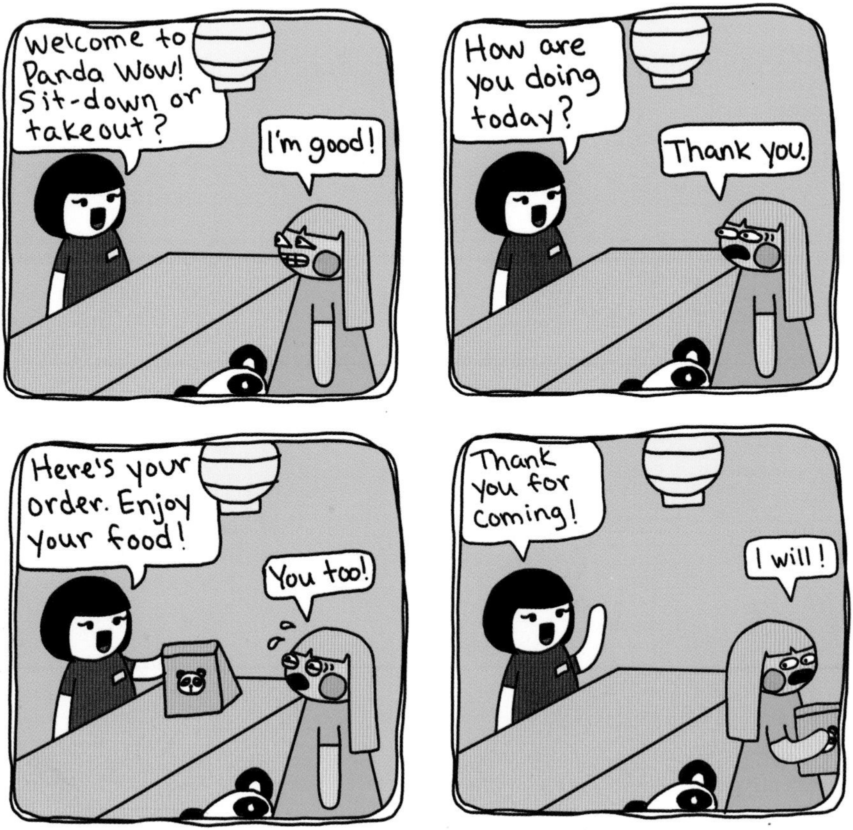
Welcome to Panda Wow! Sit-down or takeout?
I'm good!
How are you doing today?
Thank you.
Here's your order. Enjoy your food!
You too!
Thank you for coming!
I will!

ME AT THE DENTIST

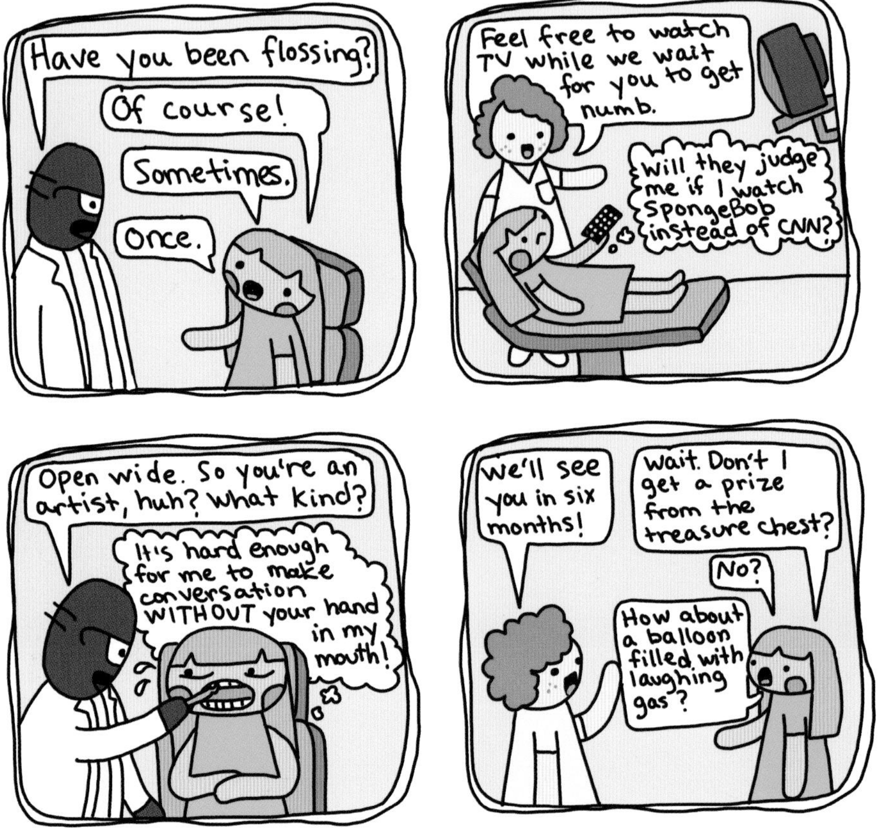
Have you been flossing?
Of course!
Sometimes.
Once.
Feel free to watch TV while we wait for you to get numb.
Will they judge me if I watch SpongeBob instead of CNN?
Open wide. So you're an artist, huh? What kind?
It's hard enough for me to make conversation WITHOUT your hand in my mouth!
We'll see you in six months!
Wait. Don't I get a prize from the treasure chest?
No?
How about a balloon filled with laughing gas?

HOW TO SURVIVE AN OFFICE JOB

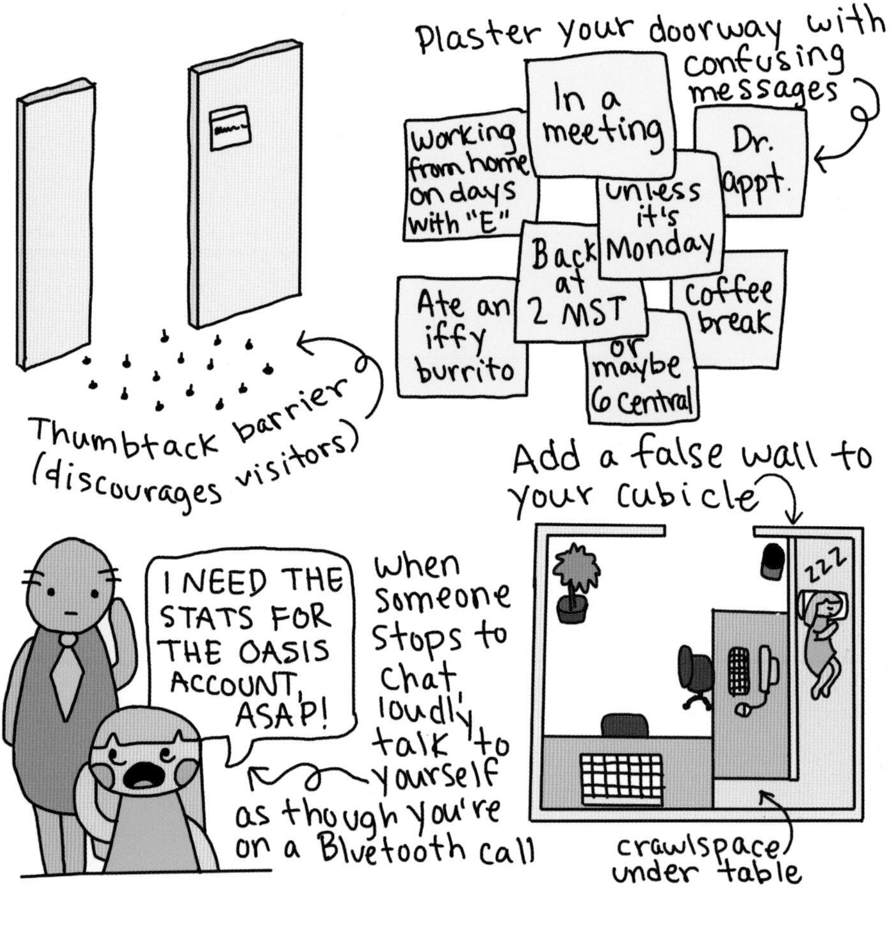
Plaster your doorway with confusing messages
Working from home on days with "E"
In a meeting
Dr. appt.
unless it's Monday
Back at 2 MST
Ate an iffy burrito
or maybe 6 Central
coffee break
Thumbtack barrier (discourages visitors)
Add a false wall to your cubicle
zzz
crawlspace under table
I NEED THE STATS FOR THE OASIS ACCOUNT, ASAP!
When someone stops to chat, loudly talk to yourself as though you're on a Bluetooth call

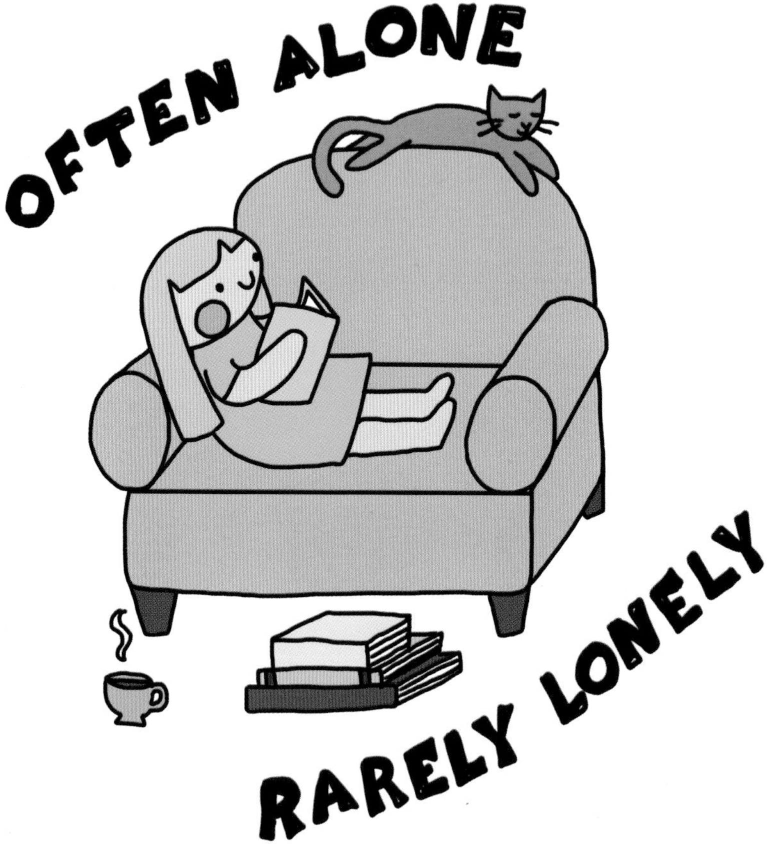
OFTEN ALONE
RARELY LONELY

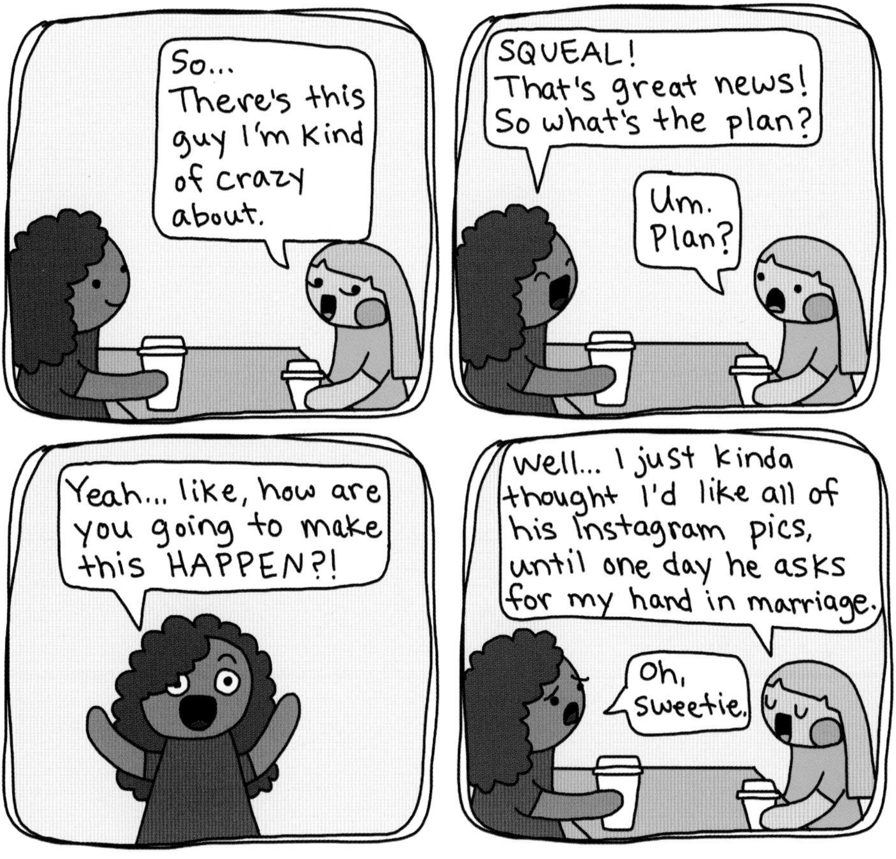
So... There's this guy I'm kind of crazy about.
SQUEAL! That's great news! So what's the plan?
Um. Plan?
Yeah... like, how are you going to make this HAPPEN?!
Well... I just kinda thought I'd like all of his Instagram pics, until one day he asks for my hand in marriage.
Oh, sweetie.

INTROVERT ON THE ROAD

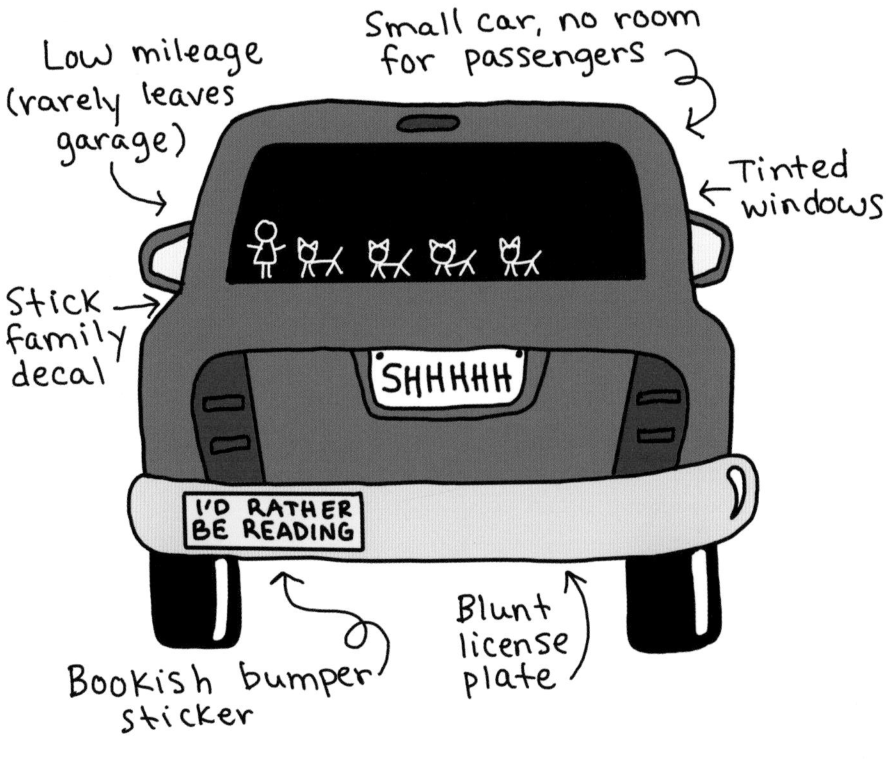

Small car, no room for passengers
Low mileage (rarely leaves garage)
Tinted windows
Stick family decal
SHHHHH
I'D RATHER BE READING
Blunt license plate
Bookish bumper sticker

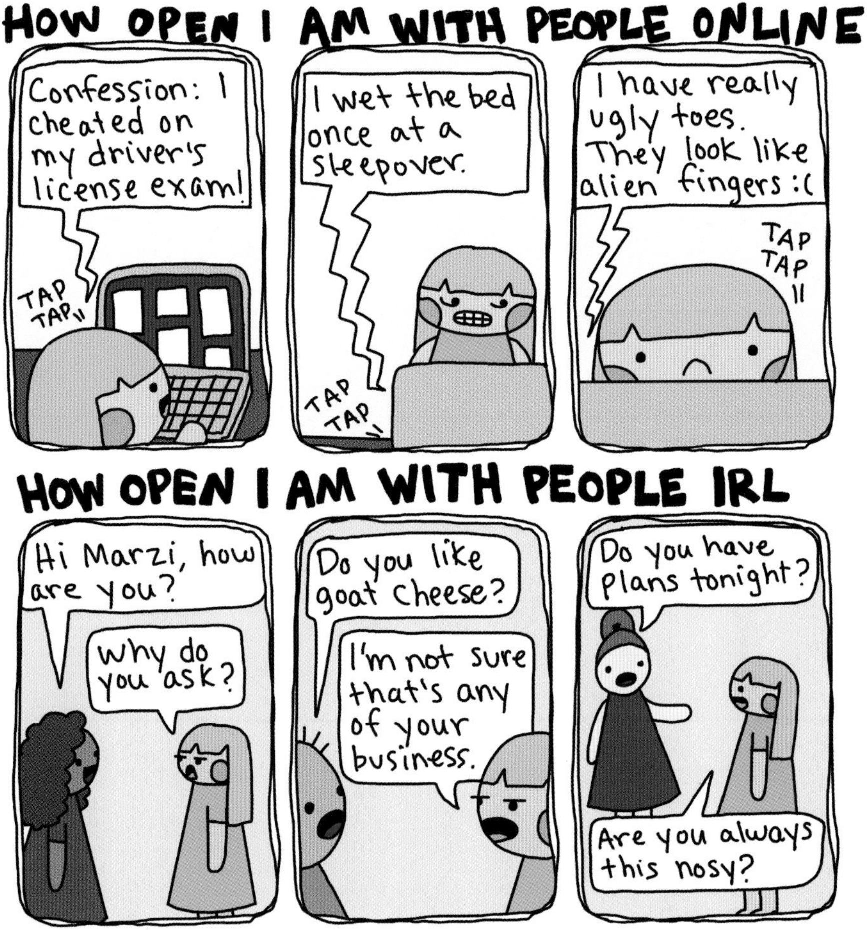
HOW OPEN I AM WITH PEOPLE ONLINE
Confession: I cheated on my driver's license exam!
TAP TAP
I wet the bed once at a sleepover.
TAP TAP
I have really ugly toes. They look like alien fingers :(
TAP TAP
HOW OPEN I AM WITH PEOPLE IRL
Hi Marzi, how are you?
Why do you ask?
Do you like goat cheese?
I'm not sure that's any of your business.
Do you have plans tonight?
Are you always this nosy?

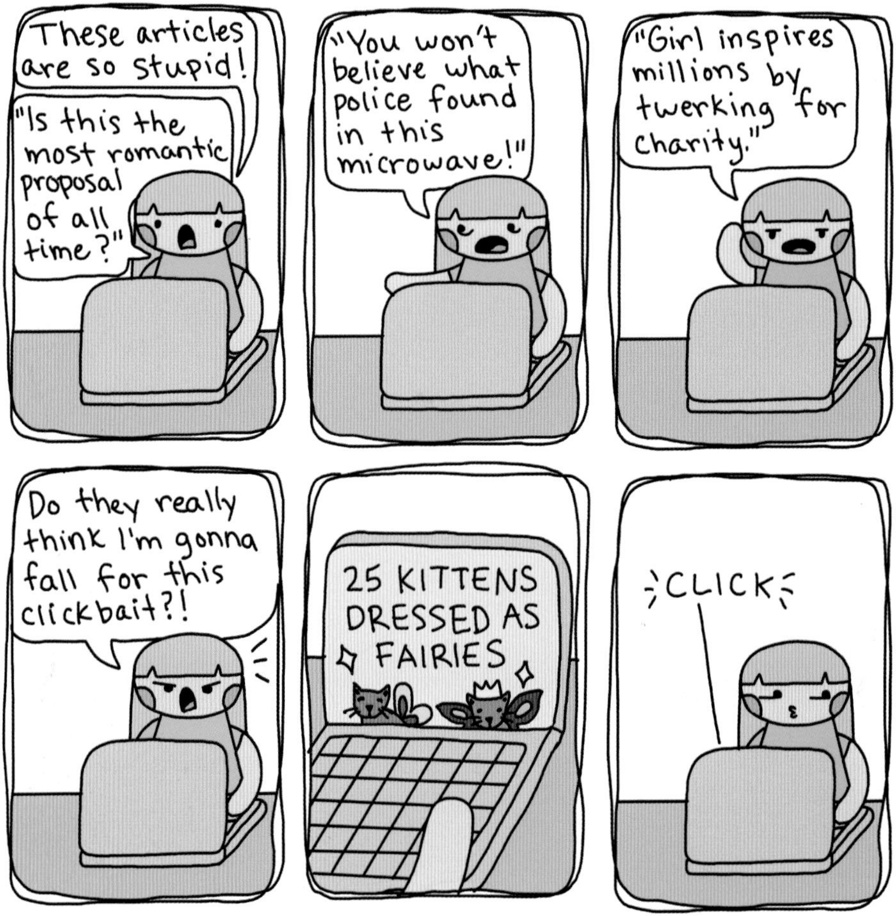
These articles are so stupid!
"Is this the most romantic proposal of all time?"
"You won't believe what police found in this microwave!"
"Girl inspires millions by twerking for charity."
Do they really think I'm gonna fall for this clickbait?!
25 KITTENS DRESSED AS FAIRIES
CLICK

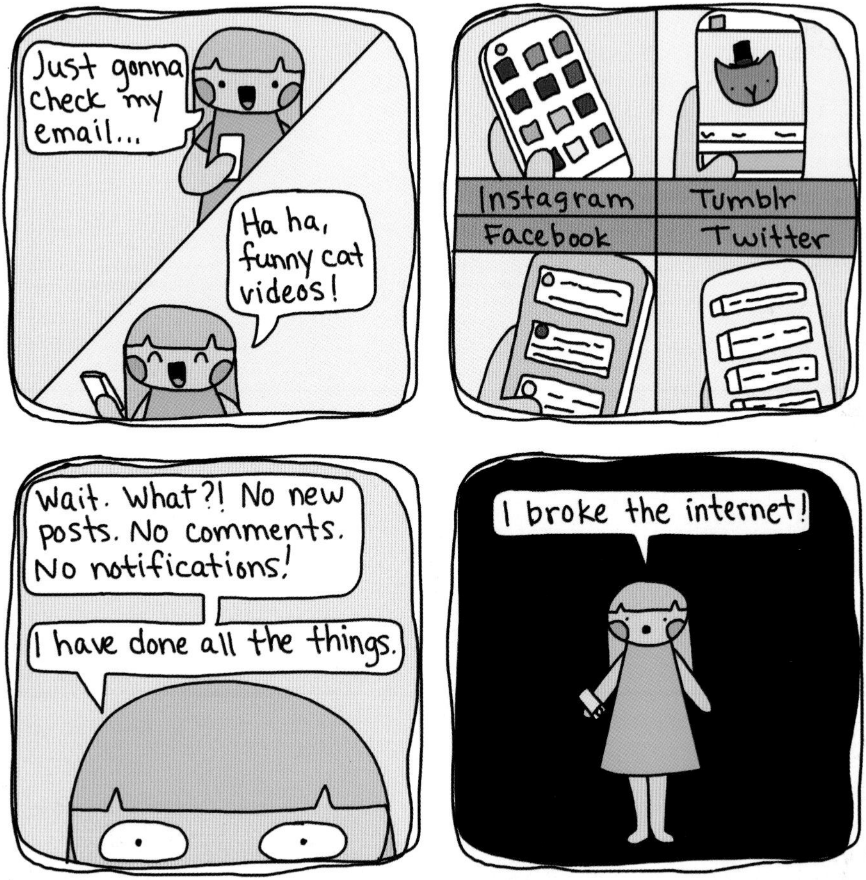
Just gonna check my email...
Ha ha, funny cat videos!
Instagram
Tumblr
Facebook
Twitter
Wait. What?! No new posts. No comments. No notifications!
I have done all the things.
I broke the internet!

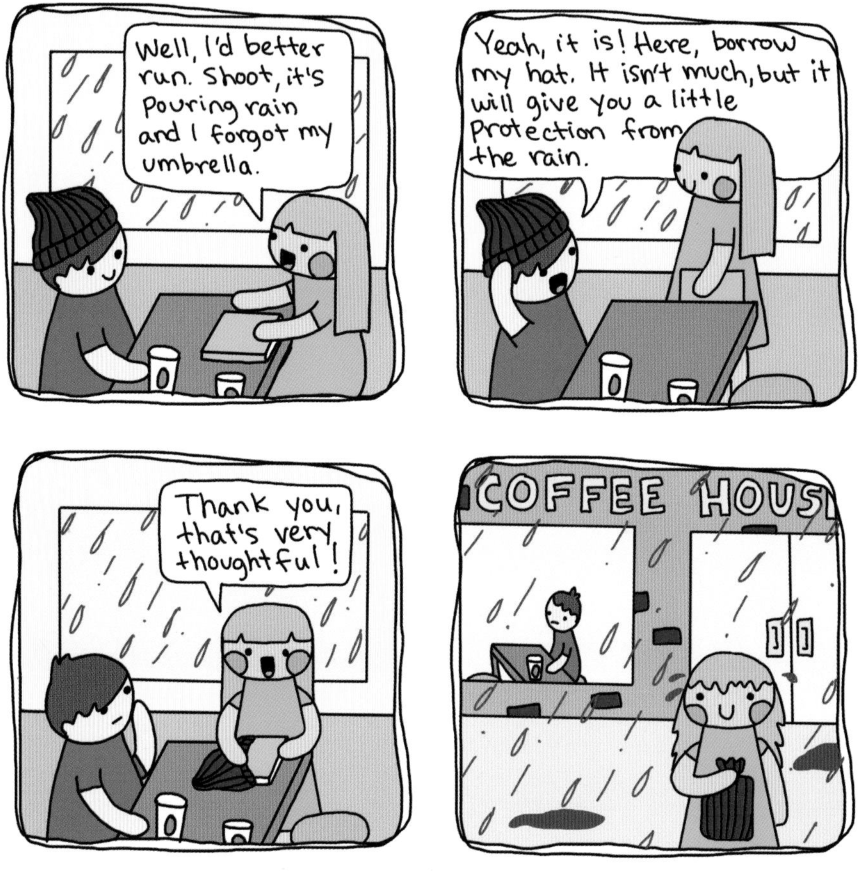
Well, I'd better run. Shoot, it's pouring rain and I forgot my umbrella.
Yeah, it is! Here, borrow my hat. It isn't much, but it will give you a little protection from the rain.
Thank you, that's very thoughtful!
COFFEE HOUS

THINGS I REFUSE TO DO

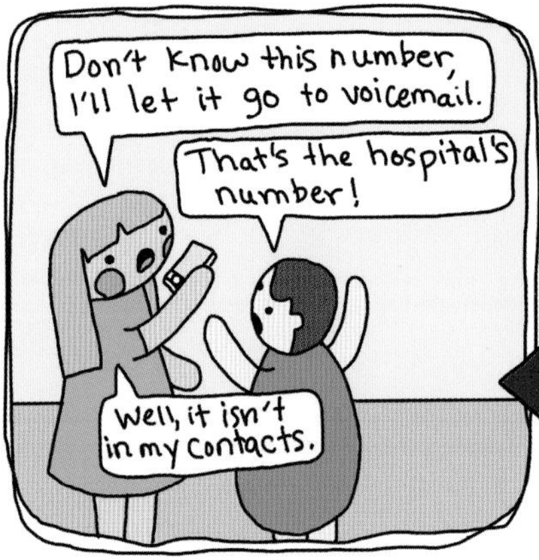
Don't know this number, I'll let it go to voicemail.
That's the hospital's number!
Well, it isn't in my contacts.

Answer a call from someone I don't know.

And sometimes not even from people I do.

Buy it from a store when I can order it online.

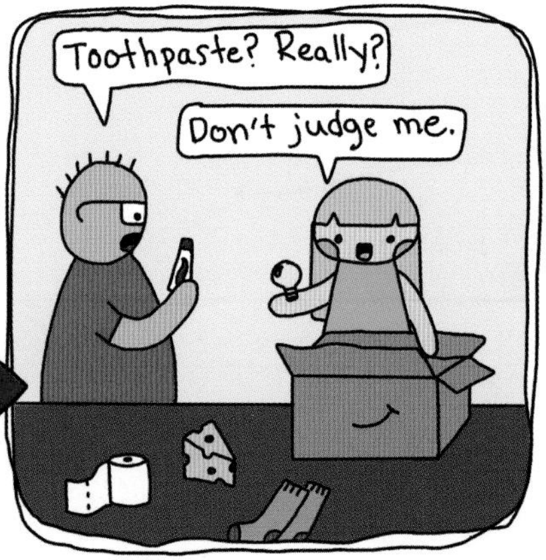
Toothpaste? Really?
Don't judge me.

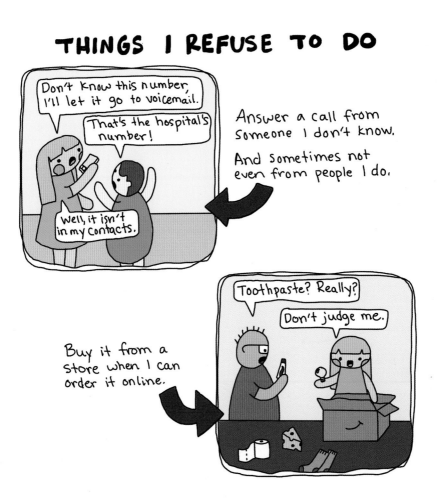

HOW TO ANNOY AN INTROVERT

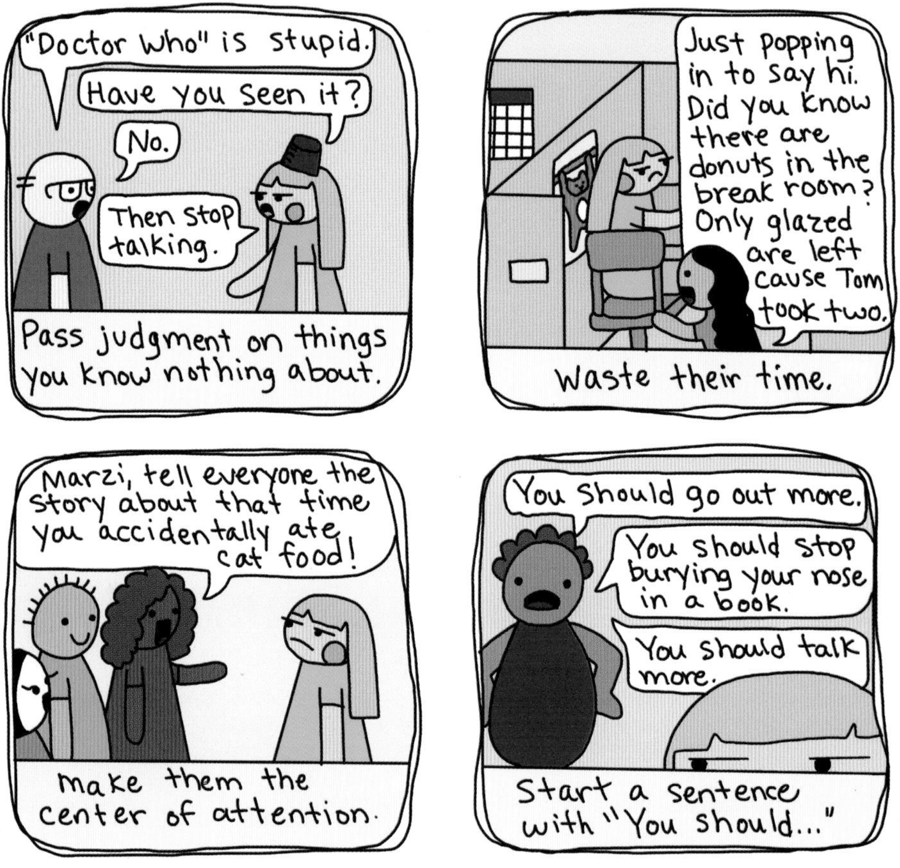
"Doctor Who" is stupid.
Have you seen it?
No.
Then stop talking.
Pass judgment on things you know nothing about.
Just popping in to say hi. Did you know there are donuts in the break room? Only glazed are left cause Tom took two.
Waste their time.
Marzi, tell everyone the story about that time you accidentally ate cat food!
Make them the center of attention.
You should go out more.
You should stop burying your nose in a book.
You should talk more.
Start a sentence with "You should..."

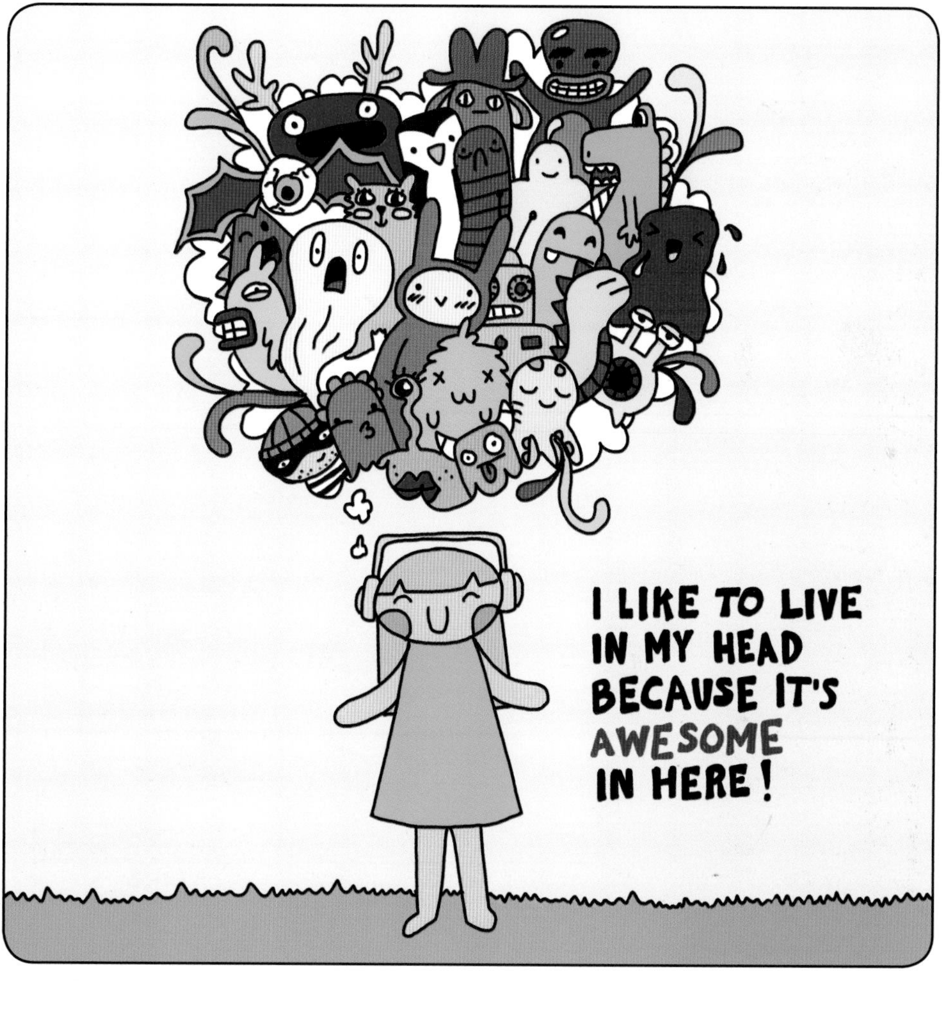
I LIKE TO LIVE
IN MY HEAD
BECAUSE IT'S
AWESOME
IN HERE!

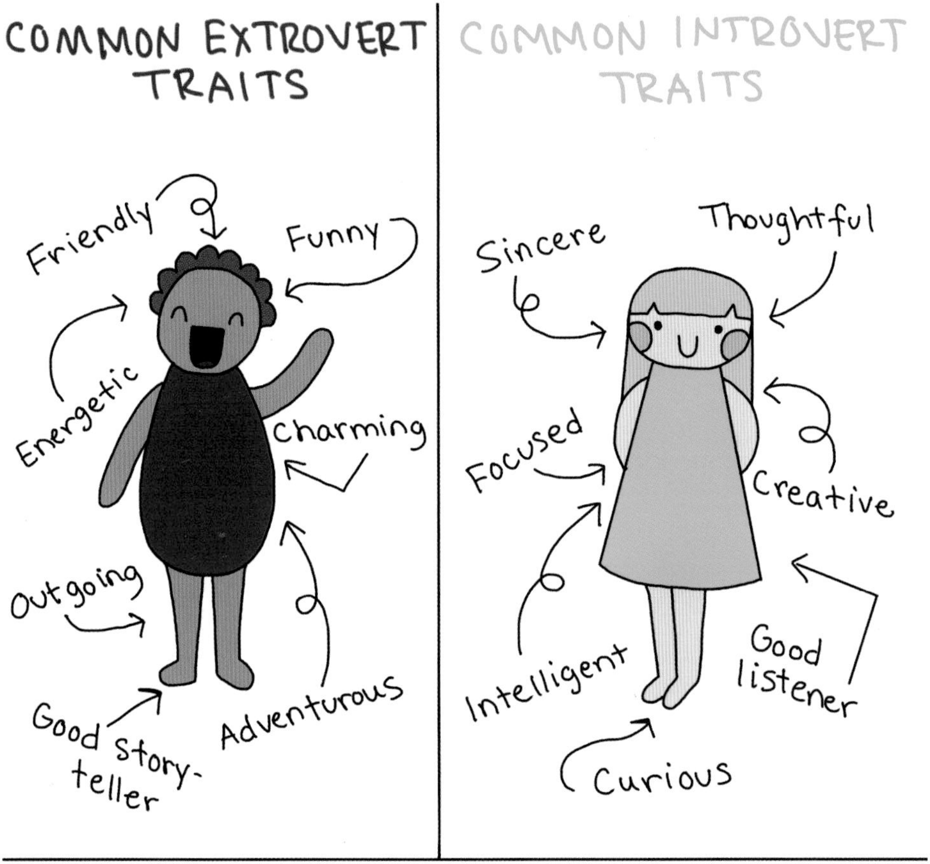
COMMON EXTROVERT TRAITS
Friendly
Funny
Energetic
Charming
Outgoing
Good story-teller
Adventurous
COMMON INTROVERT TRAITS
Sincere
Thoughtful
Focused
Creative
Intelligent
Good listener
Curious

*As introverts, our strengths may be less visible... but they are no less valuable!

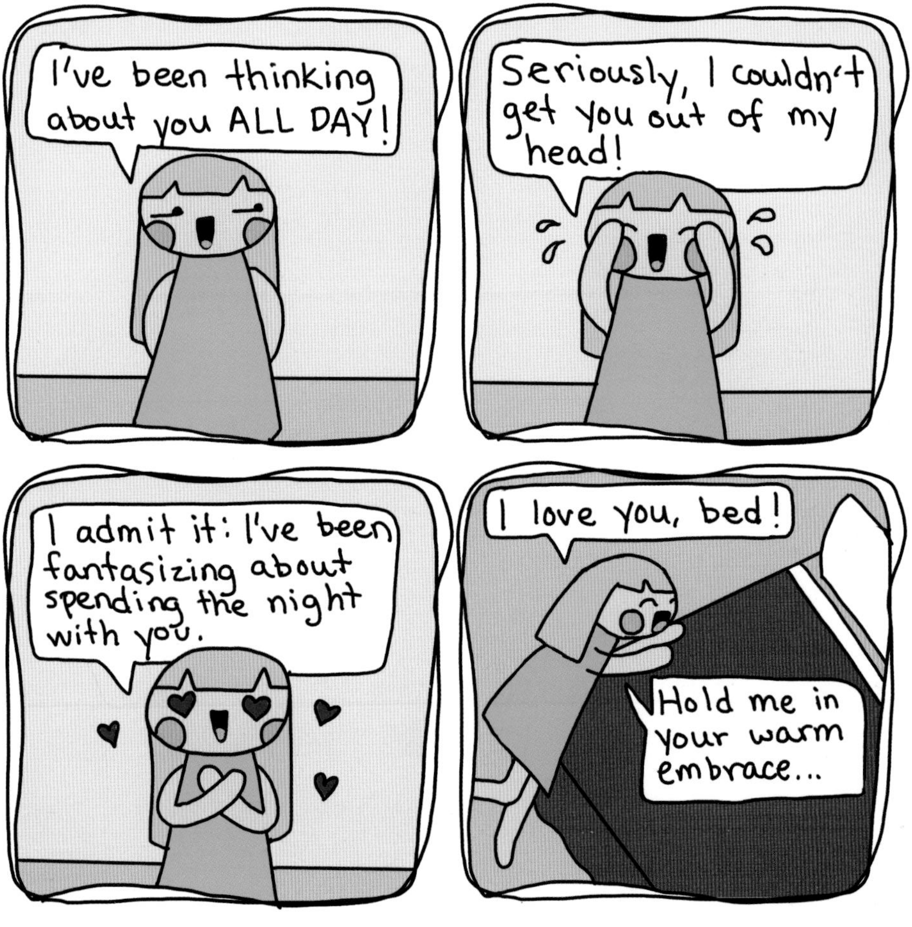
I've been thinking about you ALL DAY!
Seriously, I couldn't get you out of my head!
I admit it: I've been fantasizing about spending the night with you.
I love you, bed!
Hold me in your warm embrace...

WHAT I'M THINKING DURING A CONVERSATION

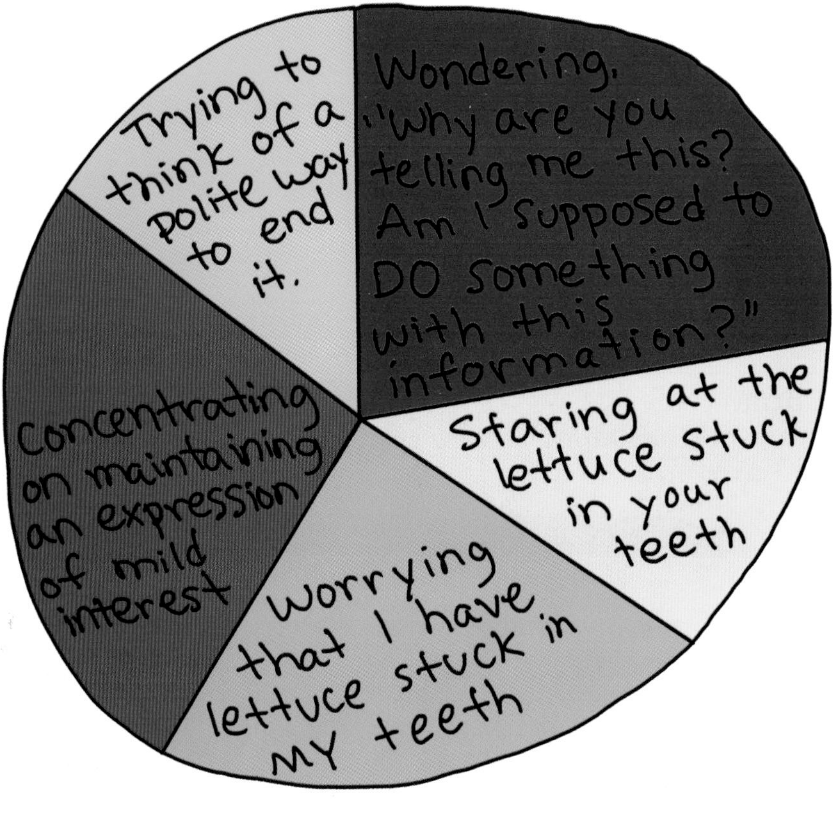
Trying to think of a polite way to end it.
Wondering, "Why are you telling me this? Am I supposed to DO something with this information?"
Staring at the lettuce stuck in your teeth
Worrying that I have lettuce stuck in my teeth
Concentrating on maintaining an expression of mild interest

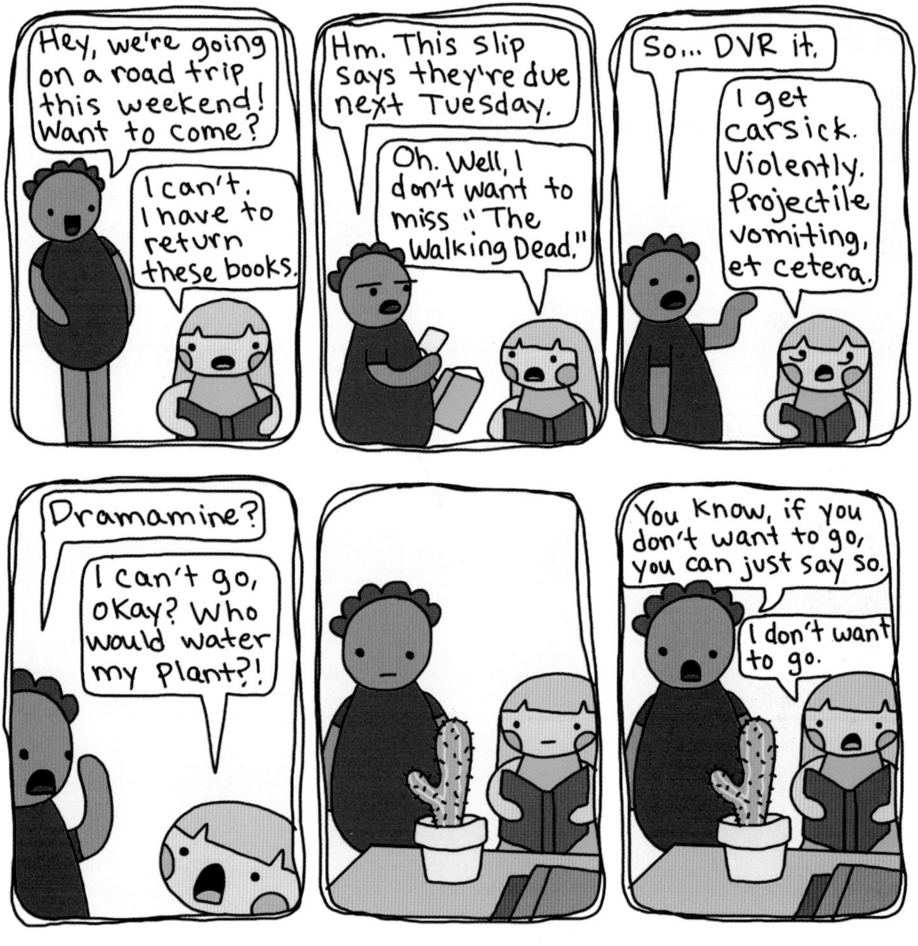
Hey, we're going on a road trip this weekend! Want to come?
I can't. I have to return these books.
Hm. This slip says they're due next Tuesday.
Oh. Well, I don't want to miss "The Walking Dead."
So... DVR it.
I get carsick. Violently. Projectile vomiting, et cetera.
Dramamine?
I can't go, okay? Who would water my plant?!
You know, if you don't want to go, you can just say so.
I don't want to go.

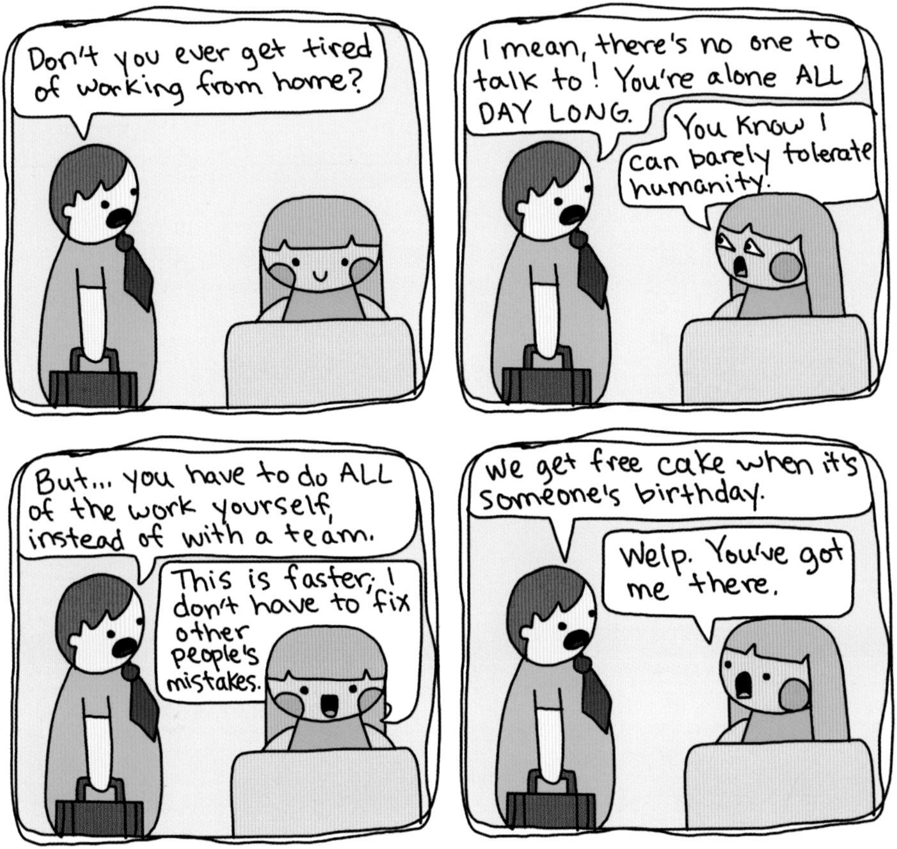

Don't you ever get tired of working from home?
I mean, there's no one to talk to! You're alone ALL DAY LONG.
You know I can barely tolerate humanity.
But... you have to do ALL of the work yourself, instead of with a team.
This is faster; I don't have to fix other people's mistakes.
We get free cake when it's someone's birthday.
Welp. You've got me there.

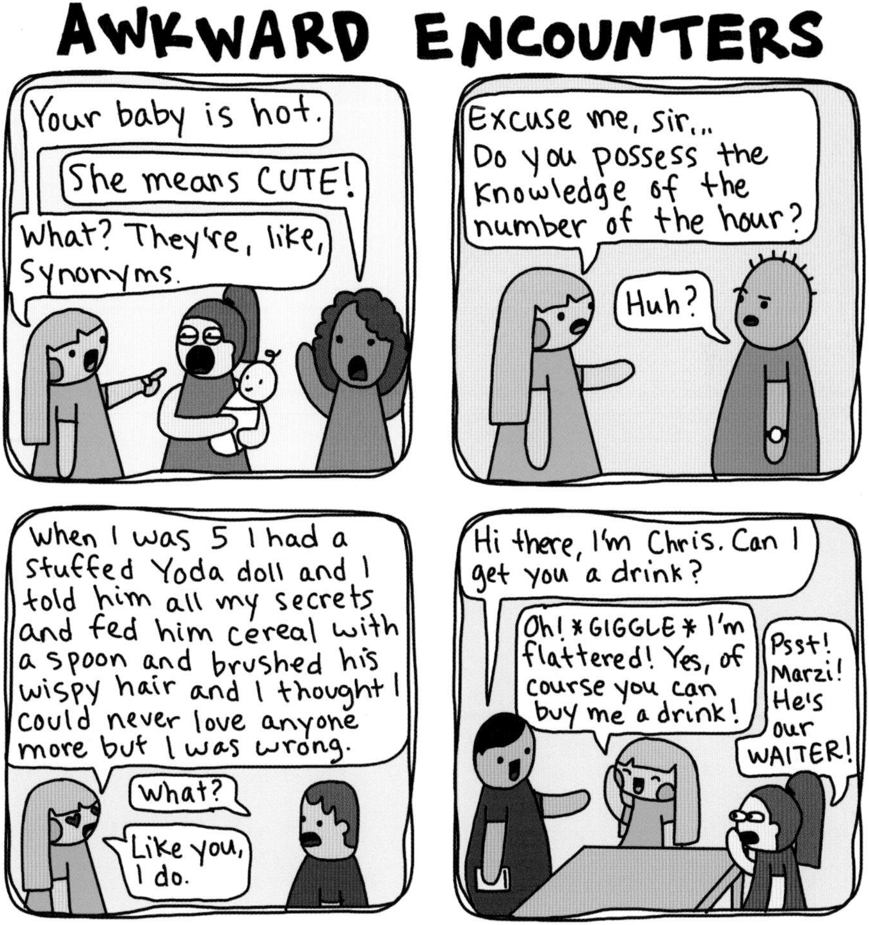
AWKWARD ENCOUNTERS
Your baby is hot.
She means CUTE!
What? They're, like, synonyms.
Excuse me, sir... Do you possess the knowledge of the number of the hour?
Huh?
When I was 5 I had a stuffed Yoda doll and I told him all my secrets and fed him cereal with a spoon and brushed his wispy hair and I thought I could never love anyone more but I was wrong.
What?
Like you, I do.
Hi there, I'm Chris. Can I get you a drink?
Oh! *GIGGLE* I'm flattered! Yes, of course you can buy me a drink!
Psst! Marzi! He's our WAITER!

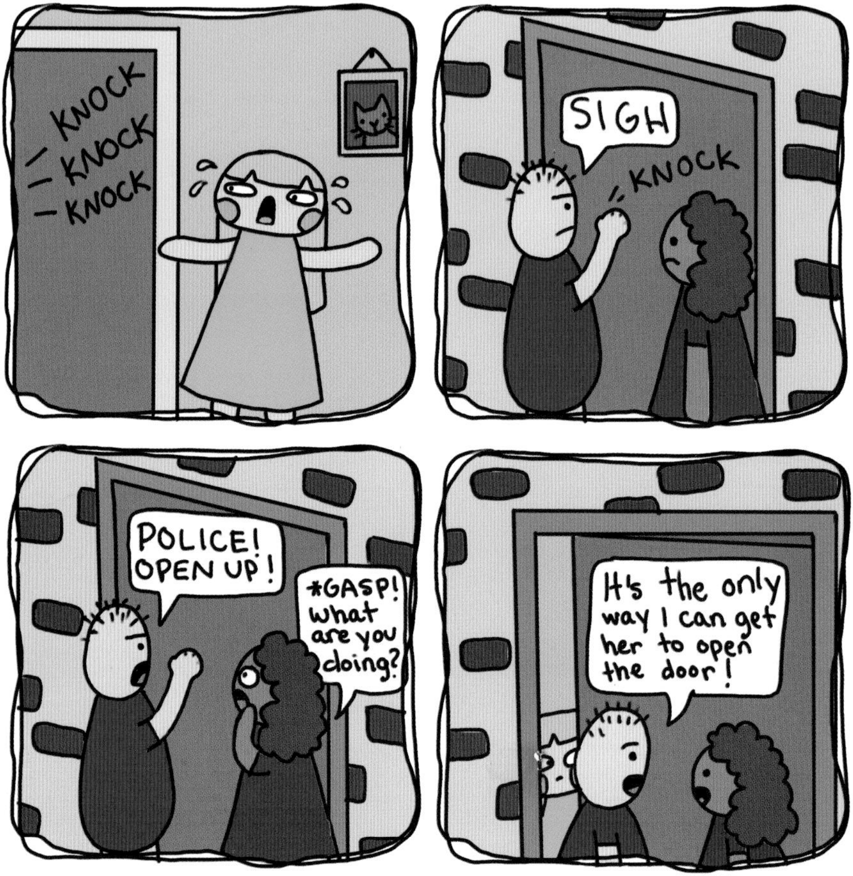
KNOCK
KNOCK
KNOCK
SIGH
KNOCK
POLICE! OPEN UP!
*GASP! what are you doing?
It's the only way I can get her to open the door!

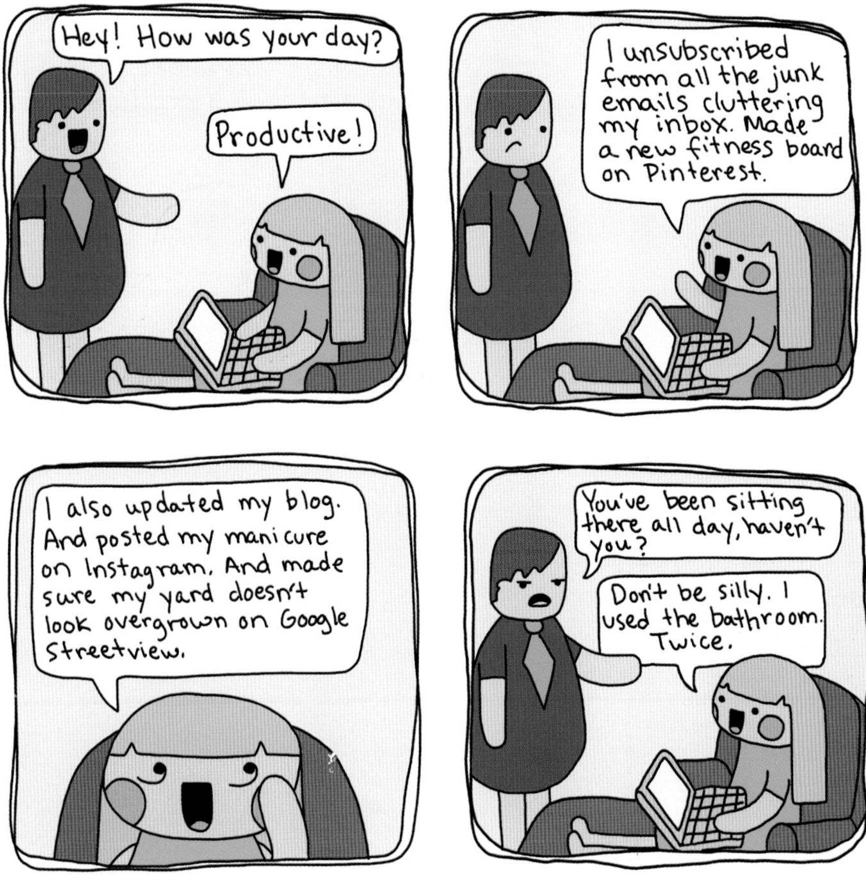
Hey! How was your day?
Productive!
I unsubscribed from all the junk emails cluttering my inbox. Made a new fitness board on Pinterest.
I also updated my blog. And posted my manicure on Instagram. And made sure my yard doesn't look overgrown on Google Streetview.
You've been sitting there all day, haven't you?
Don't be silly. I used the bathroom. Twice.

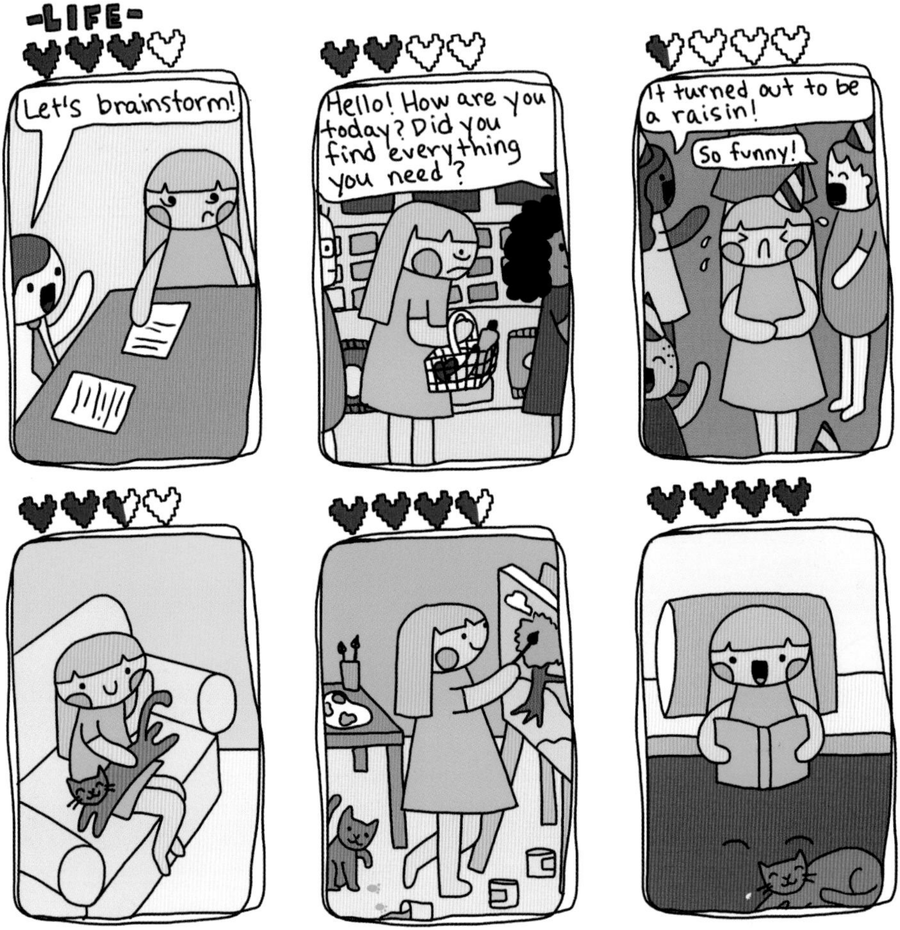
-LIFE-
Let's brainstorm!
Hello! How are you today? Did you find everything you need?
It turned out to be a raisin!
So funny!

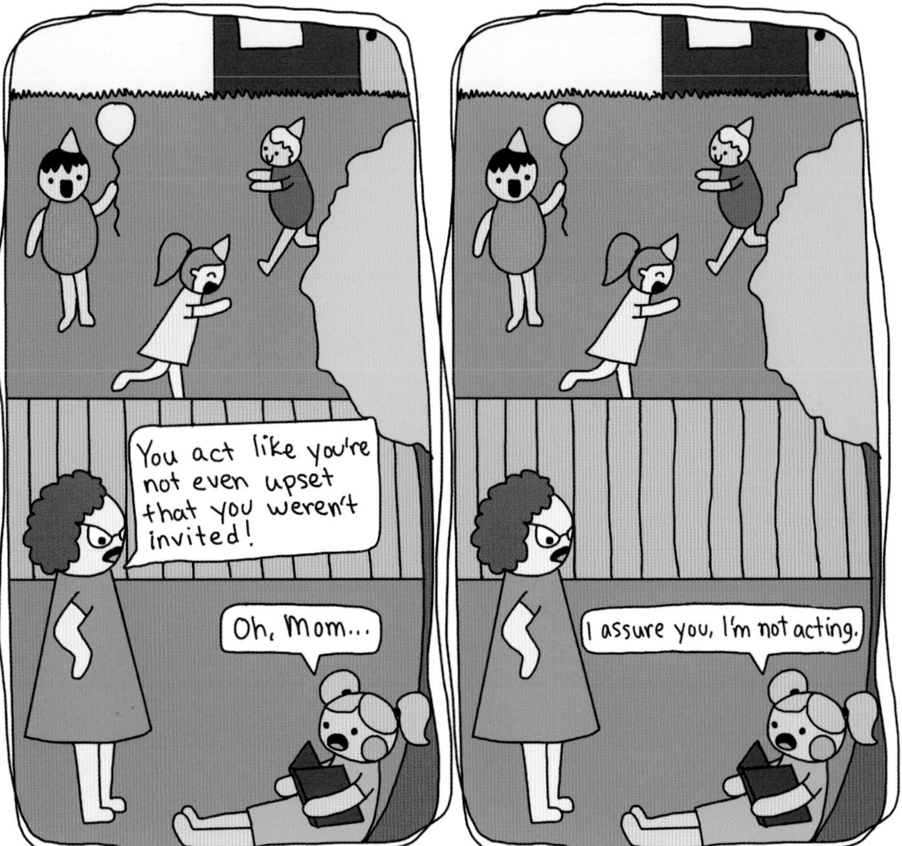
You act like you're not even upset that you weren't invited!
Oh, Mom...
I assure you, I'm not acting.

HOW TO GET RID OF GUESTS

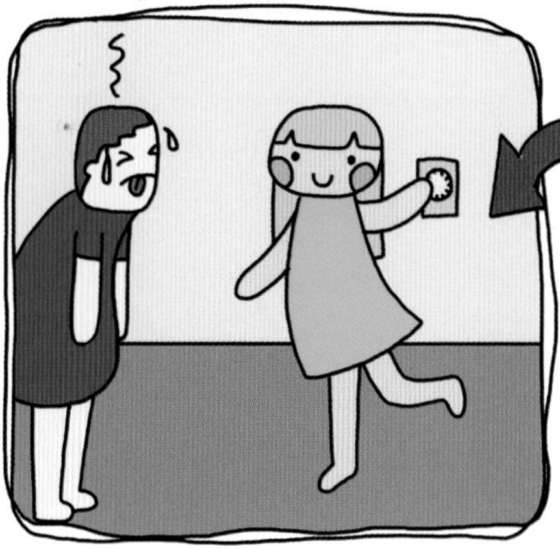

Discreetly turn up the thermostat. 90°F should do it.

Show them your vacation pics. From 1998.

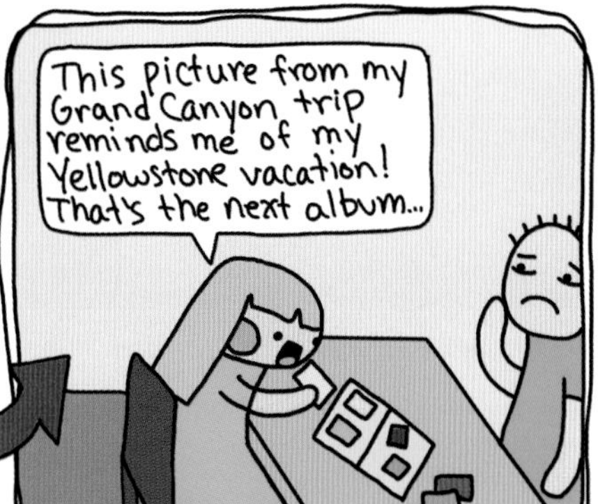
This picture from my Grand Canyon trip reminds me of my Yellowstone vacation! That's the next album...

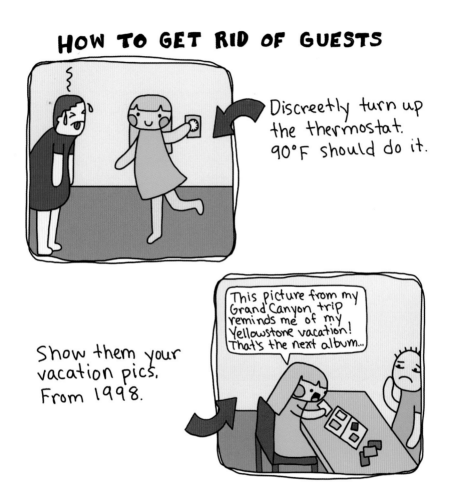

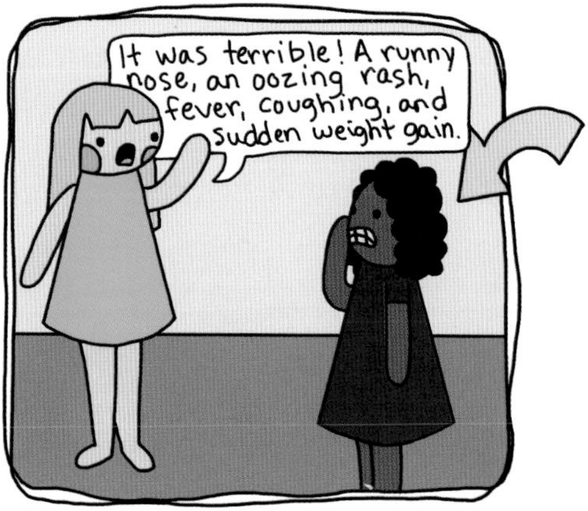
It was terrible! A runny nose, an oozing rash, fever, coughing, and sudden weight gain.

Tell them all the symptoms of your recent illness.

Include your deceased great-grandmother in the conversation.

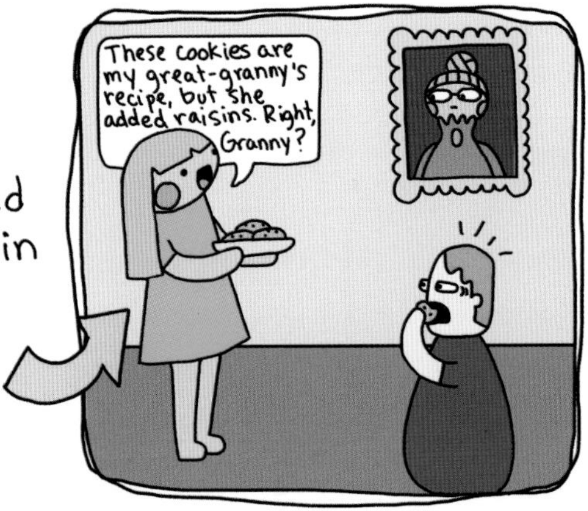
These cookies are my great-granny's recipe, but she added raisins. Right, Granny?

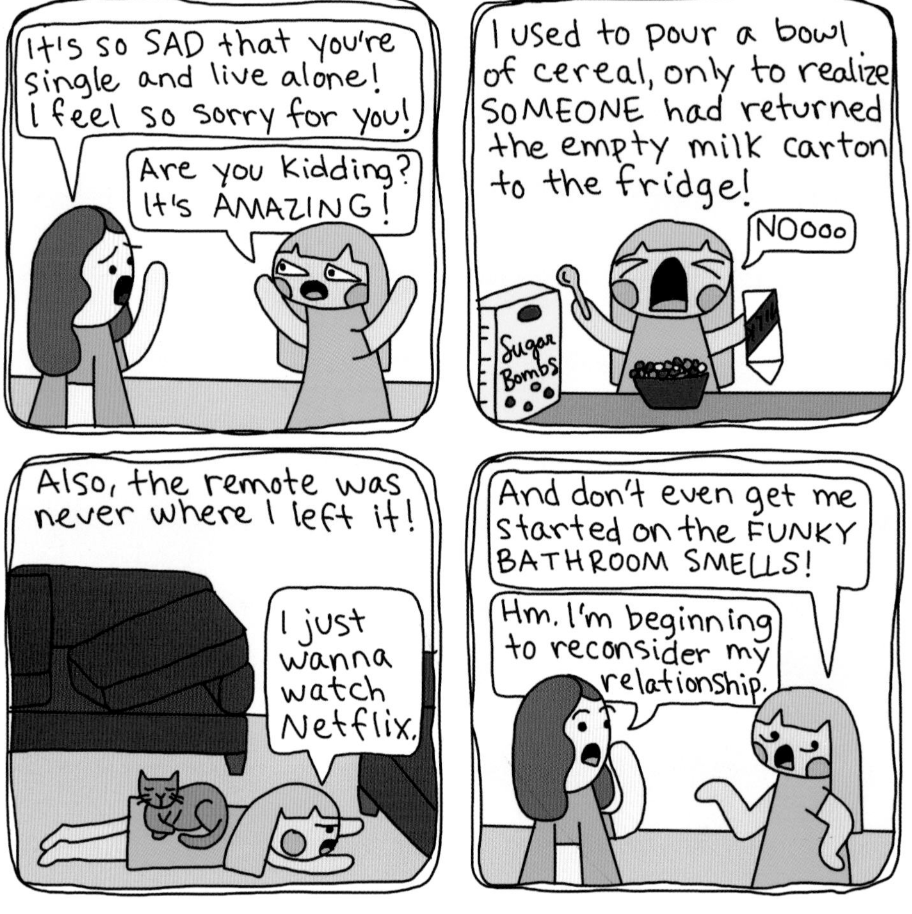

It's so SAD that you're single and live alone! I feel so sorry for you!
Are you kidding? It's AMAZING!
I used to pour a bowl of cereal, only to realize SOMEONE had returned the empty milk carton to the fridge!
NOooo
Sugar Bombs
Also, the remote was never where I left it!
I just wanna watch Netflix.
And don't even get me started on the FUNKY BATHROOM SMELLS!
Hm. I'm beginning to reconsider my relationship.

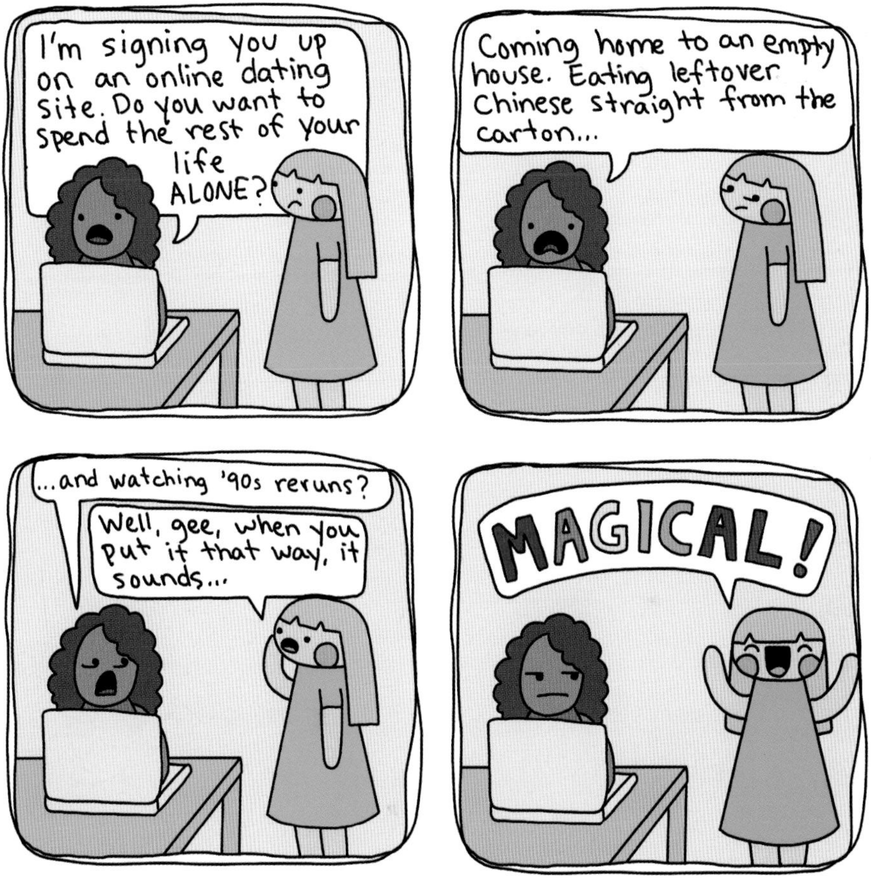
I'm signing you up on an online dating site. Do you want to spend the rest of your life ALONE?
Coming home to an empty house. Eating leftover Chinese straight from the carton...
...and watching '90s reruns?
Well, gee, when you put it that way, it sounds...
MAGICAL!

ITEMS THAT ARE PROBABLY INTROVERTS 'CAUSE THEY'RE ALMOST ALWAYS ALONE

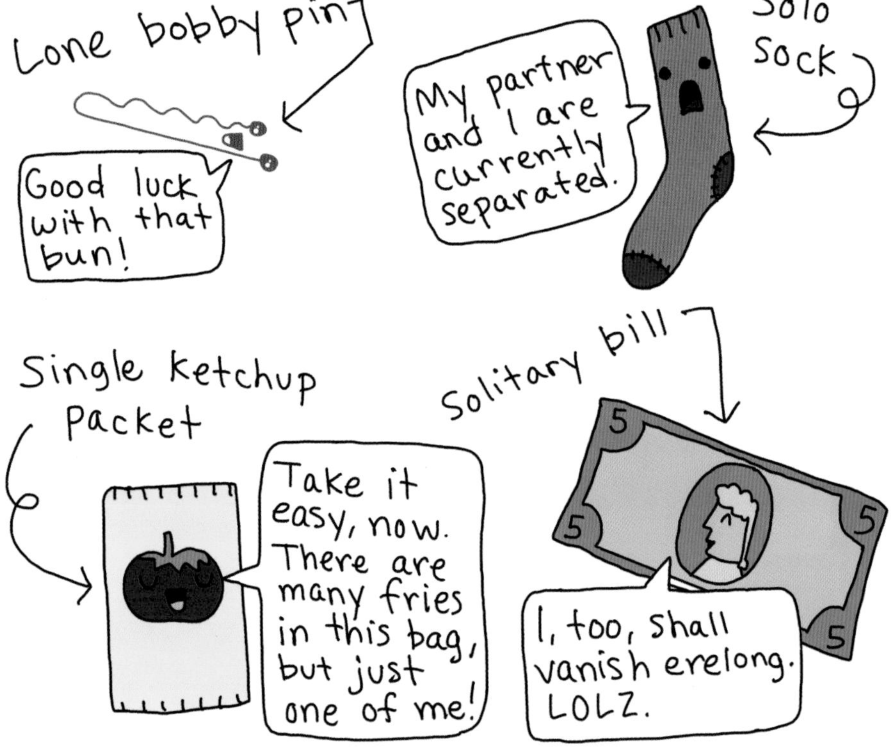
Lone bobby pin
Good luck with that bun!
My partner and I are currently separated.
Solo sock
Single ketchup packet
Take it easy, now. There are many fries in this bag, but just one of me!
Solitary bill
I, too, shall vanish erelong. LOLZ.
5

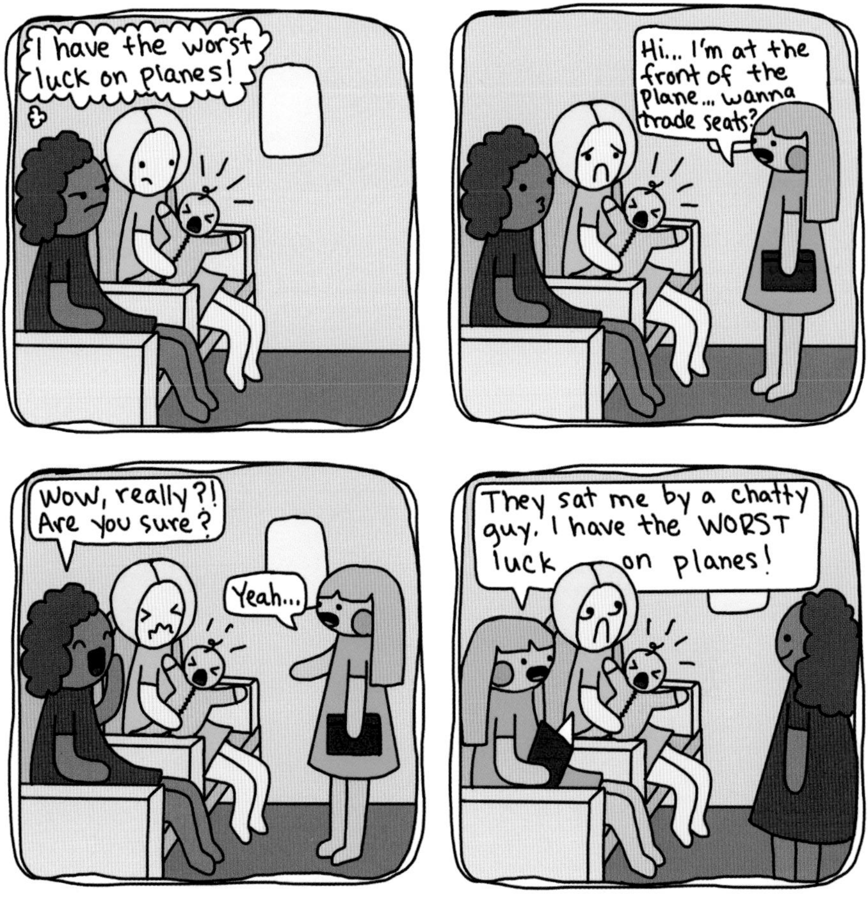
I have the worst luck on planes!
Hi... I'm at the front of the plane... wanna trade seats?
Wow, really?! Are you sure?
Yeah...
They sat me by a chatty guy. I have the WORST luck on planes!

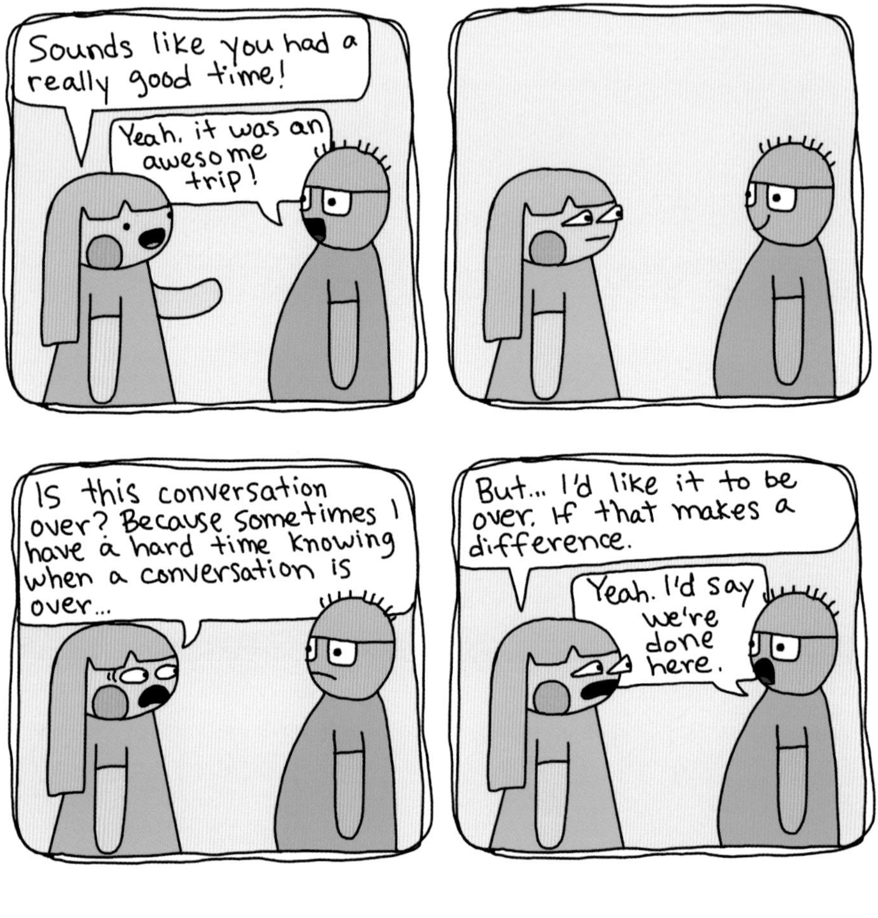

Sounds like you had a really good time!
Yeah, it was an awesome trip!
Is this conversation over? Because sometimes I have a hard time knowing when a conversation is over...
But... I'd like it to be over, if that makes a difference.
Yeah. I'd say we're done here.

PIE CHART OF MY SOUL

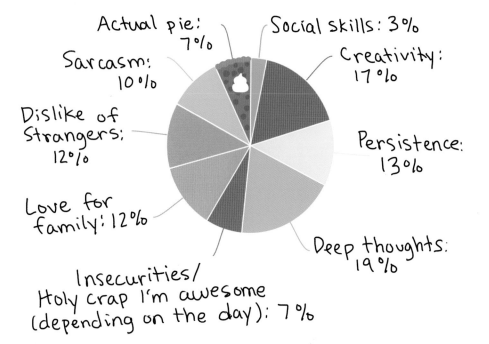

Actual pie: 7%

Social skills: 3%

Sarcasm: 10%

Creativity: 17%

Dislike of Strangers: 12%

Persistence: 13%

Love for family: 12%

Deep thoughts: 19%

Insecurities/
Holy crap I'm awesome
(depending on the day): 7%

INCOMING TEXT
I'm tired of dealing with humans. I do not understand them.
They say one thing but mean another.
INCOMING TEXT
They hate their bodies, but post a new selfie every day.
INCOMING TEXT
They laugh when they see someone get hurt or humiliated.
I think the human race is doomed.
OUTGOING TEXT
I Know how you feel.
Finally! Somebody GETS it. I wonder if he's single...?

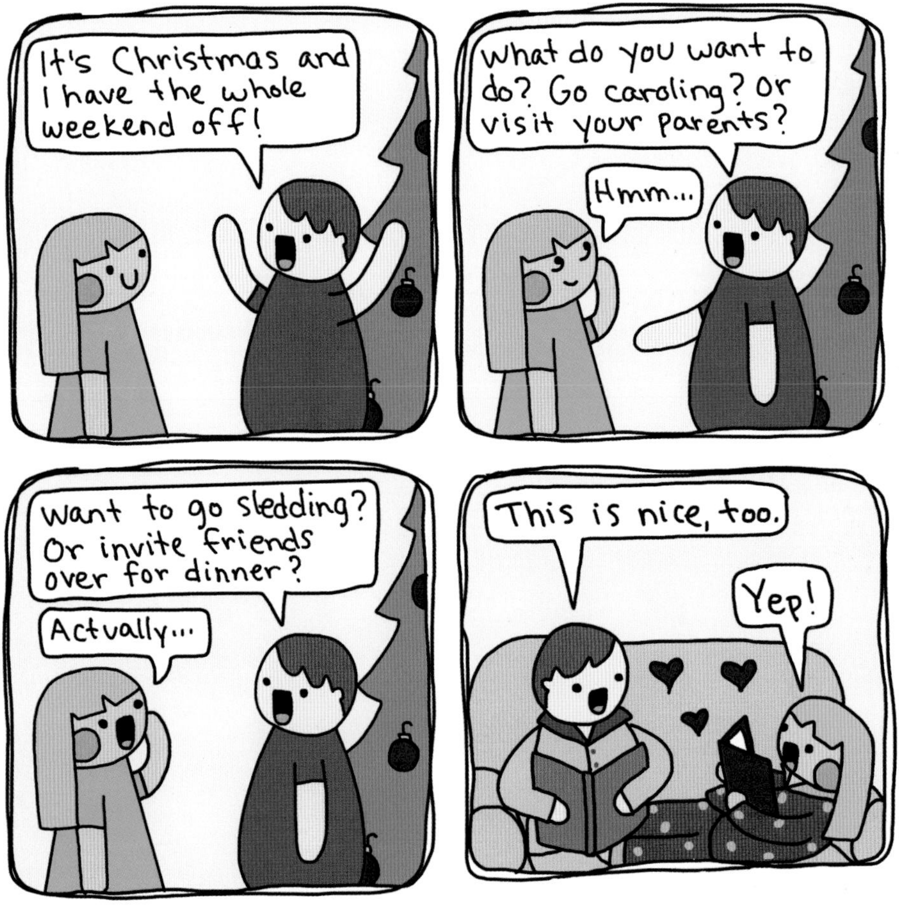
It's Christmas and I have the whole weekend off!
What do you want to do? Go caroling? Or visit your parents?
Hmm...
Want to go sledding? Or invite friends over for dinner?
Actually...
This is nice, too.
Yep!

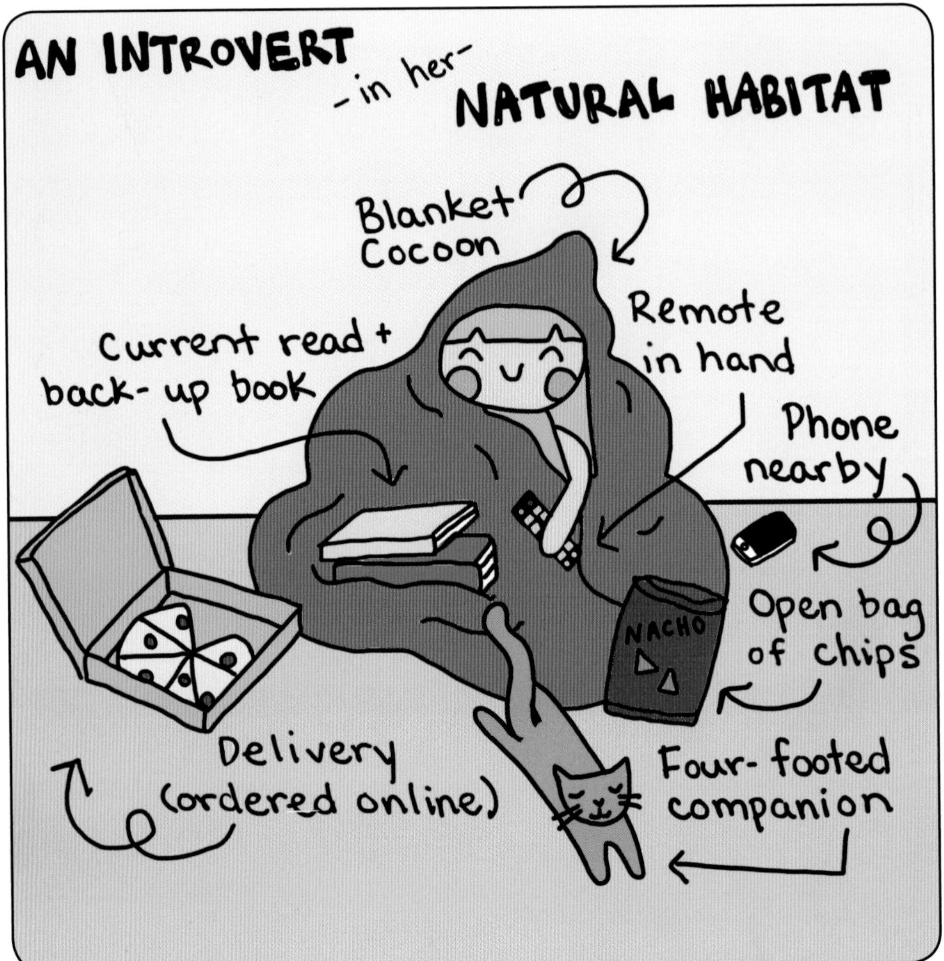
AN INTROVERT
-in her-
NATURAL HABITAT
Blanket Cocoon
Remote in hand
Current read + back-up book
Phone nearby
Open bag of chips
NACHO
Delivery (ordered online)
Four-footed companion

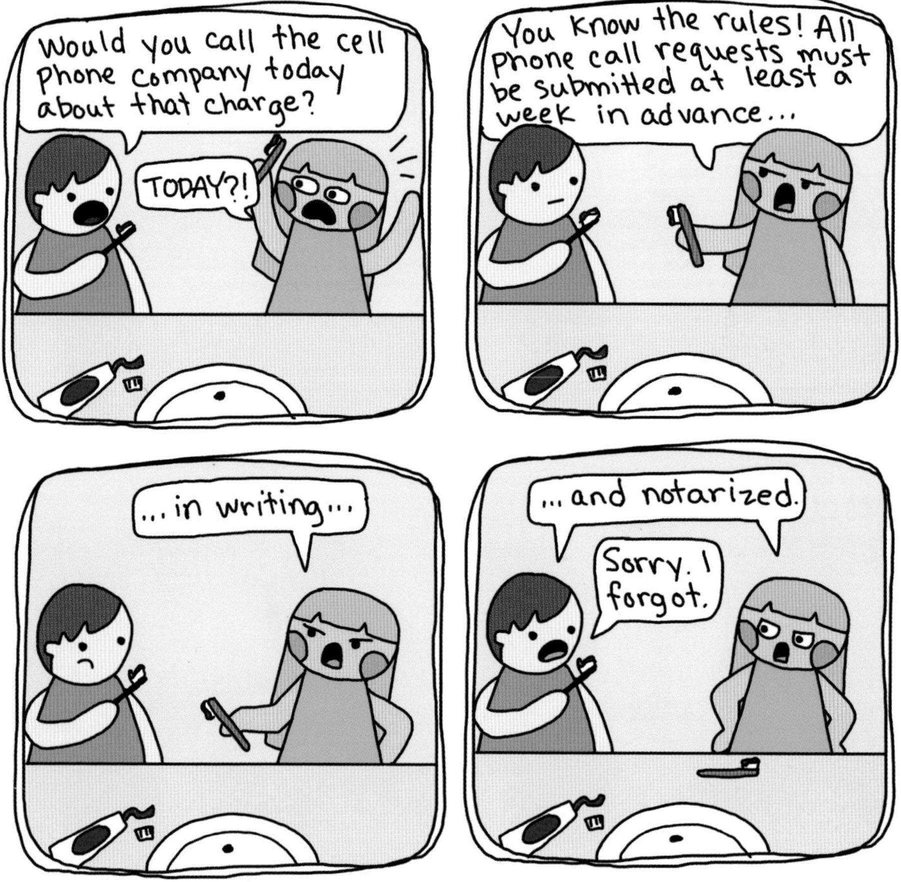
Would you call the cell phone company today about that charge?
TODAY?!
You know the rules! All phone call requests must be submitted at least a week in advance...
...in writing...
...and notarized.
Sorry. I forgot.

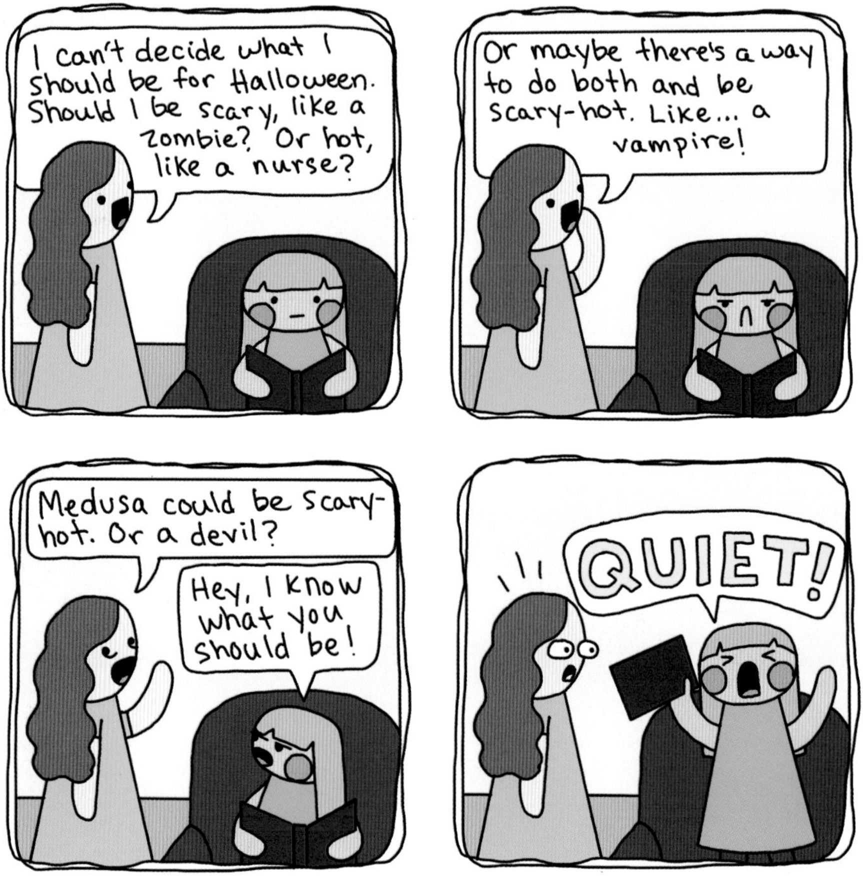
I can't decide what I should be for Halloween. Should I be scary, like a zombie? Or hot, like a nurse?
Or maybe there's a way to do both and be scary-hot. Like... a vampire!
Medusa could be scary-hot. Or a devil?
Hey, I know what you should be!
QUIET!

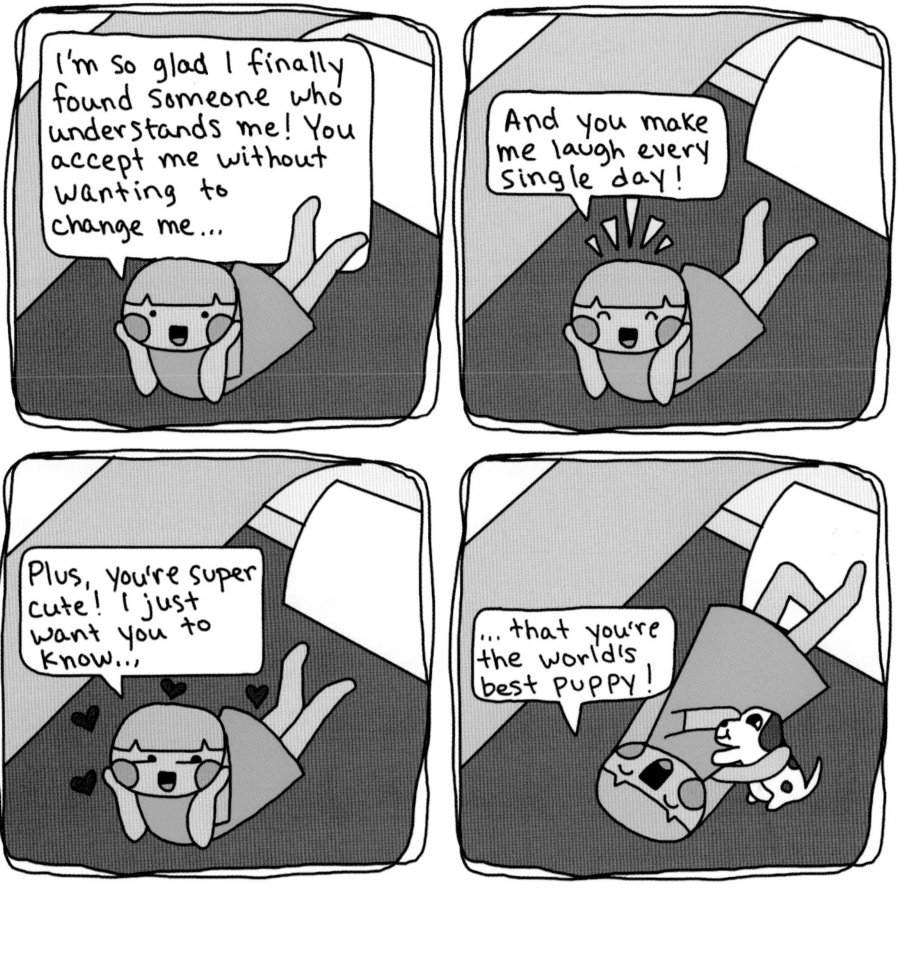
I'm so glad I finally found someone who understands me! You accept me without wanting to change me...
And you make me laugh every single day!
Plus, you're super cute! I just want you to know...,
... that you're the world's best puppy!

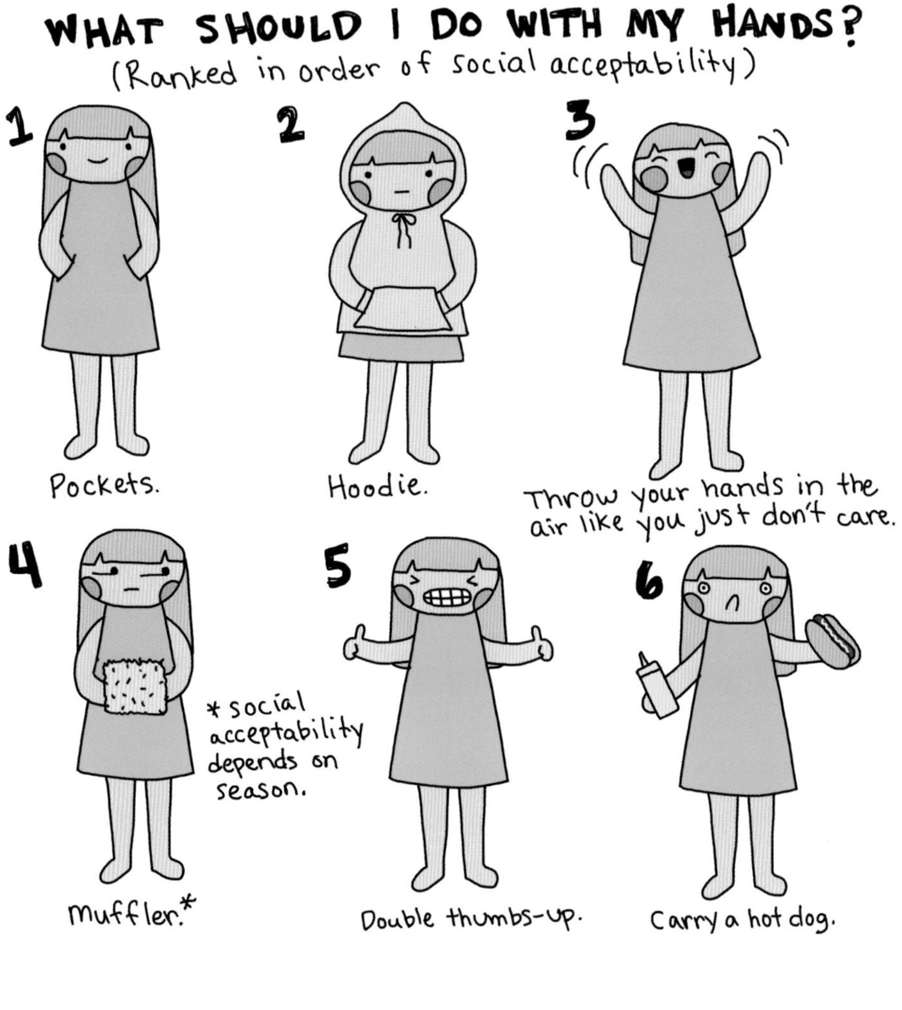
WHAT SHOULD I DO WITH MY HANDS?
(Ranked in order of social acceptability)
1
Pockets.
2
Hoodie.
3
Throw your hands in the air like you just don't care.
4
Muffler.*
* social acceptability depends on season.
5
Double thumbs-up.
6
Carry a hot dog.

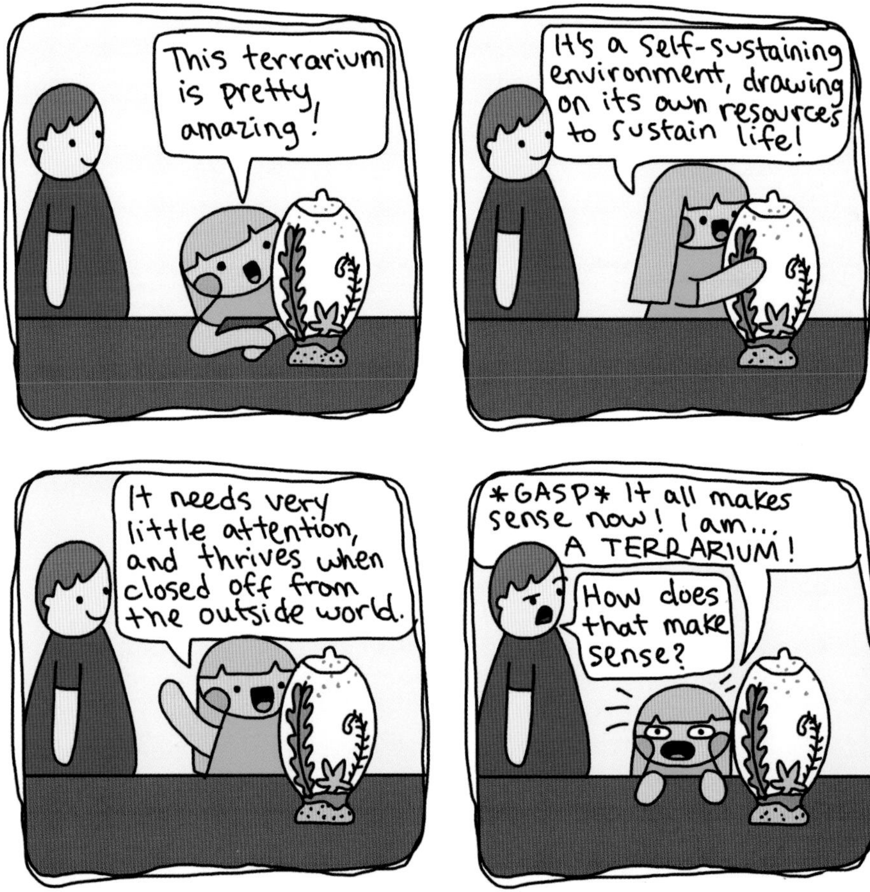
This terrarium is pretty amazing!
It's a self-sustaining environment, drawing on its own resources to sustain life!
It needs very little attention, and thrives when closed off from the outside world.
GASP It all makes sense now! I am... A TERRARIUM!
How does that make sense?

HOW TO WRAP UP A CONVERSATION

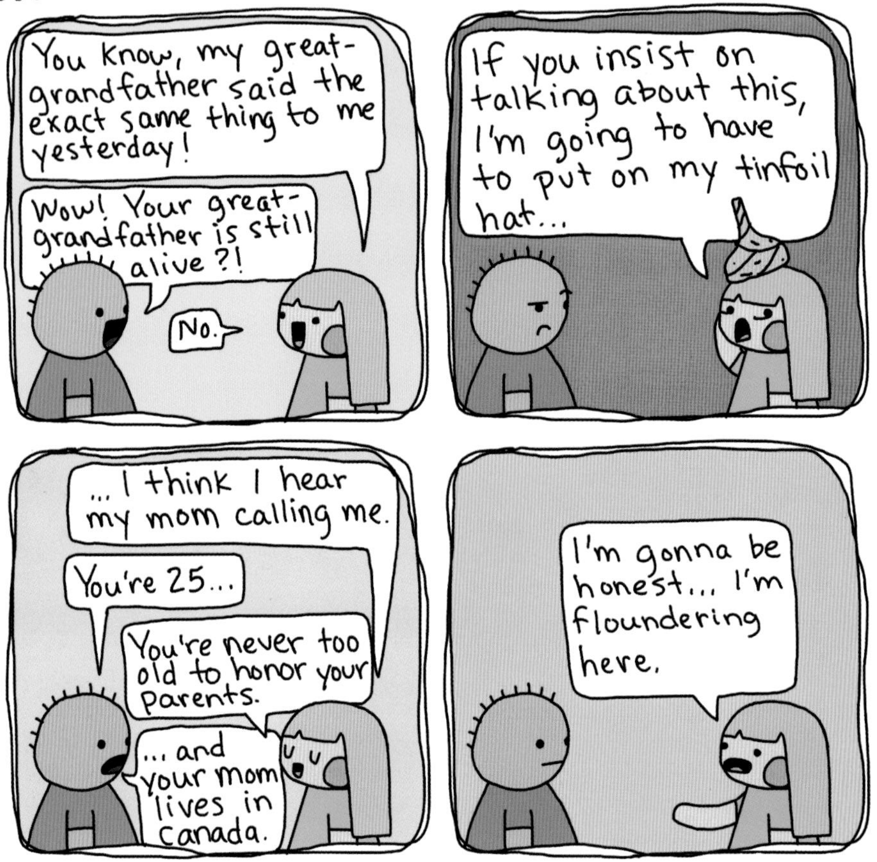
You know, my great-grandfather said the exact same thing to me yesterday!
Wow! Your great-grandfather is still alive?!
No.
If you insist on talking about this, I'm going to have to put on my tinfoil hat...
...I think I hear my mom calling me.
You're 25...
You're never too old to honor your parents.
...and your mom lives in canada.
I'm gonna be honest... I'm floundering here.

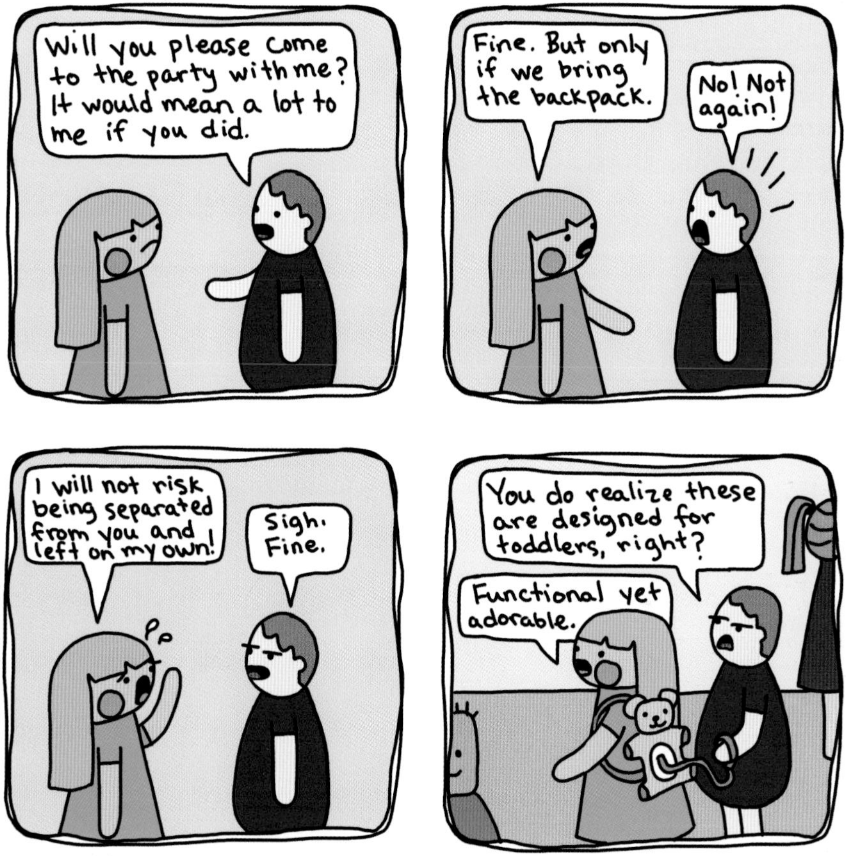
Will you please come to the party with me? It would mean a lot to me if you did.
Fine. But only if we bring the backpack.
No! Not again!
I will not risk being separated from you and left on my own!
Sigh. Fine.
You do realize these are designed for toddlers, right?
Functional yet adorable.

THOUGHTS I HAVE AT THE LIBRARY

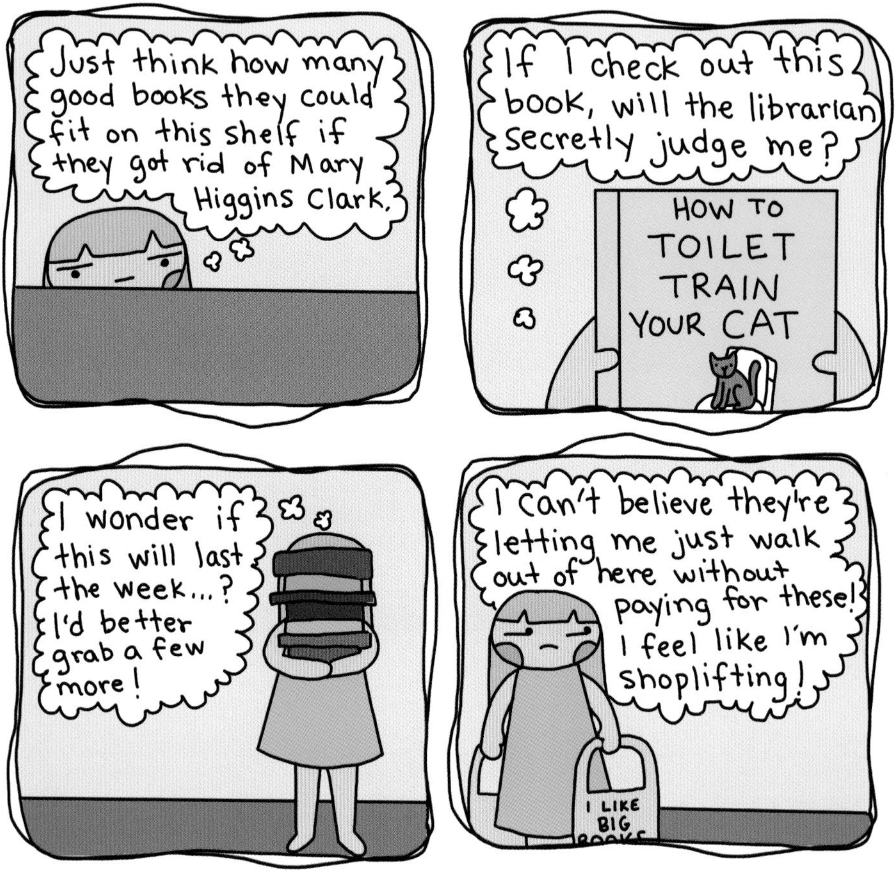

Just think how many good books they could fit on this shelf if they got rid of Mary Higgins Clark.
If I check out this book, will the librarian secretly judge me?
HOW TO TOILET TRAIN YOUR CAT
I wonder if this will last the week...? I'd better grab a few more!
I can't believe they're letting me just walk out of here without paying for these! I feel like I'm shoplifting!
I LIKE BIG

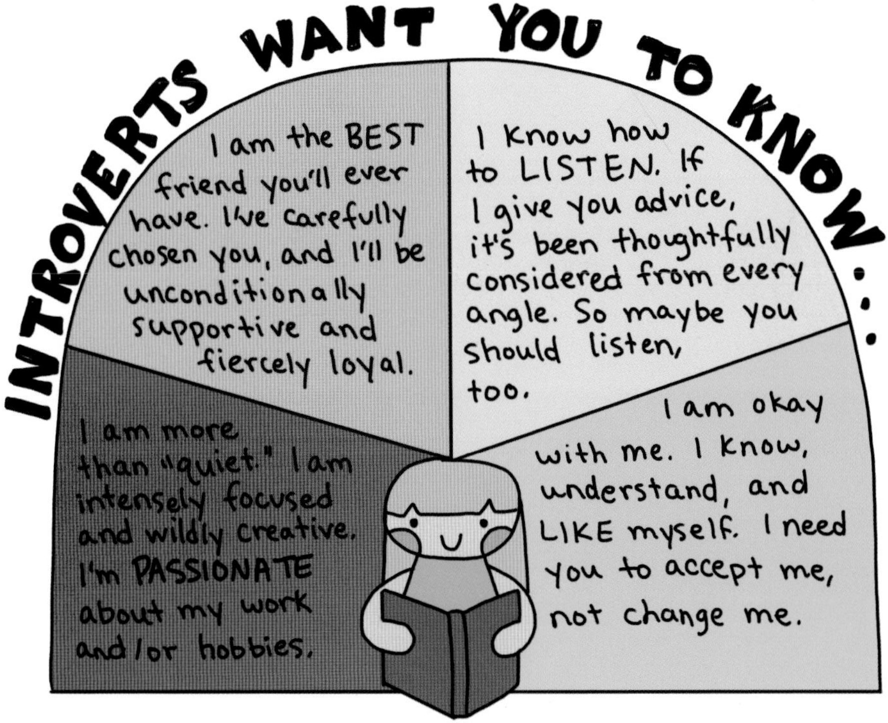
INTROVERTS WANT YOU TO KNOW...
I am the BEST friend you'll ever have. I've carefully chosen you, and I'll be unconditionally supportive and fiercely loyal.
I know how to LISTEN. If I give you advice, it's been thoughtfully considered from every angle. So maybe you should listen, too.
I am more than "quiet." I am intensely focused and wildly creative. I'm PASSIONATE about my work and/or hobbies.
I am okay with me. I know, understand, and LIKE myself. I need you to accept me, not change me.

WHY MY LAPTOP IS MY SOULMATE

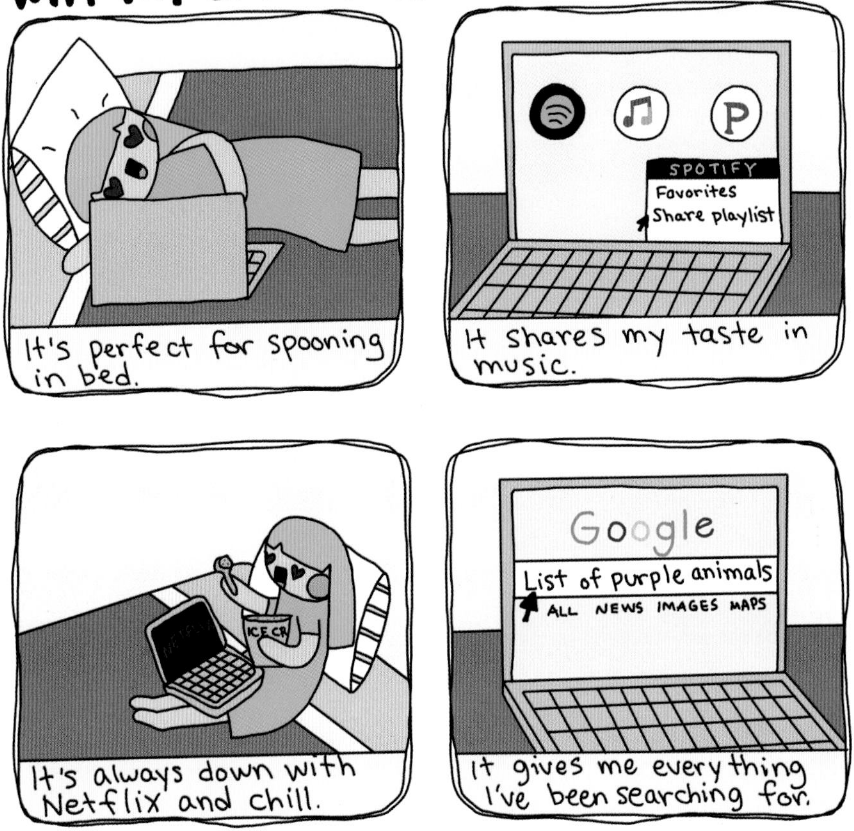
It's perfect for spooning in bed.
SPOTIFY
Favorites
Share playlist
It shares my taste in music.
ICE CR
It's always down with Netflix and chill.
Google
List of purple animals
ALL NEWS IMAGES MAPS
It gives me everything I've been searching for.

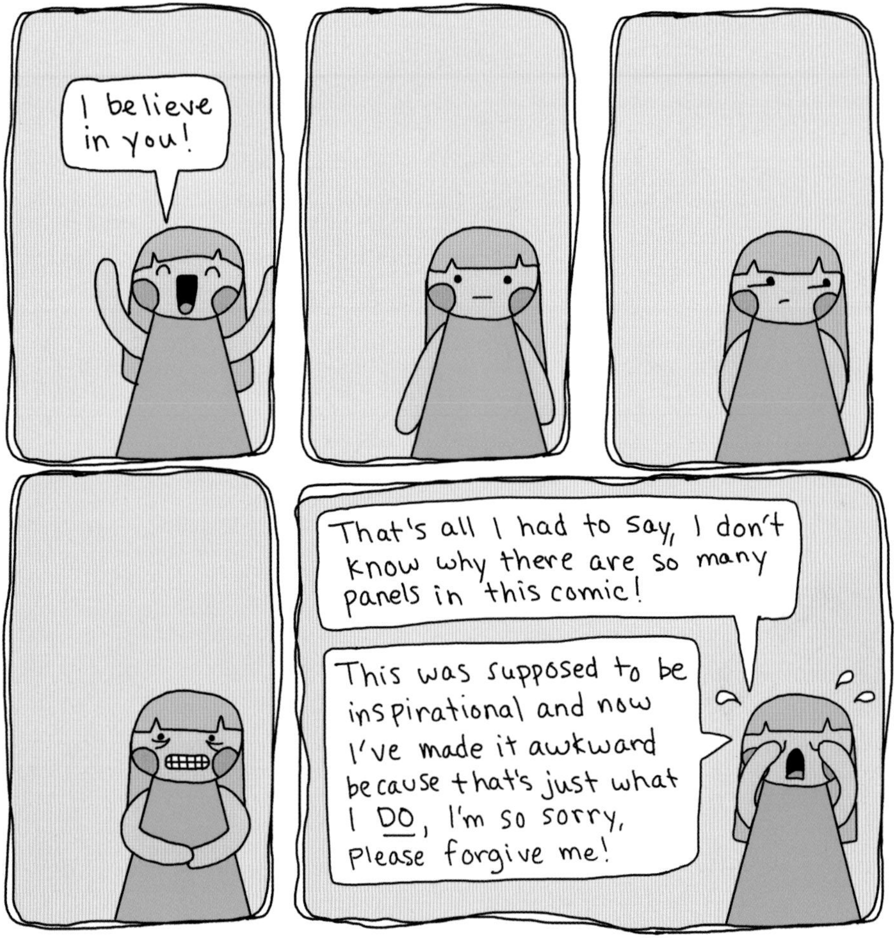
I believe in you!
That's all I had to say, I don't know why there are so many panels in this comic!
This was supposed to be inspirational and now I've made it awkward because that's just what I DO, I'm so sorry, please forgive me!

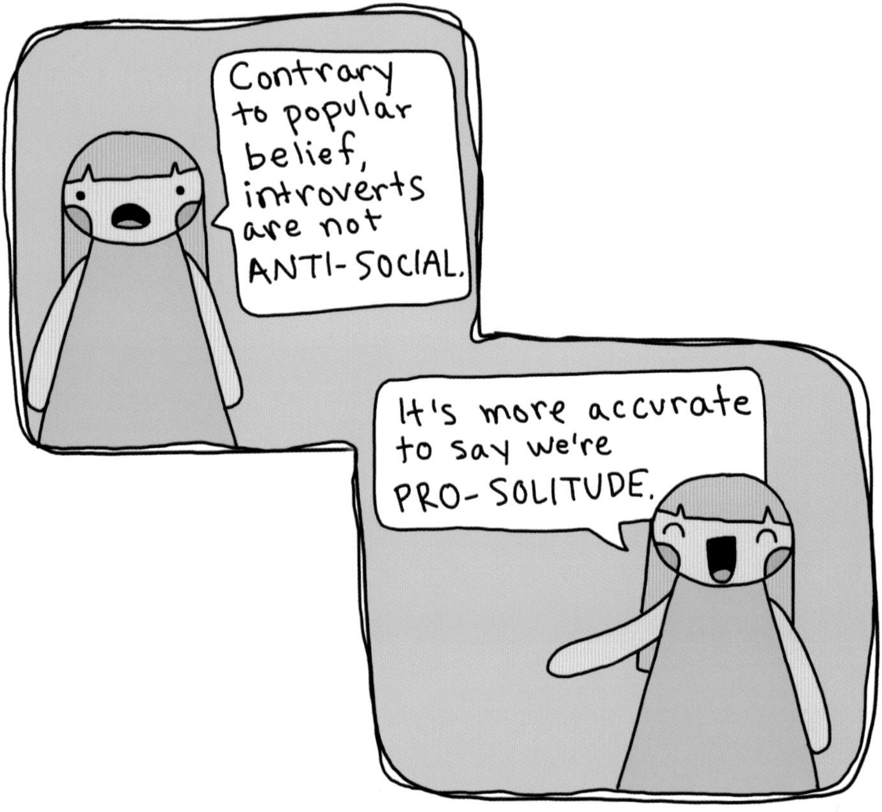
Contrary to popular belief, introverts are not ANTI-SOCIAL.
It's more accurate to say we're PRO-SOLITUDE.

HOW TO TORTURE AN INTROVERT

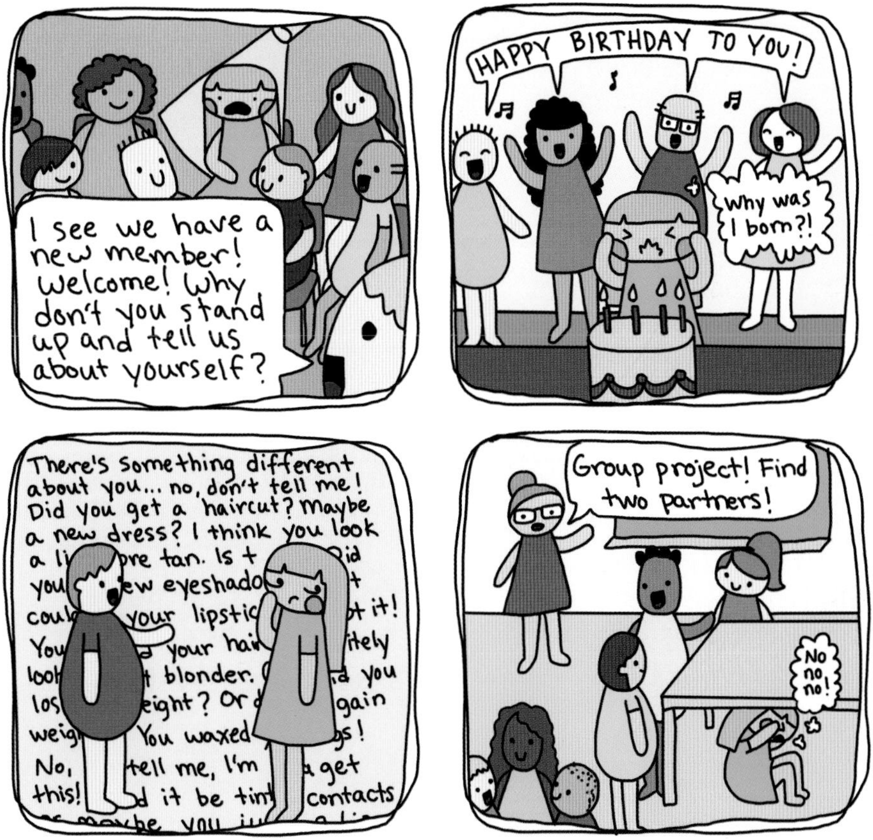
I see we have a new member! Welcome! Why don't you stand up and tell us about yourself?
HAPPY BIRTHDAY TO YOU!
Why was I born?!
There's something different about you... no, don't tell me! Did you get a haircut? Maybe a new dress? I think you look
re tan. Is
ew eyeshado
your lipstic
your hai
blonder.
you
eight? Or
gain
You waxed
No,
tell me, I'm
get
this!
it be
contacts
Group project! Find two partners!
No no no!

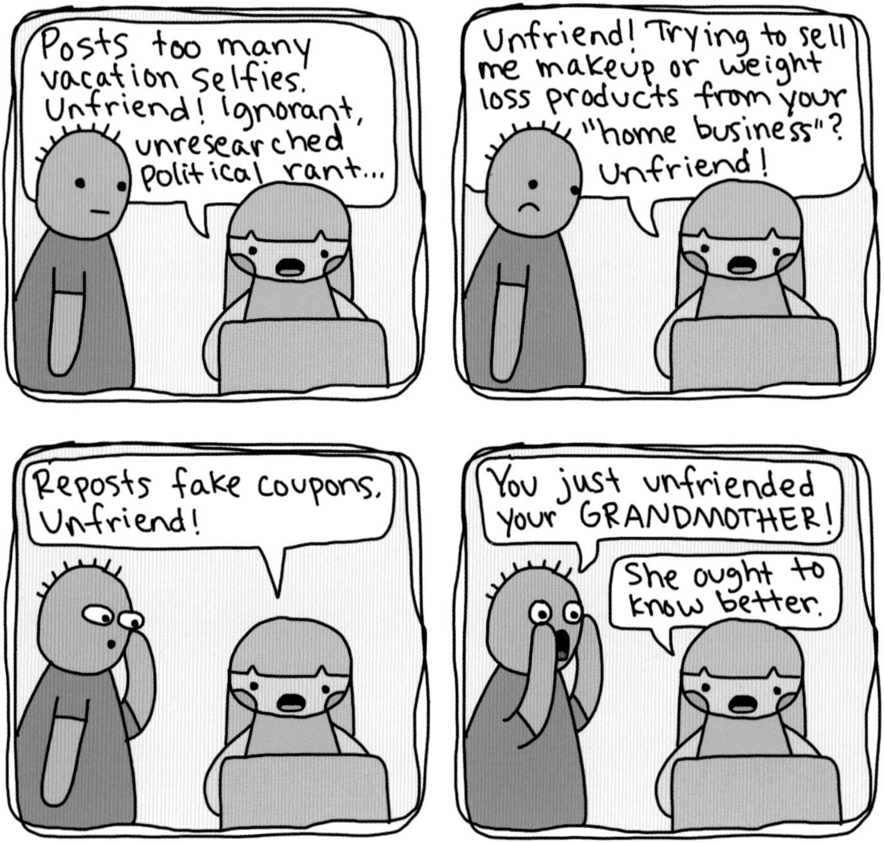
Posts too many vacation selfies. Unfriend! Ignorant, unresearched political rant...
Unfriend! Trying to sell me makeup or weight loss products from your "home business"? Unfriend!
Reposts fake coupons. Unfriend!
You just unfriended your GRANDMOTHER!
She ought to know better.

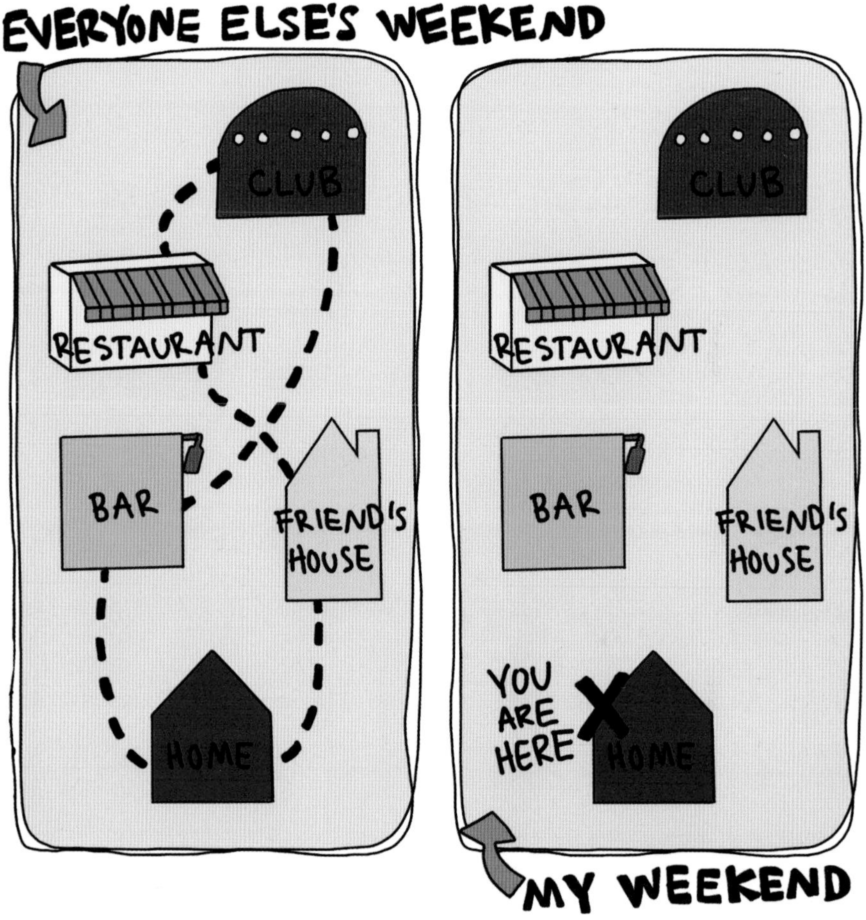
EVERYONE ELSE'S WEEKEND
CLUB
RESTAURANT
BAR
FRIEND'S HOUSE
HOME
CLUB
RESTAURANT
BAR
FRIEND'S HOUSE
YOU ARE HERE
HOME
MY WEEKEND

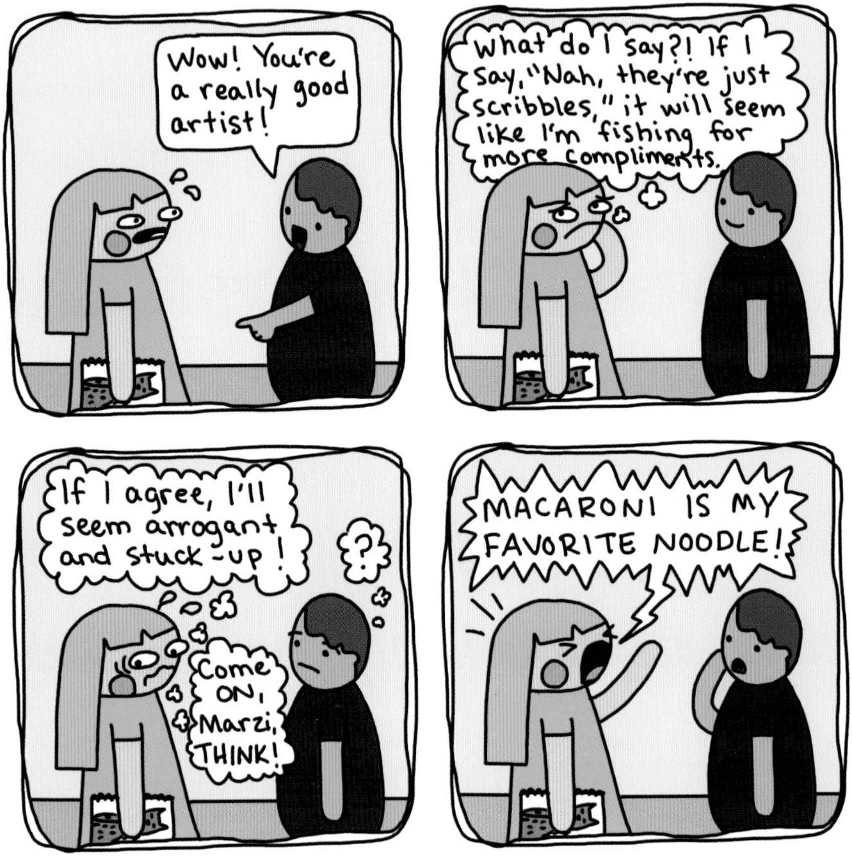
Wow! You're a really good artist!
What do I say?! If I say, "Nah, they're just scribbles," it will seem like I'm fishing for more compliments.
If I agree, I'll seem arrogant and stuck-up!
?
Come ON, Marzi, THINK!
MACARONI IS MY FAVORITE NOODLE!

WHEN YOUR MOUTH BETRAYS YOU

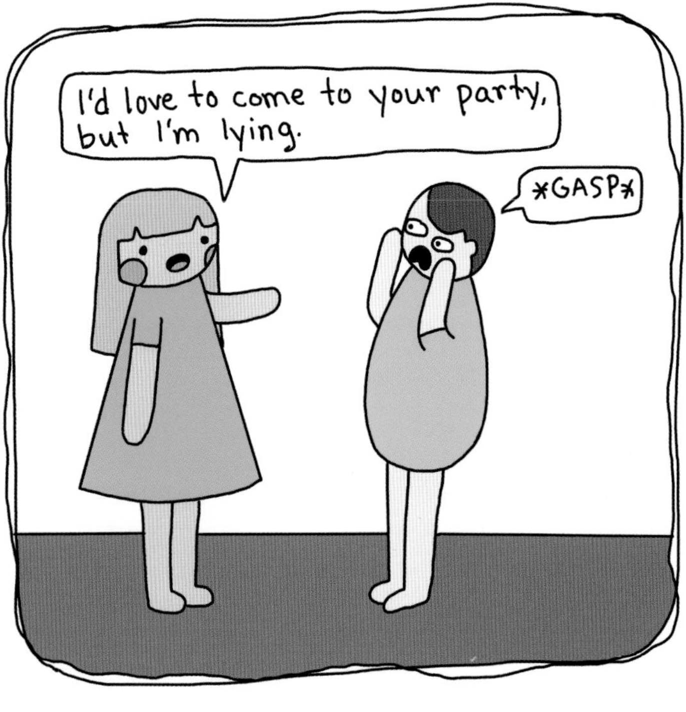
I'd love to come to your party, but I'm lying.
GASP

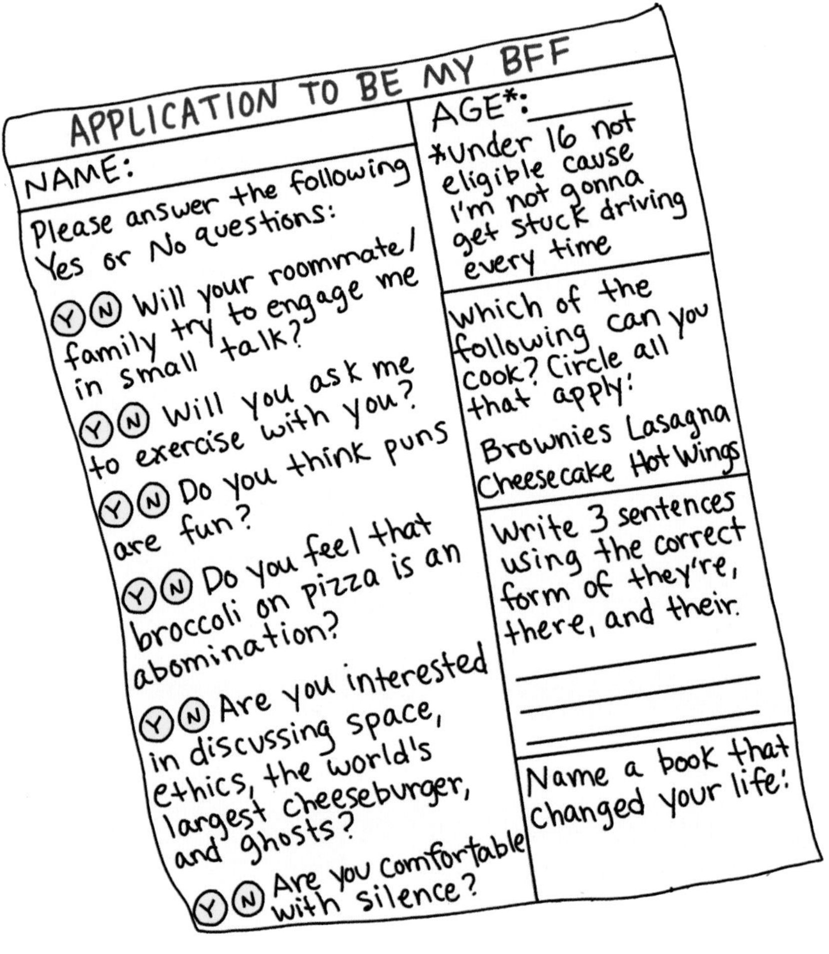
APPLICATION TO BE MY BFF
NAME:
Please answer the following Yes or No questions:
Y N Will your roommate/family try to engage me in small talk?
Y N Will you ask me to exercise with you?
Y N Do you think puns are fun?
Y N Do you feel that broccoli on pizza is an abomination?
Y N Are you interested in discussing space, ethics, the world's largest cheeseburger, and ghosts?
Y N Are you comfortable with silence?
AGE*:
*Under 16 not eligible cause I'm not gonna get stuck driving every time
Which of the following can you cook? Circle all that apply:
Brownies Lasagna
Cheesecake Hot Wings
Write 3 sentences using the correct form of they're, there, and their.
Name a book that changed your life:

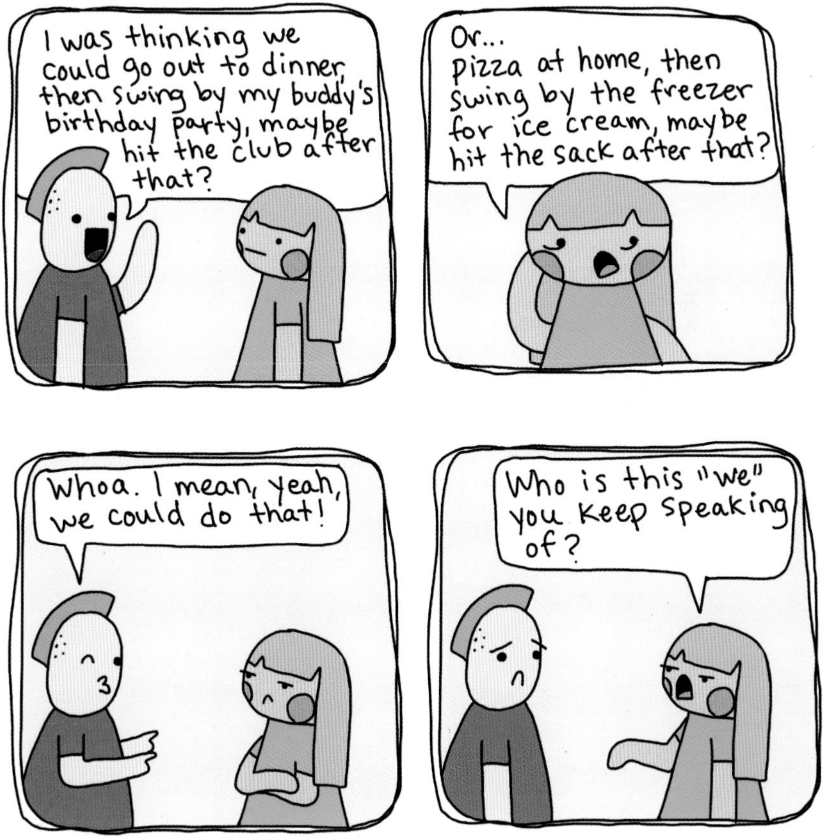
I was thinking we could go out to dinner, then swing by my buddy's birthday party, maybe hit the club after that?
Or... pizza at home, then swing by the freezer for ice cream, maybe hit the sack after that?
Whoa. I mean, yeah, we could do that!
Who is this "we" you keep speaking of?

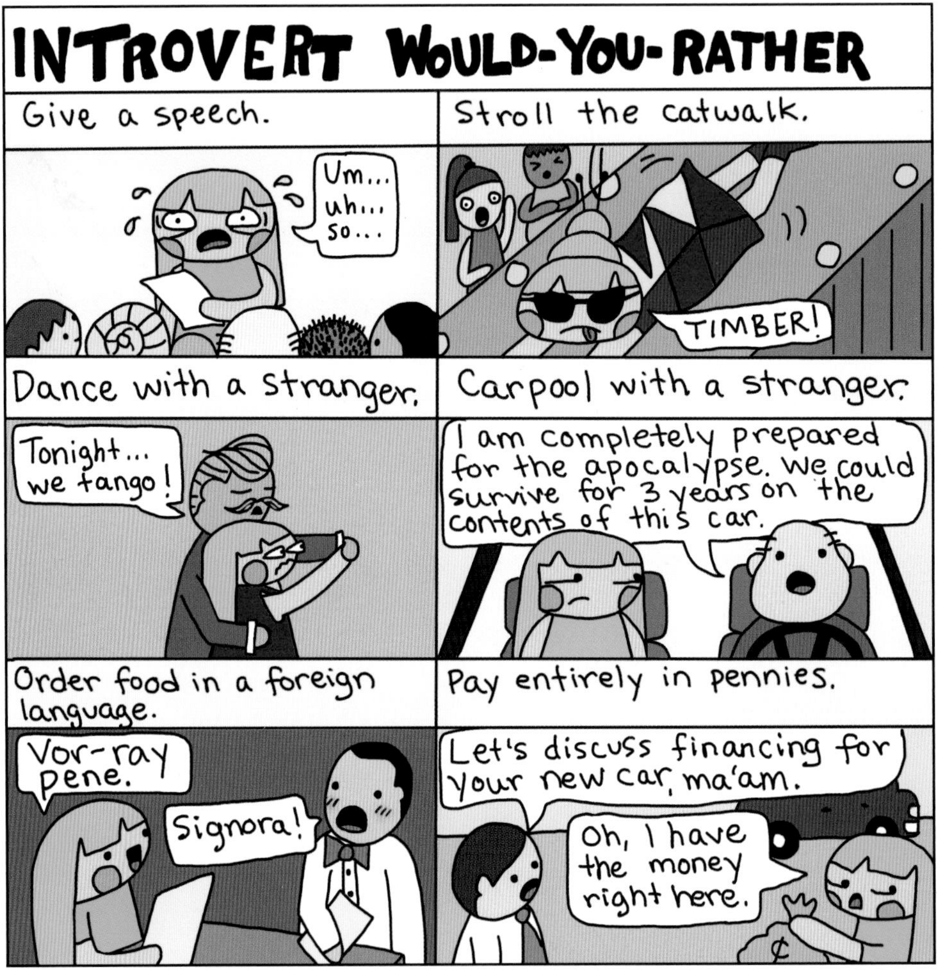
INTROVERT WOULD-YOU-RATHER
Give a speech.
Um... uh... so...
Stroll the catwalk.
TIMBER!
Dance with a stranger.
Tonight... we tango!
Carpool with a stranger.
I am completely prepared for the apocalypse. We could survive for 3 years on the contents of this car.
Order food in a foreign language.
Vor-ray pene.
Signora!
Pay entirely in pennies.
Let's discuss financing for your new car, ma'am.
Oh, I have the money right here.
¢

WHY INTROVERTS ARE QUIET

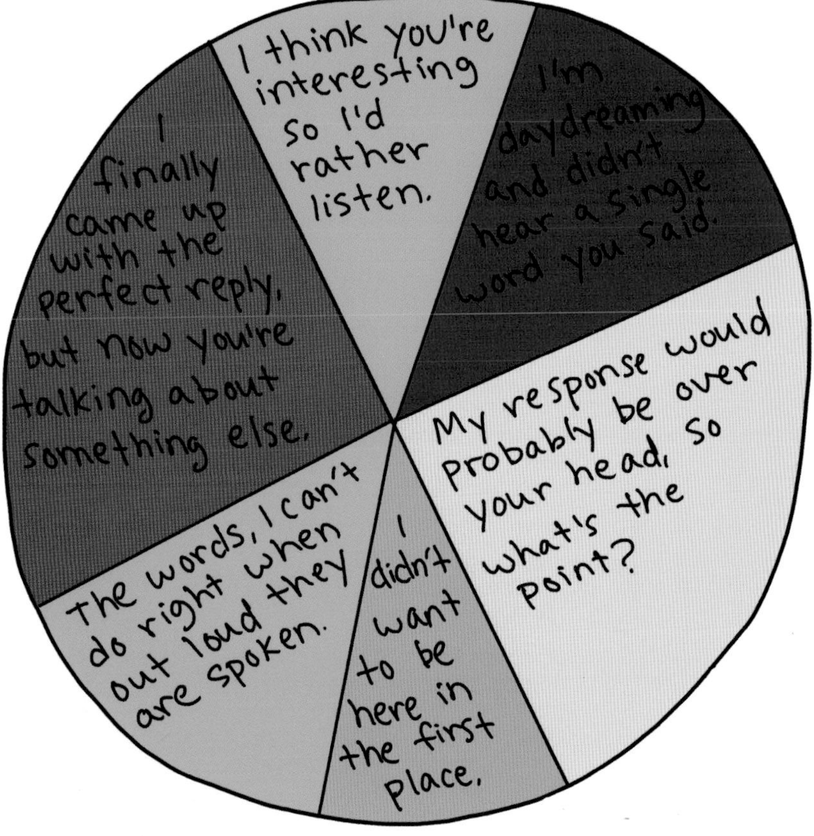

I think you're interesting so I'd rather listen.
I'm daydreaming and didn't hear a single word you said.
My response would probably be over your head, so what's the point?
I didn't want to be here in the first place.
The words, I can't do right when out loud they are spoken.
I finally came up with the perfect reply, but now you're talking about something else.

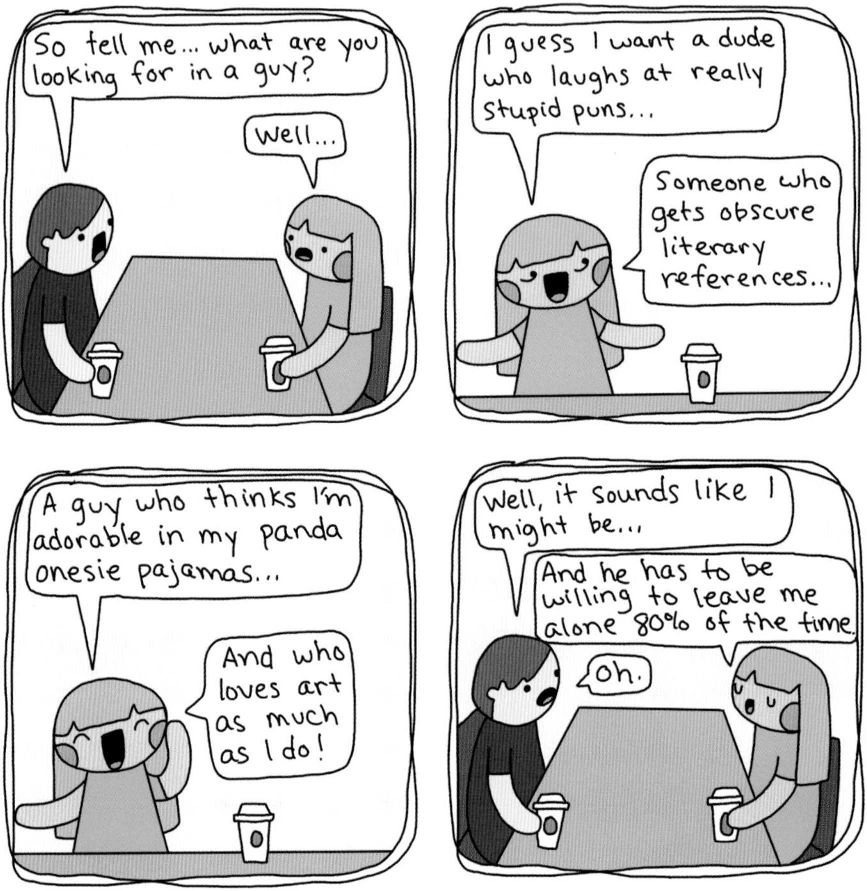
So tell me... what are you looking for in a guy?
Well...
I guess I want a dude who laughs at really stupid puns...
Someone who gets obscure literary references...
A guy who thinks I'm adorable in my panda onesie pajamas...
And who loves art as much as I do!
Well, it sounds like I might be...
And he has to be willing to leave me alone 80% of the time.
Oh.

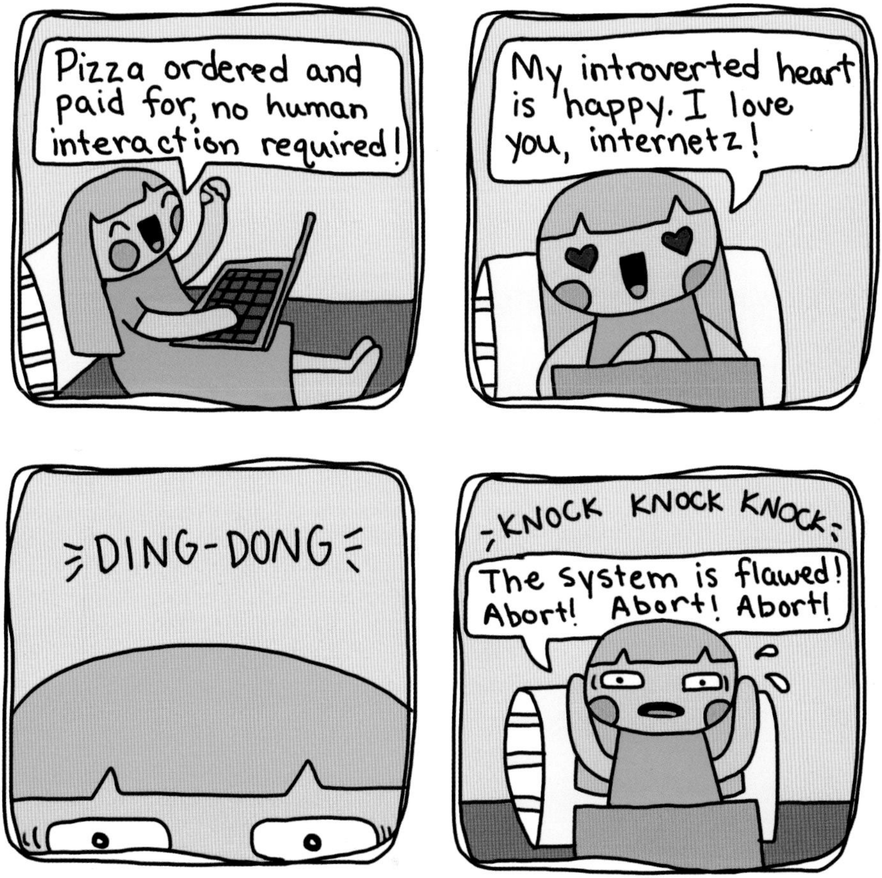
Pizza ordered and paid for, no human interaction required!
My introverted heart is happy. I love you, internetz!
DING-DONG
KNOCK KNOCK KNOCK
The system is flawed! Abort! Abort! Abort!

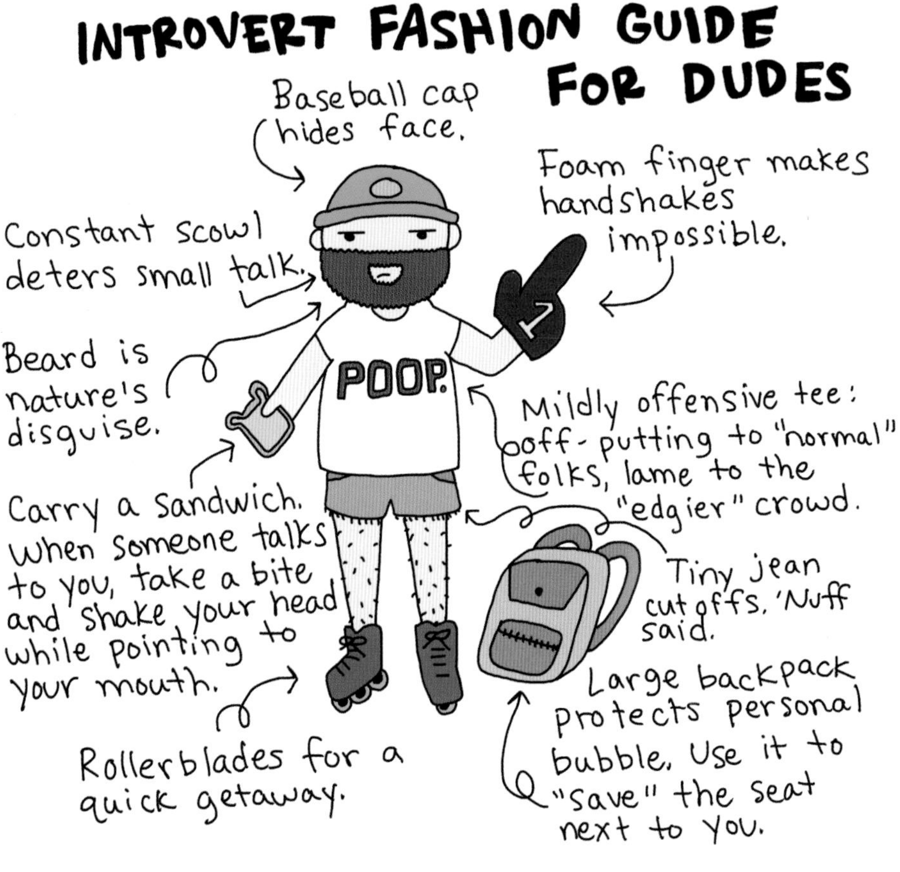
INTROVERT FASHION GUIDE FOR DUDES
Baseball cap hides face.
Foam finger makes handshakes impossible.
Constant scowl deters small talk.
Beard is nature's disguise.
POOP.
1
Mildly offensive tee: off-putting to "normal" folks, lame to the "edgier" crowd.
Carry a sandwich. When someone talks to you, take a bite and shake your head while pointing to your mouth.
Tiny jean cutoffs. 'Nuff said.
Large backpack protects personal bubble. Use it to "save" the seat next to you.
Rollerblades for a quick getaway.

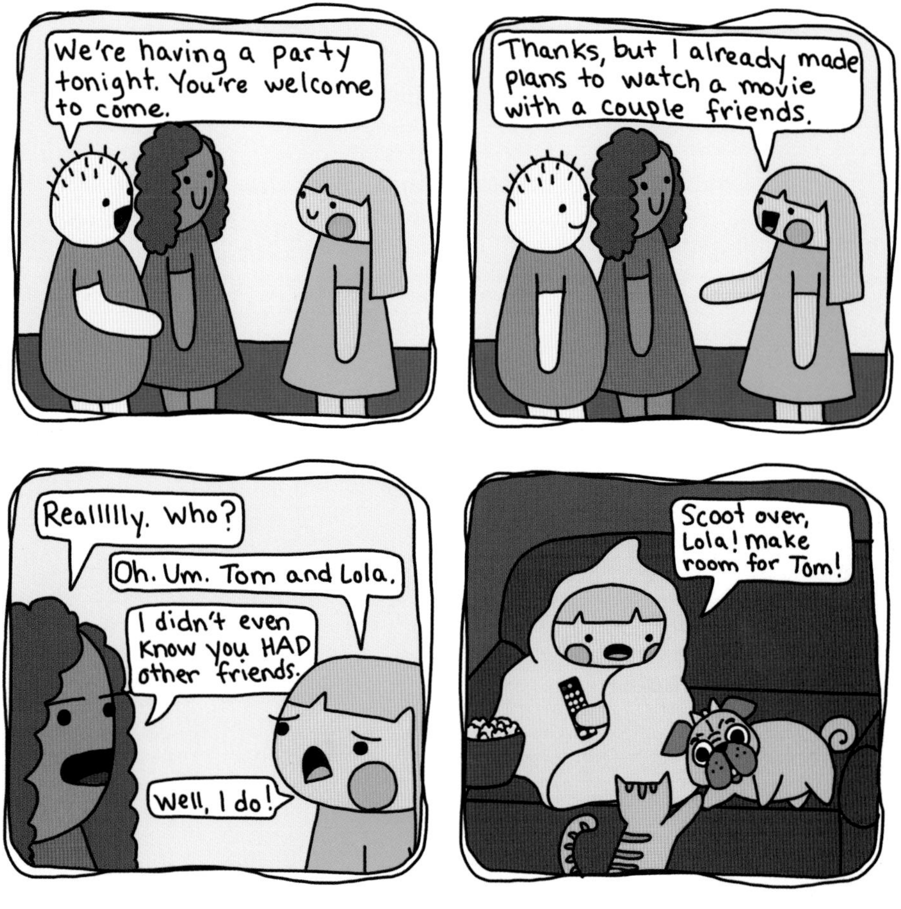
We're having a party tonight. You're welcome to come.
Thanks, but I already made plans to watch a movie with a couple friends.
Reallllly. Who?
Oh. Um. Tom and Lola.
I didn't even know you HAD other friends.
Well, I do!
Scoot over, Lola! make room for Tom!

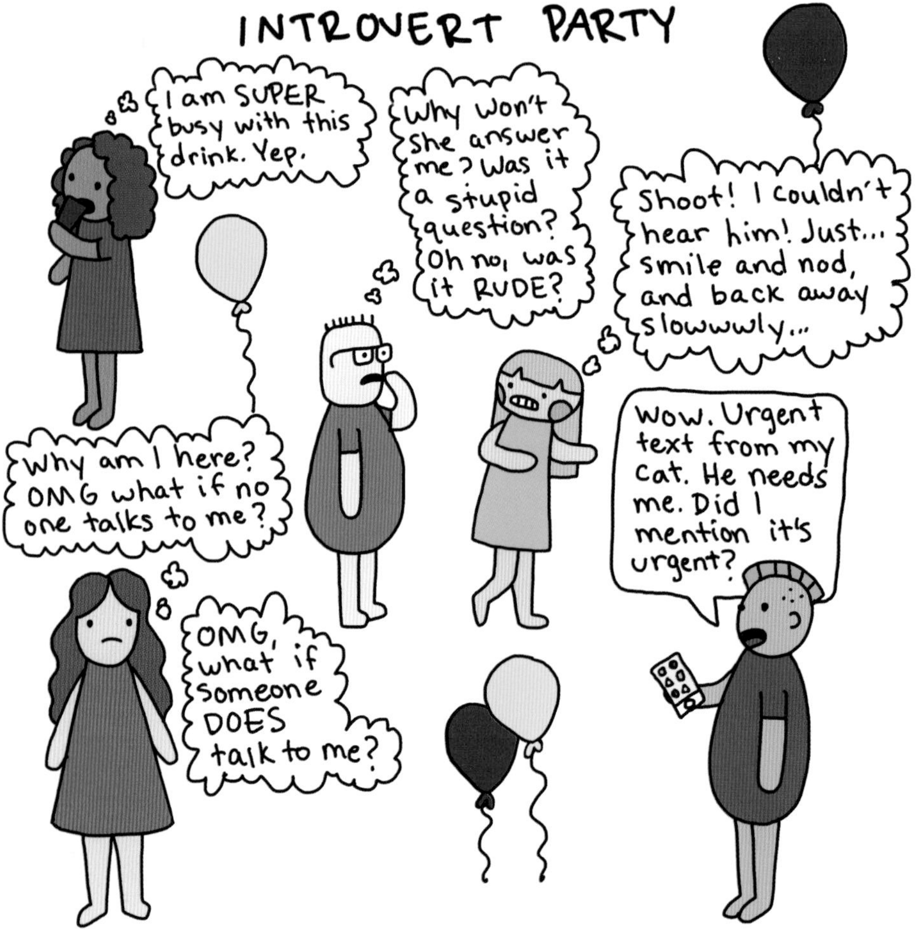
INTROVERT PARTY
I am SUPER busy with this drink. Yep.
Why won't she answer me? Was it a stupid question? Oh no, was it RUDE?
Shoot! I couldn't hear him! Just... smile and nod, and back away slowwwly...
Why am I here? OMG what if no one talks to me?
OMG, what if someone DOES talk to me?
Wow. Urgent text from my cat. He needs me. Did I mention it's urgent?

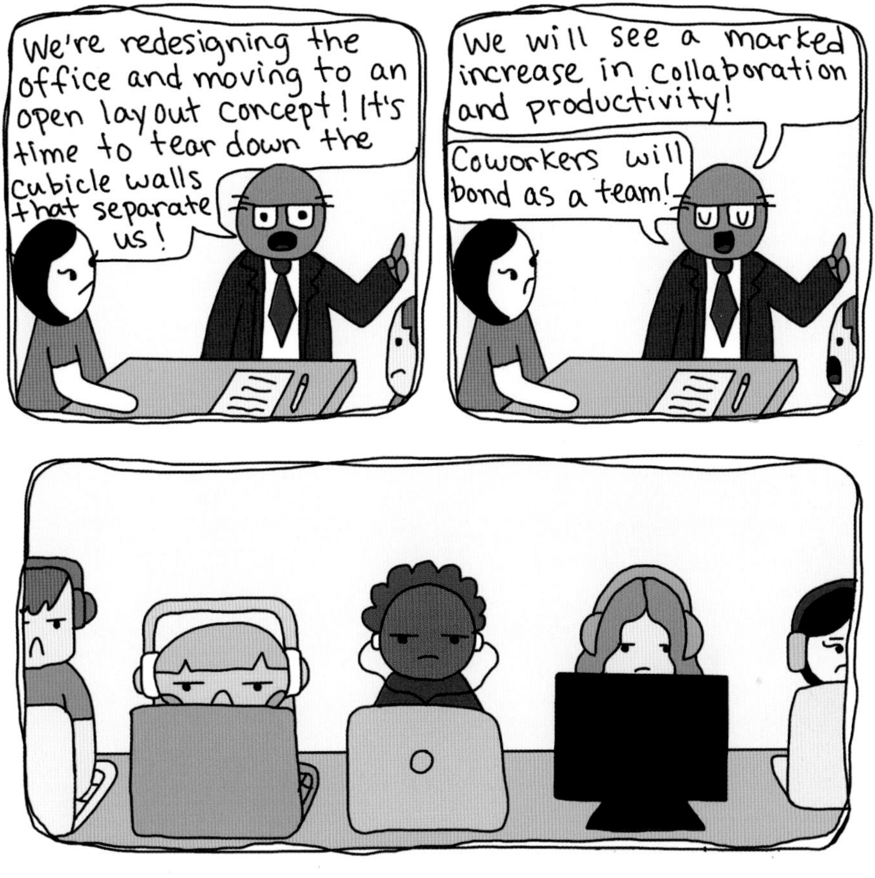
We're redesigning the office and moving to an open layout concept! It's time to tear down the cubicle walls that separate us!
We will see a marked increase in collaboration and productivity!
Coworkers will bond as a team!

REASONS TO ♥ THE HOLIDAYS

EXTROVERTS	INTROVERTS
Shopping at stores decked out for the holidays	Christmas shopping online
Peppermint mocha coffee dates →	Homemade hot chocolate with baby marshmallows
Cute boots	Fuzzy slippers
Christmas parties	Reading in the glow of the Christmas tree
Snowball fights	Quiet walks in the snow
Going Christmas caroling ♪ ♩	Listening to Christmas music while sipping cider

WHY I HATE THE MALL

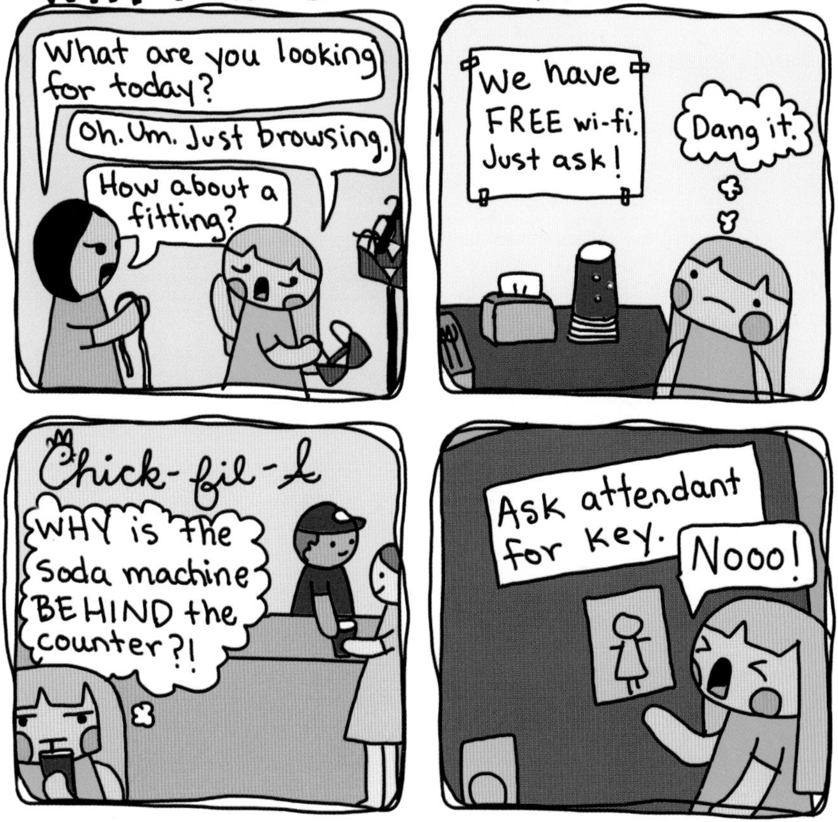
What are you looking for today?
Oh. Um. Just browsing.
How about a fitting?
We have FREE wi-fi. Just ask!
Dang it.
Chick-fil-A
WHY is the soda machine BEHIND the counter?!
Ask attendant for key.
Nooo!

MY TALENTS

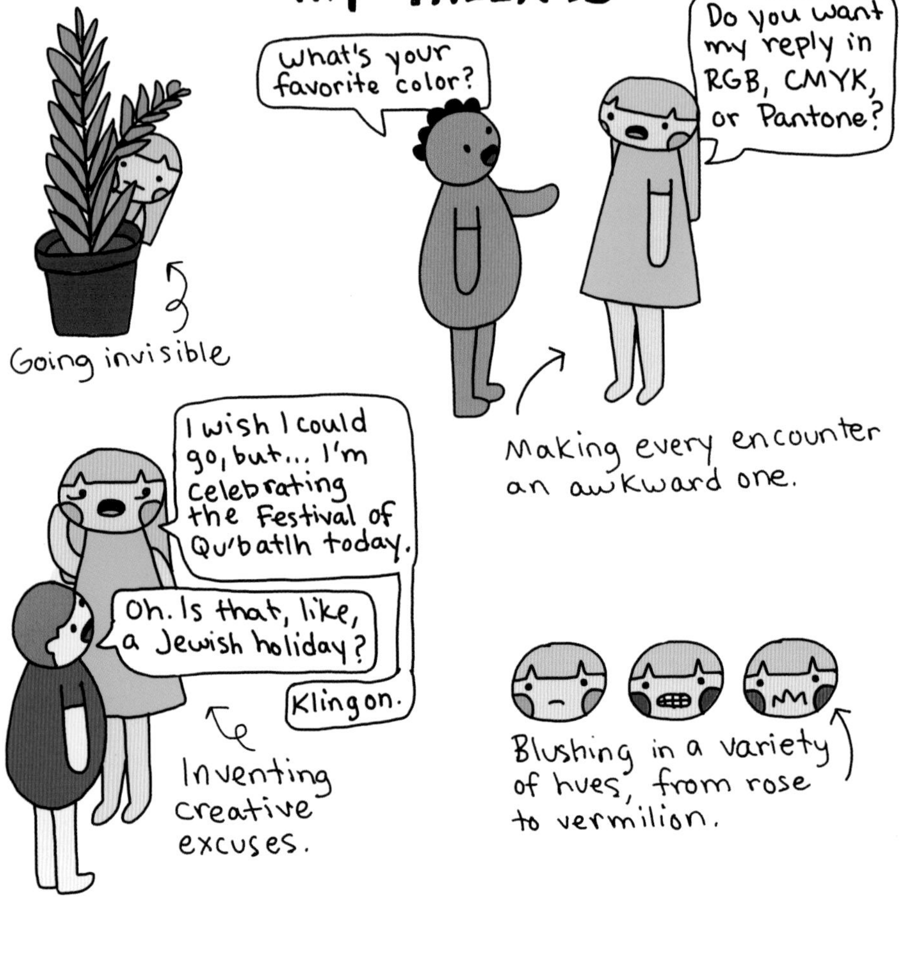
Going invisible
What's your favorite color?
Do you want my reply in RGB, CMYK, or Pantone?
Making every encounter an awkward one.
I wish I could go, but... I'm celebrating the Festival of Qu'batlh today.
Oh. Is that, like, a Jewish holiday?
Klingon.
Inventing creative excuses.
Blushing in a variety of hues, from rose to vermilion.

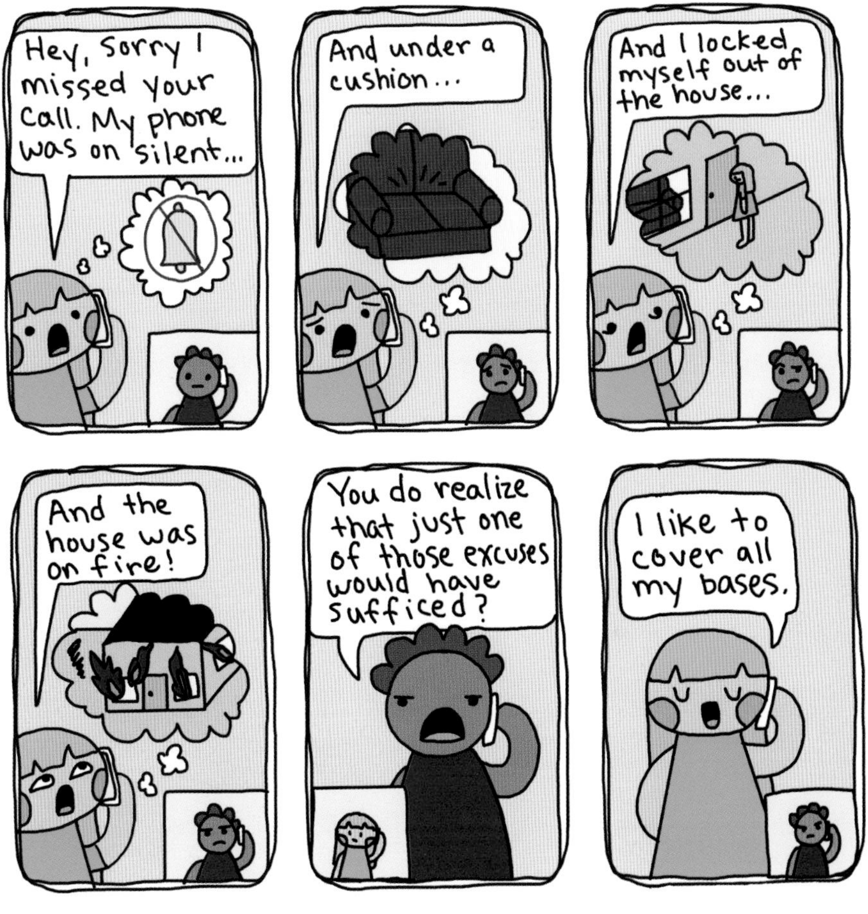
Hey, Sorry! missed your call. My phone was on silent...
And under a cushion...
And I locked myself out of the house...
And the house was on fire!
You do realize that just one of those excuses would have sufficed?
I like to cover all my bases.

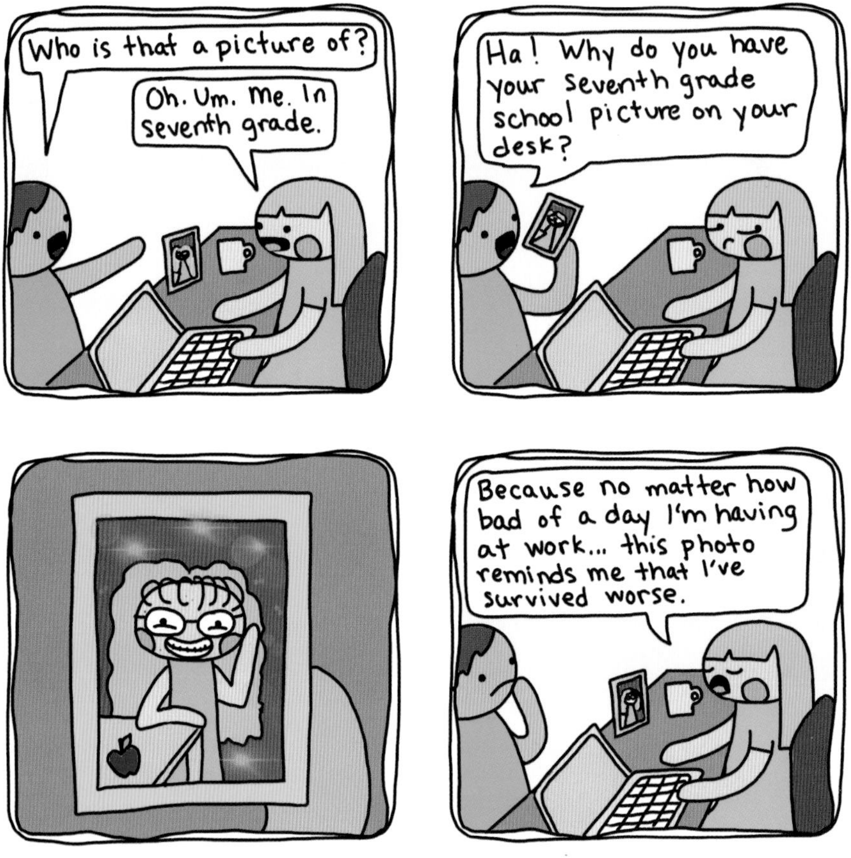
Who is that a picture of?
Oh. Um. Me. In seventh grade.
Ha! Why do you have your seventh grade school picture on your desk?
Because no matter how bad of a day I'm having at work... this photo reminds me that I've survived worse.

WHEN YOU MAKE A

NEW BFF ONLINE

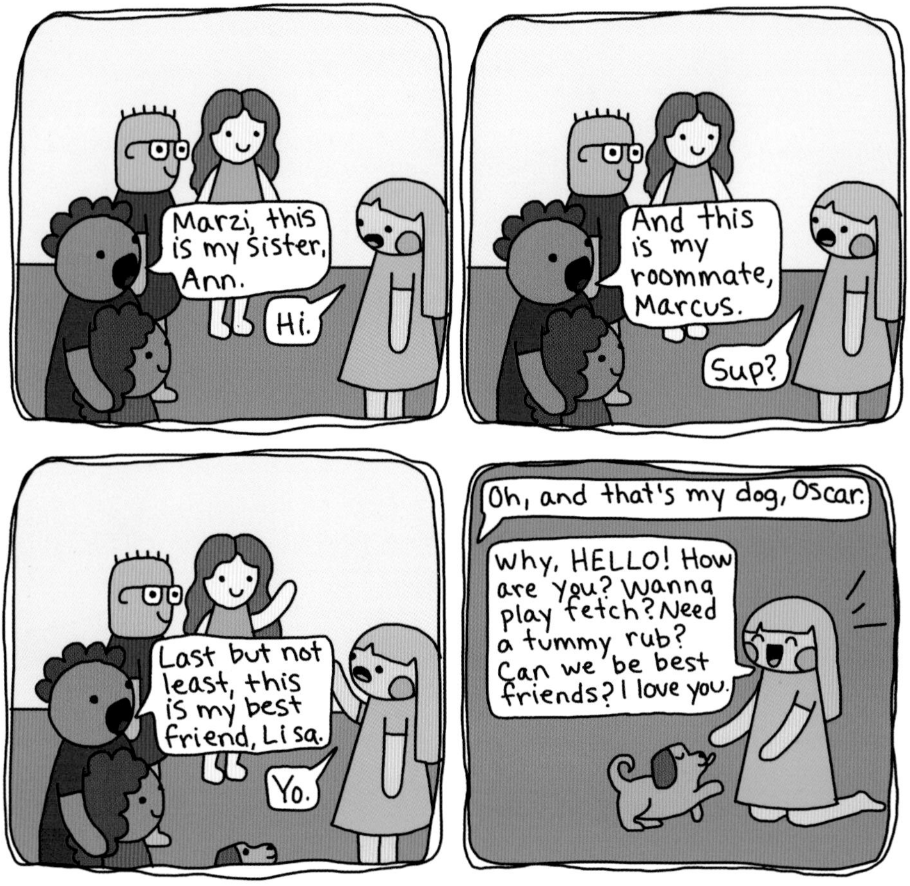
Marzi, this is my sister, Ann.
Hi.
And this is my roommate, Marcus.
Sup?
Last but not least, this is my best friend, Lisa.
Yo.
Oh, and that's my dog, Oscar.
Why, HELLO! How are you? Wanna play fetch? Need a tummy rub? Can we be best friends? I love you.

PEOPLE AS PLANTS

EXTROVERT

Colorful and hard to get rid of. Most often found in groups.

AMBIVERT

Lovely and sweet most of the time, but can also be unexpectedly thorny.

INTROVERT

Hoards life-sustaining water within. Stands alone; don't get too close!

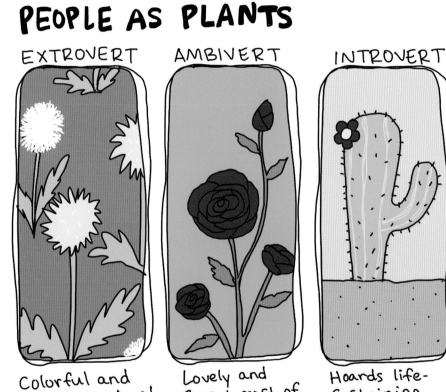

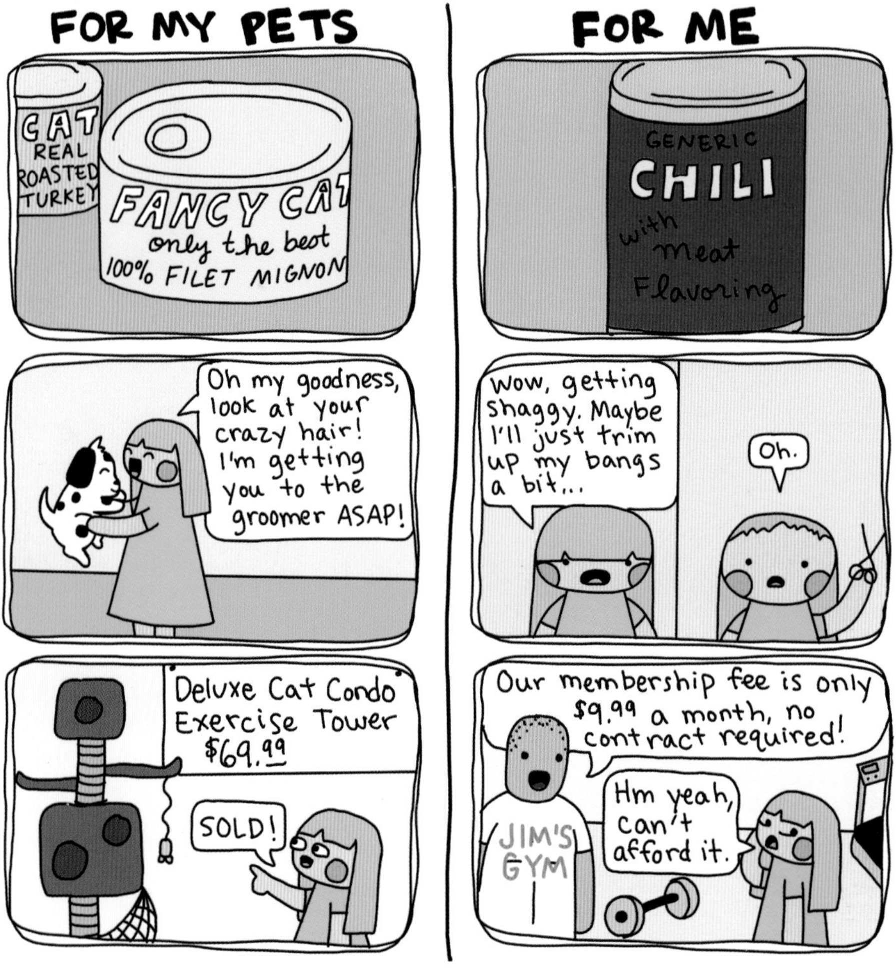
FOR MY PETS
FOR ME
CAT REAL ROASTED TURKEY
FANCY CAT only the best 100% FILET MIGNON
GENERIC CHILI with meat Flavoring
Oh my goodness, look at your crazy hair! I'm getting you to the groomer ASAP!
Wow, getting shaggy. Maybe I'll just trim up my bangs a bit...
Oh.
Deluxe Cat Condo Exercise Tower $69.99
SOLD!
Our membership fee is only $9.99 a month, no contract required!
JIM'S GYM
Hm yeah, can't afford it.

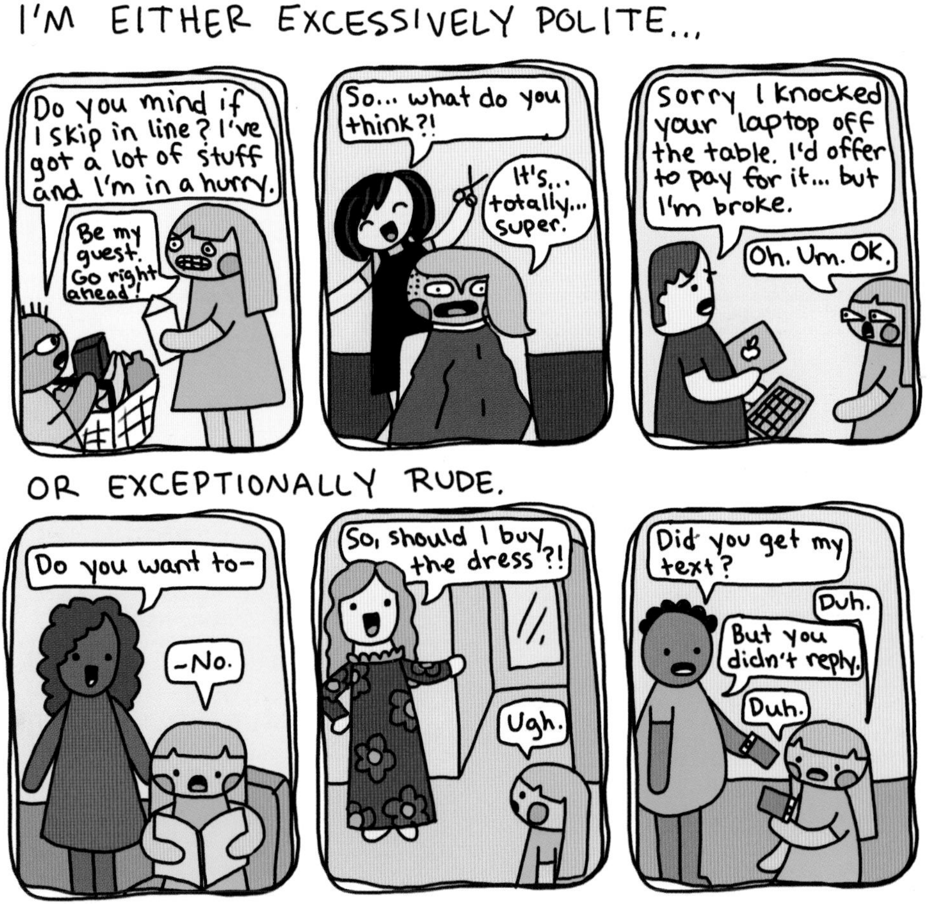
I'M EITHER EXCESSIVELY POLITE...
Do you mind if I skip in line? I've got a lot of stuff and I'm in a hurry.
Be my guest. Go right ahead!
So... what do you think?!
It's... totally... super.
Sorry I knocked your laptop off the table. I'd offer to pay for it... but I'm broke.
Oh. Um. OK.
OR EXCEPTIONALLY RUDE.
Do you want to-
-No.
So, should I buy the dress?!
Ugh.
Did you get my text?
Duh.
But you didn't reply.
Duh.

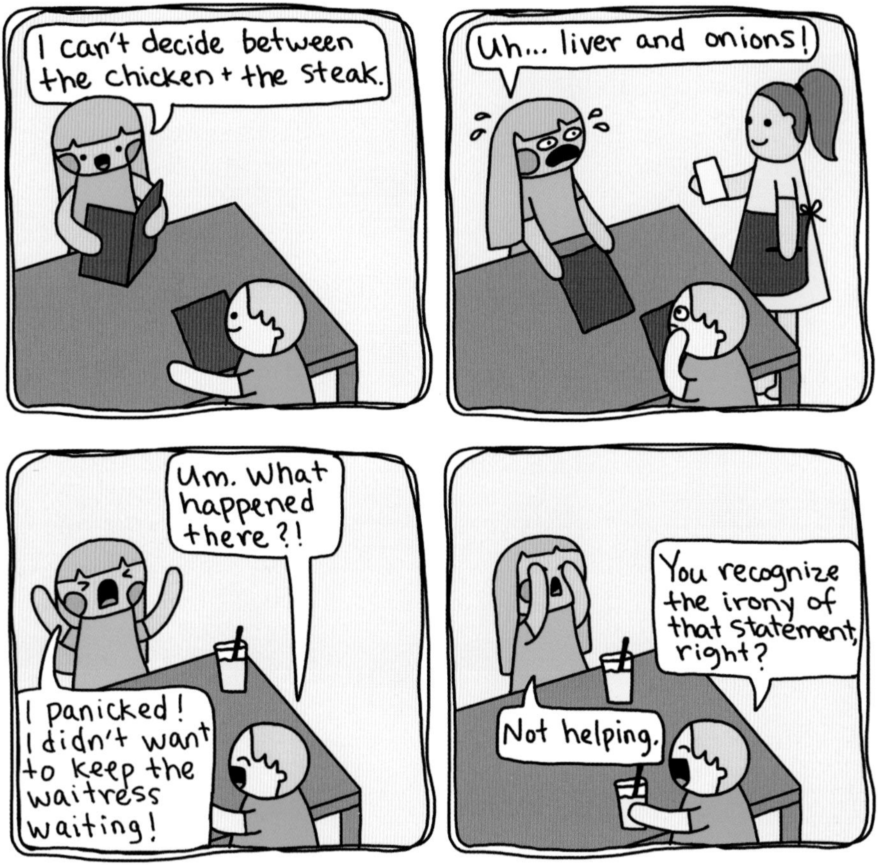
I can't decide between the chicken + the steak.
Uh... liver and onions!
Um. What happened there?!
I panicked! I didn't want to keep the waitress waiting!
You recognize the irony of that statement, right?
Not helping.

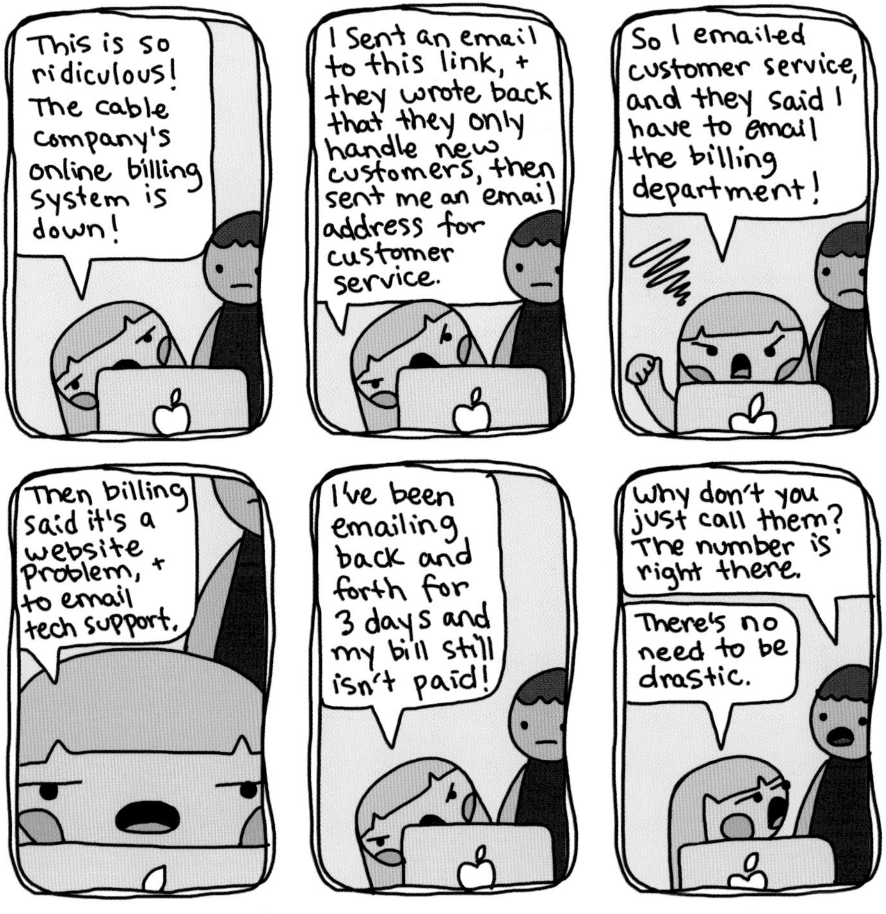
This is so ridiculous! The cable company's online billing system is down!
I Sent an email to this link, + they wrote back that they only handle new customers, then sent me an email address for customer service.
So I emailed customer service, and they said I have to email the billing department!
Then billing said it's a website problem, + to email tech support.
I've been emailing back and forth for 3 days and my bill still isn't paid!
Why don't you just call them? The number is right there.
There's no need to be drastic.

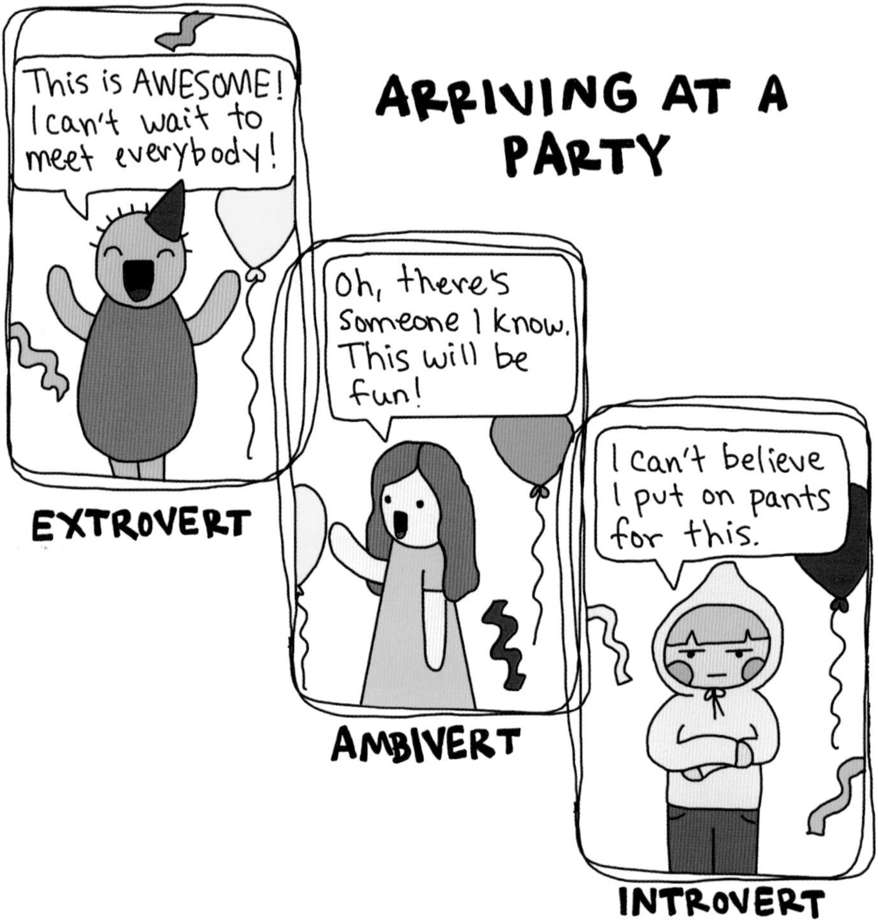
ARRIVING AT A PARTY
This is AWESOME! I can't wait to meet everybody!
EXTROVERT
Oh, there's someone I know. This will be fun!
AMBIVERT
I can't believe I put on pants for this.
INTROVERT

ACTUAL REASONS I'VE BEEN LATE

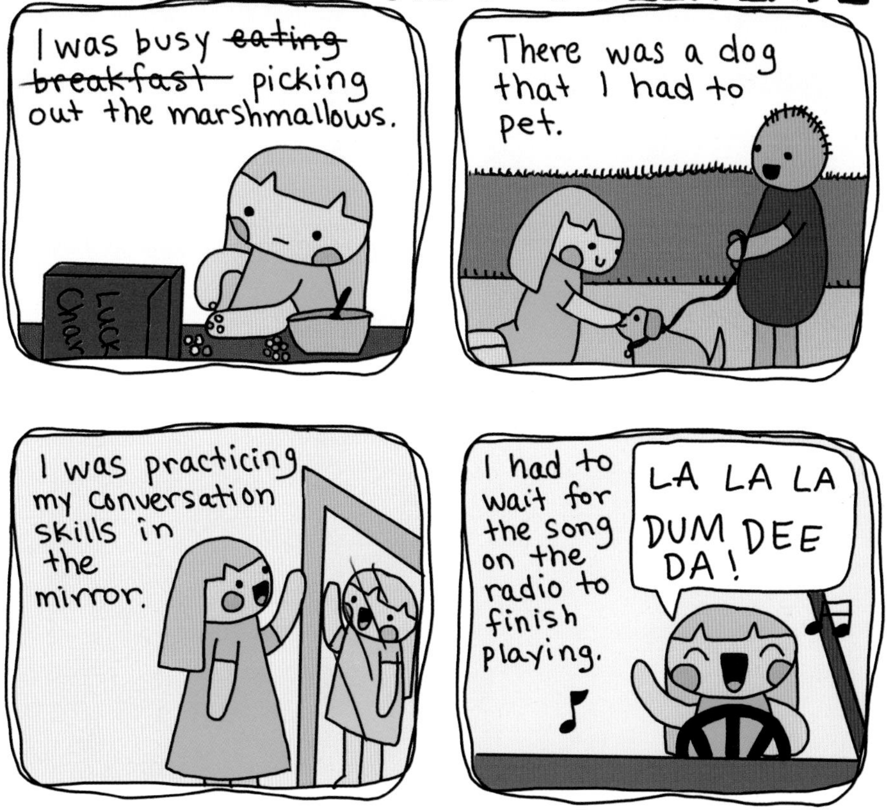
I was busy ~~eating breakfast~~ picking out the marshmallows.
LUCK Char
There was a dog that I had to pet.
I was practicing my conversation skills in the mirror.
I had to wait for the song on the radio to finish playing.
LA LA LA DUM DEE DA!

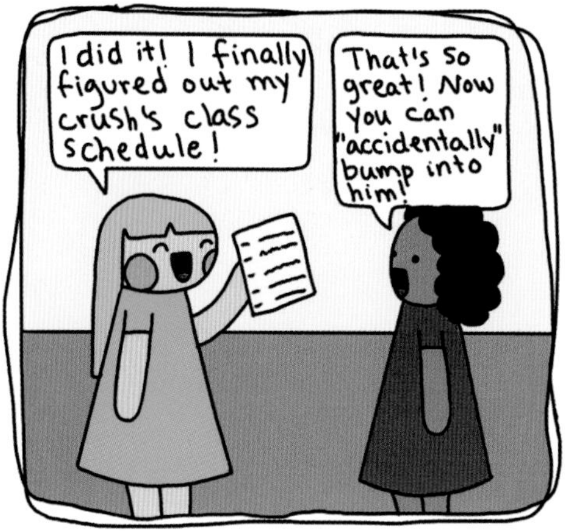
I did it! I finally figured out my crush's class schedule!
That's so great! Now you can "accidentally" bump into him!

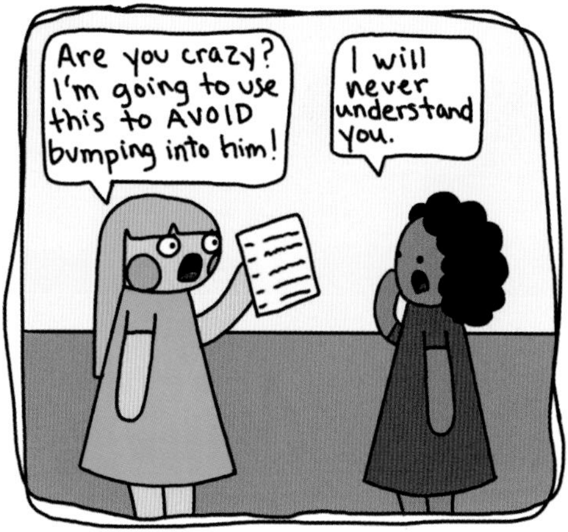
Are you crazy? I'm going to use this to AVOID bumping into him!
I will never understand you.

HOW TO GAIN MY TRUST

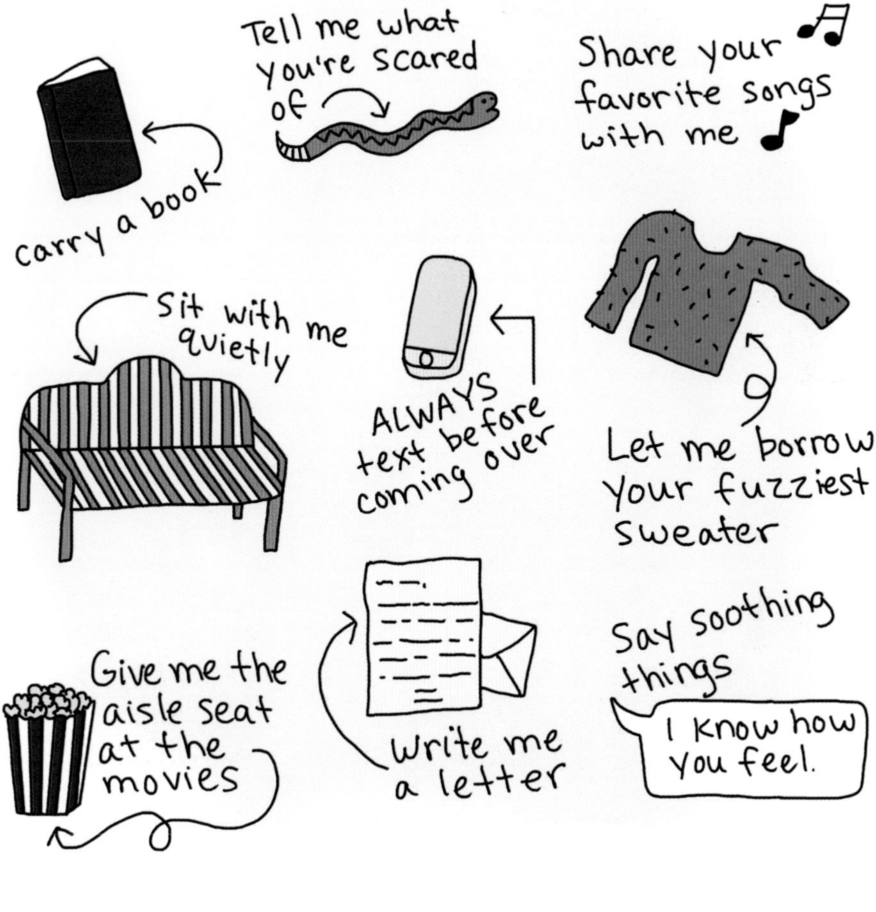
Carry a book
Tell me what you're scared of
Share your favorite songs with me
Sit with me quietly
ALWAYS text before coming over
Let me borrow your fuzziest sweater
Give me the aisle seat at the movies
Write me a letter
Say soothing things
I know how you feel.

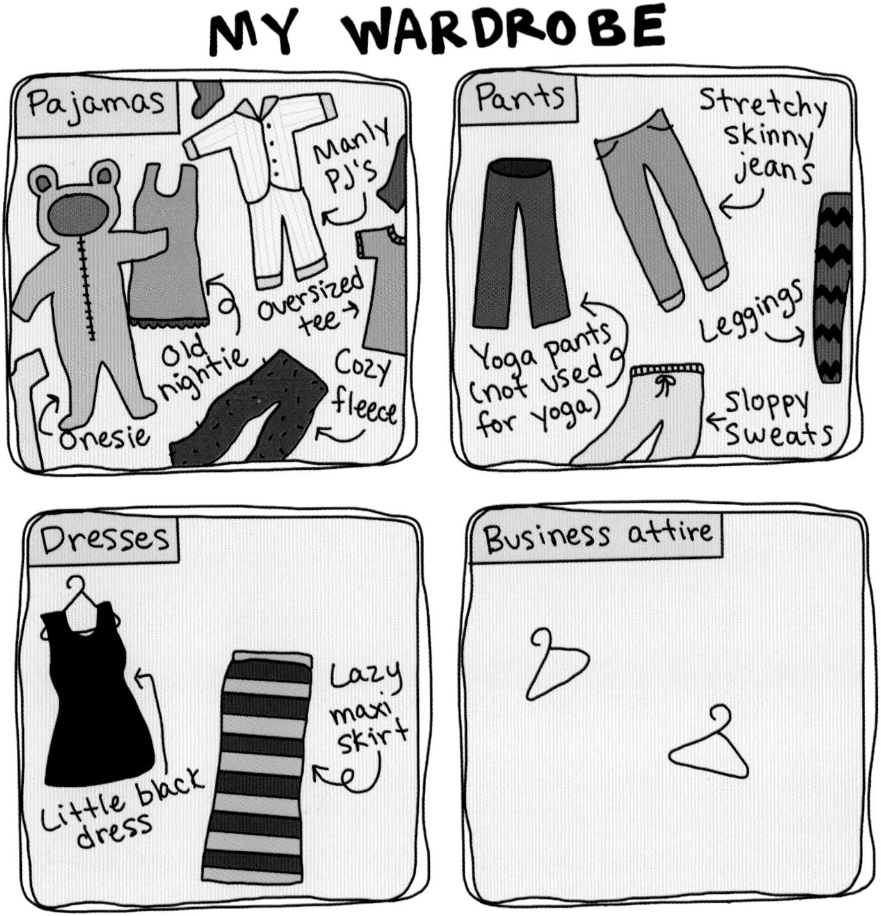
MY WARDROBE
Pajamas
Manly PJ's
Onesie
Old nightie
oversized tee
Cozy fleece
Pants
Stretchy skinny jeans
Yoga pants (not used for yoga)
Leggings
Sloppy Sweats
Dresses
Little black dress
Lazy maxi skirt
Business attire

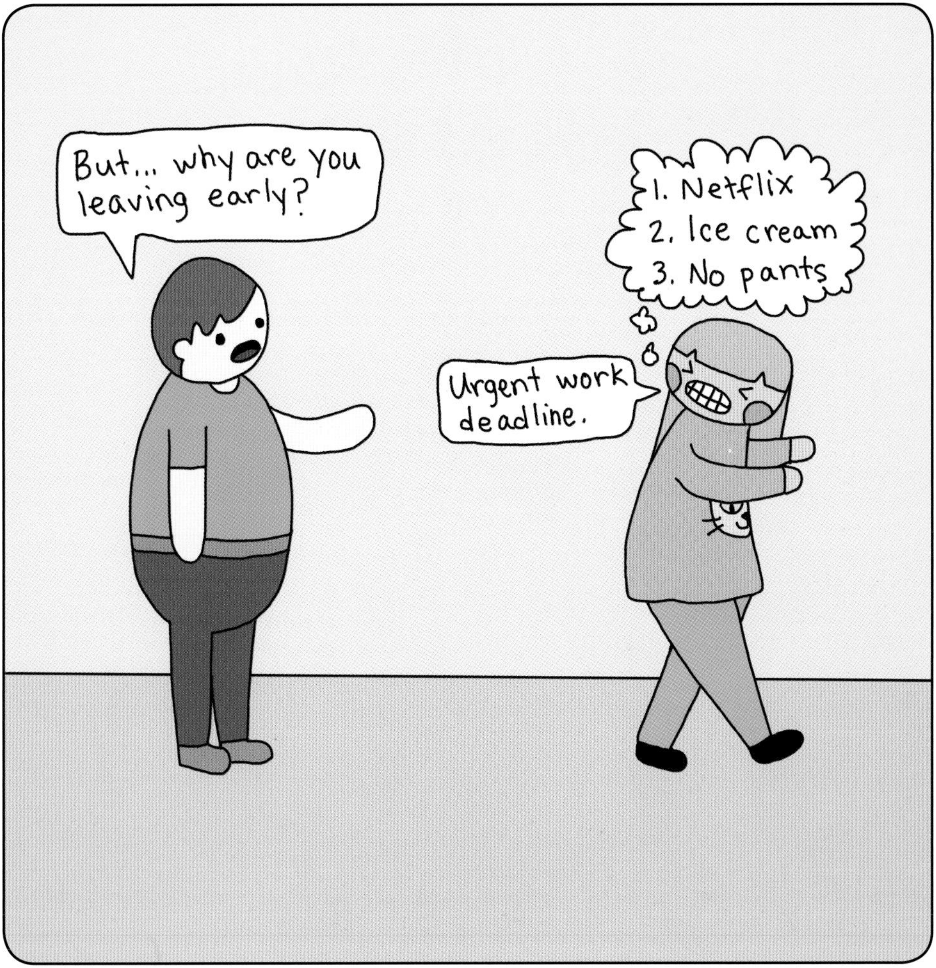
But... why are you leaving early?
1. Netflix
2. Ice cream
3. No pants
Urgent work deadline.

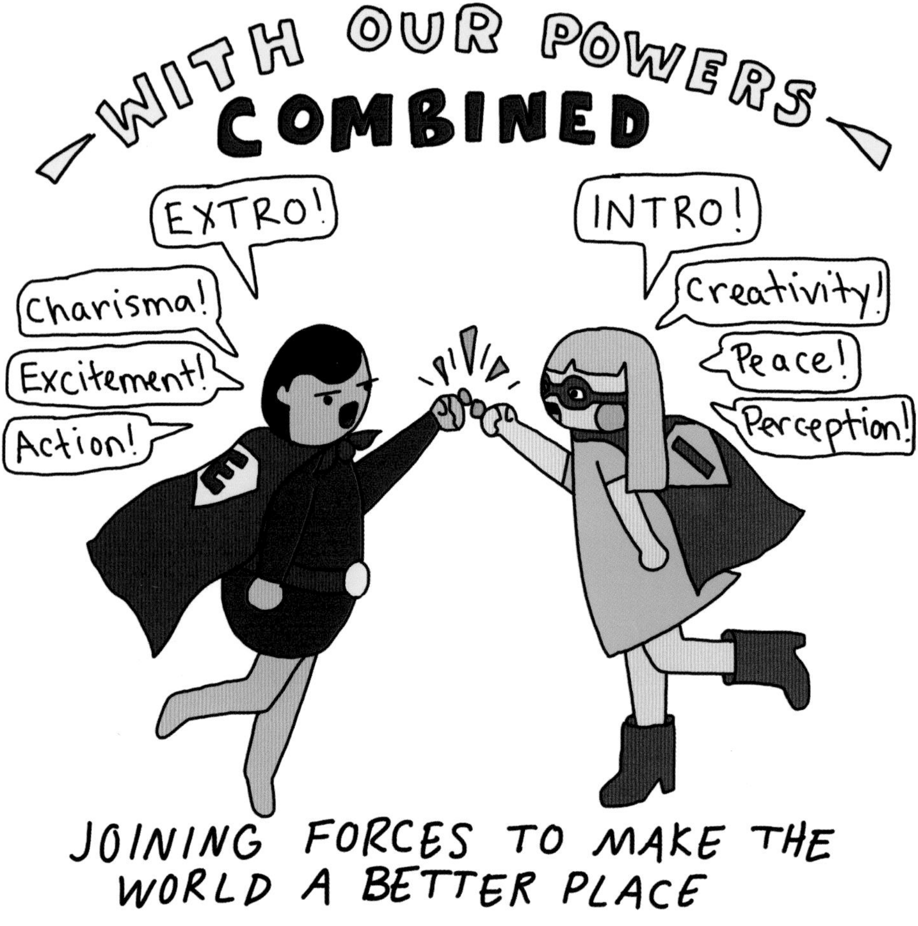
WITH OUR POWERS
COMBINED
EXTRO!
Charisma!
Excitement!
Action!
E
INTRO!
Creativity!
Peace!
Perception!
I
JOINING FORCES TO MAKE THE WORLD A BETTER PLACE

THINGS TO SAY WHEN YOU DON'T KNOW WHAT TO SAY

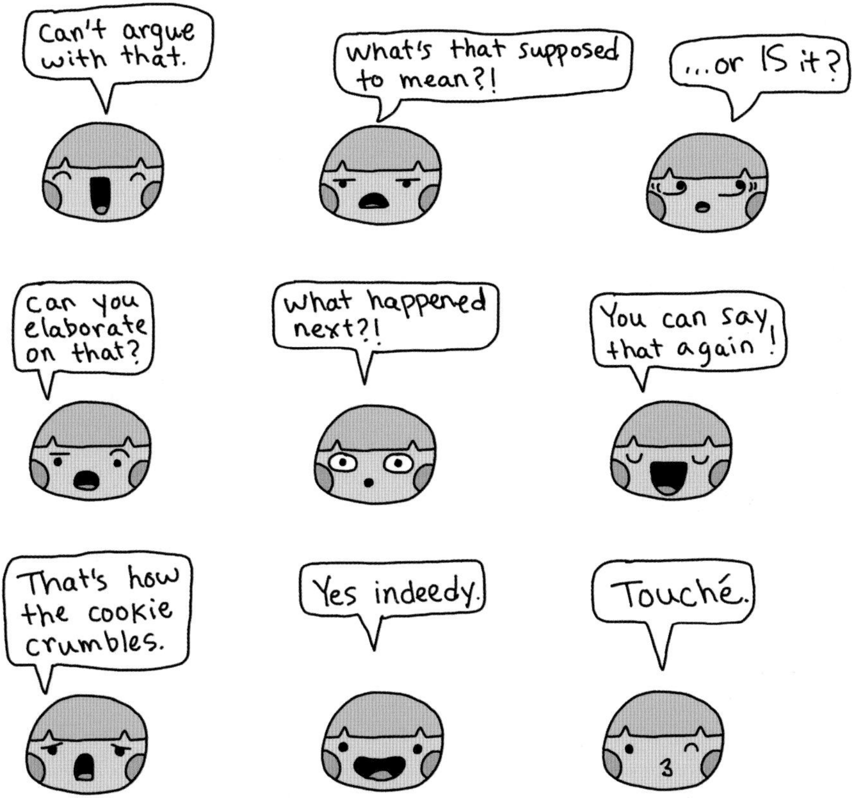
Can't argue with that.
What's that supposed to mean?!
...or IS it?
Can you elaborate on that?
What happened next?!
You can say that again!
That's how the cookie crumbles.
Yes indeedy.
Touché.
3

INTROVERT TRUTH-OR-DARE

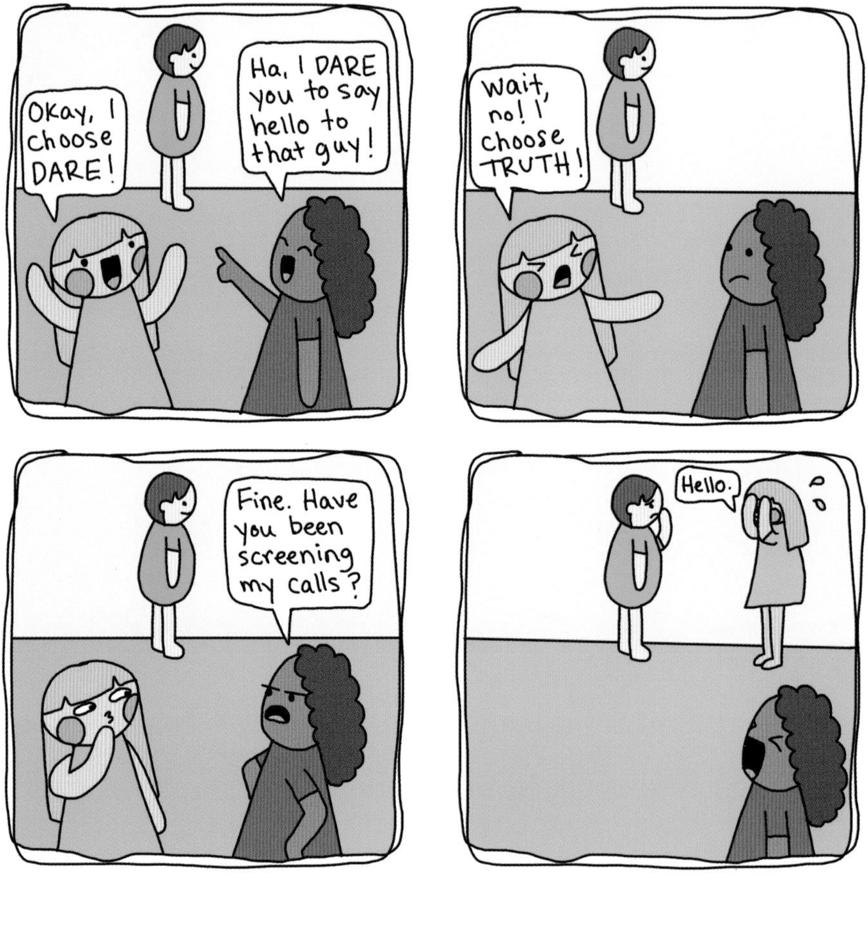
Okay, I choose DARE!
Ha, I DARE you to say hello to that guy!
Wait, no! I choose TRUTH!
Fine. Have you been screening my calls?
Hello.

INTROVERT VACATION SUGGESTIONS

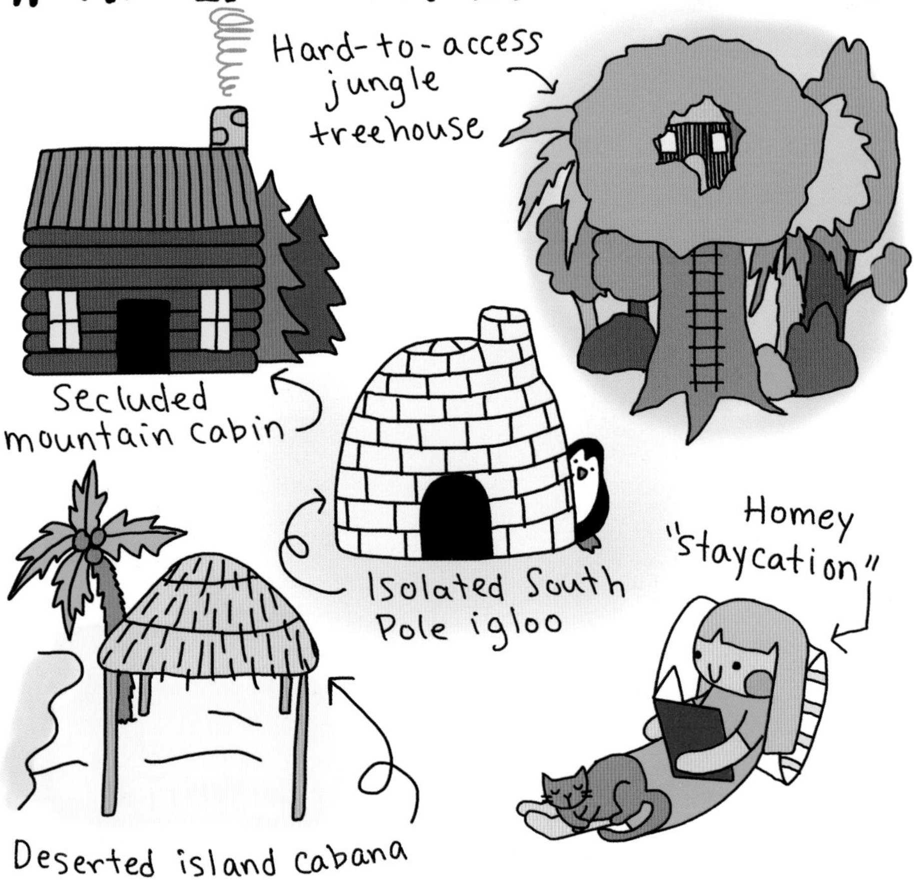

Hard-to-access jungle treehouse
Secluded mountain cabin
Isolated South Pole igloo
Homey "staycation"
Deserted island cabana

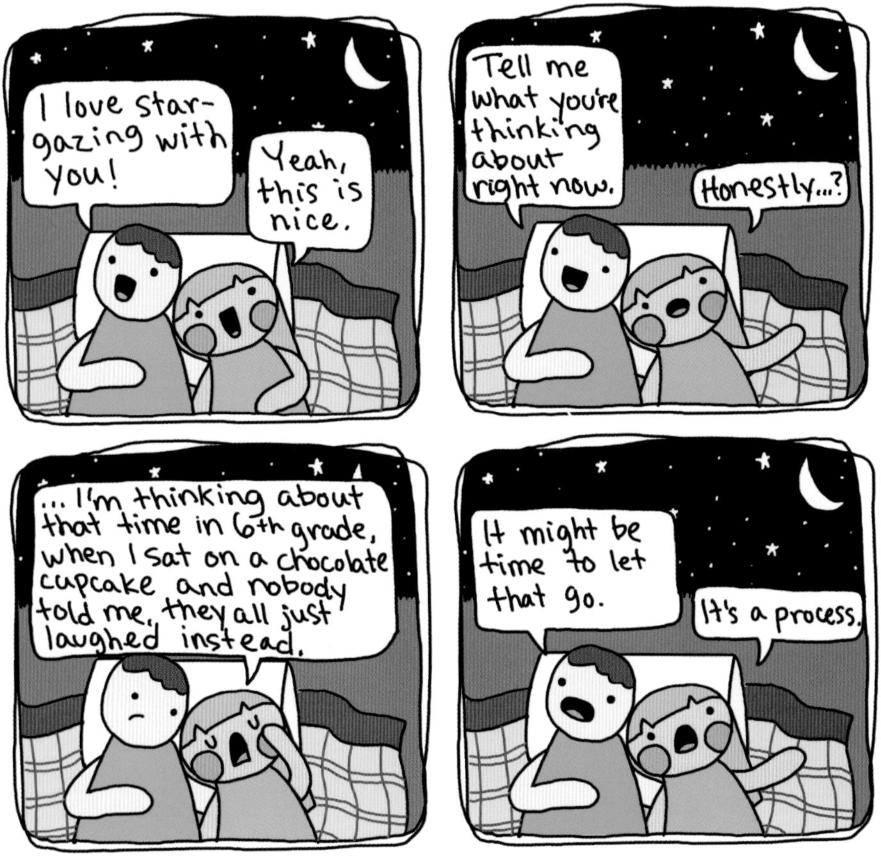
I love star-gazing with you!
Yeah, this is nice.
Tell me what you're thinking about right now.
Honestly...?
... I'm thinking about that time in 6th grade, when I sat on a chocolate cupcake and nobody told me, they all just laughed instead.
It might be time to let that go.
It's a process.

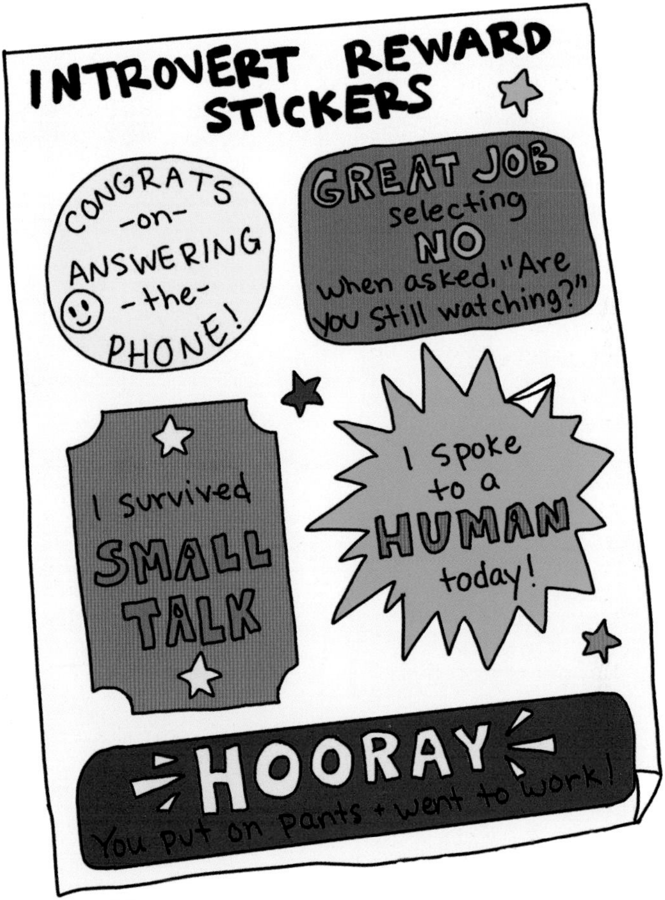
INTROVERT REWARD STICKERS
CONGRATS -on- ANSWERING -the- PHONE!
GREAT JOB selecting NO when asked, "Are you still watching?"
I survived SMALL TALK
I spoke to a HUMAN today!
HOORAY
You put on pants + went to work!

THE INTERNET HAS RUINED ME

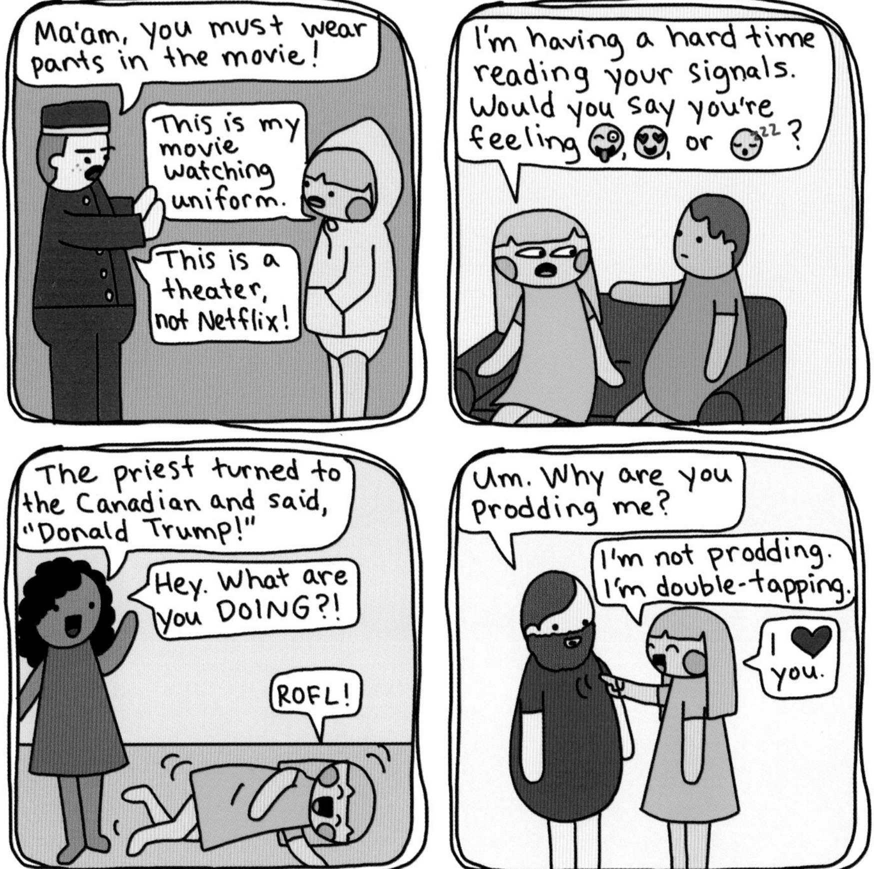

Ma'am, you must wear pants in the movie!
This is my movie watching uniform.
This is a theater, not Netflix!
I'm having a hard time reading your signals. Would you say you're feeling 😜, 😍, or 😴?
The priest turned to the Canadian and said, "Donald Trump!"
Hey. What are you DOING?!
ROFL!
Um. Why are you prodding me?
I'm not prodding. I'm double-tapping.
I ❤ you.

ME ON A DATING APP

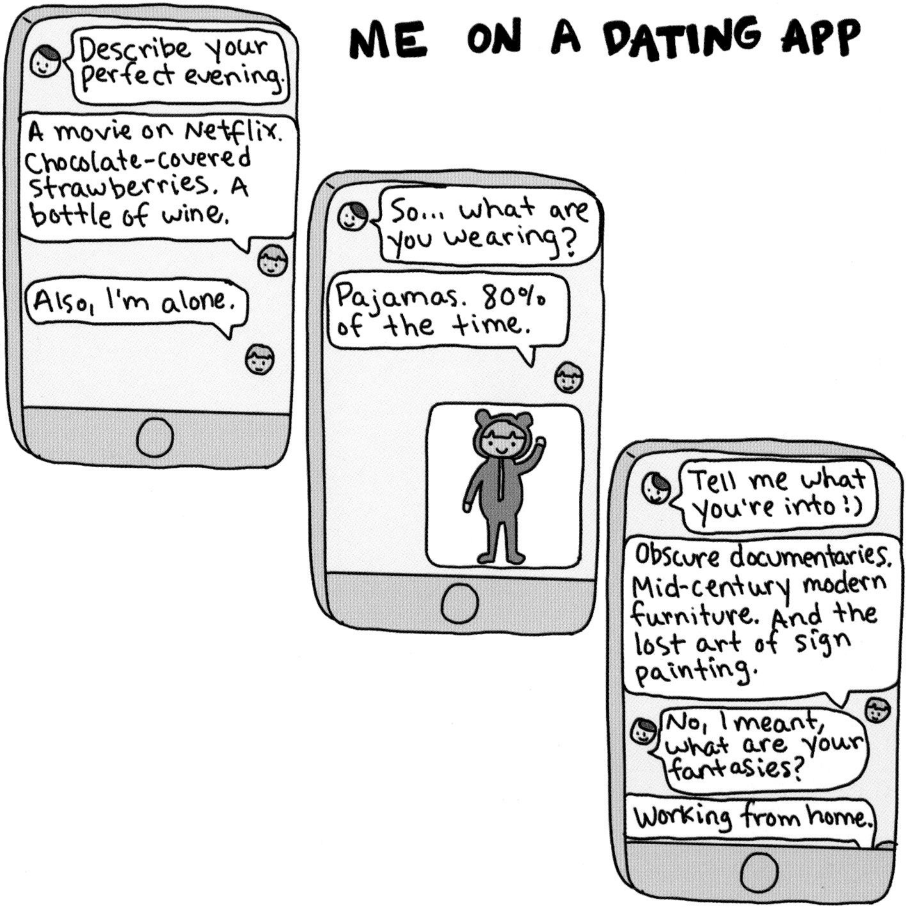

Describe your perfect evening.
A movie on Netflix. Chocolate-covered strawberries. A bottle of wine.
Also, I'm alone.
So... what are you wearing?
Pajamas. 80% of the time.
Tell me what you're into :)
Obscure documentaries. Mid-century modern furniture. And the lost art of sign painting.
No, I meant, what are your fantasies?
Working from home.

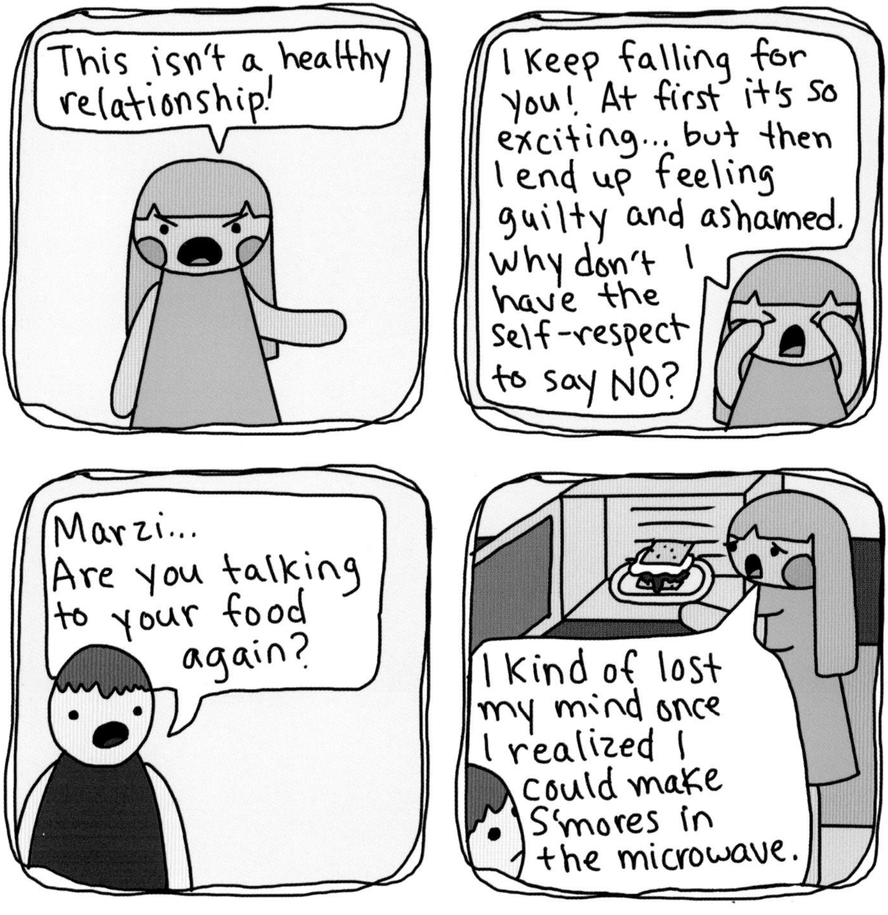
This isn't a healthy relationship!
I keep falling for you! At first it's so exciting... but then I end up feeling guilty and ashamed.
Why don't I have the self-respect to say NO?
Marzi... Are you talking to your food again?
I kind of lost my mind once I realized I could make S'mores in the microwave.

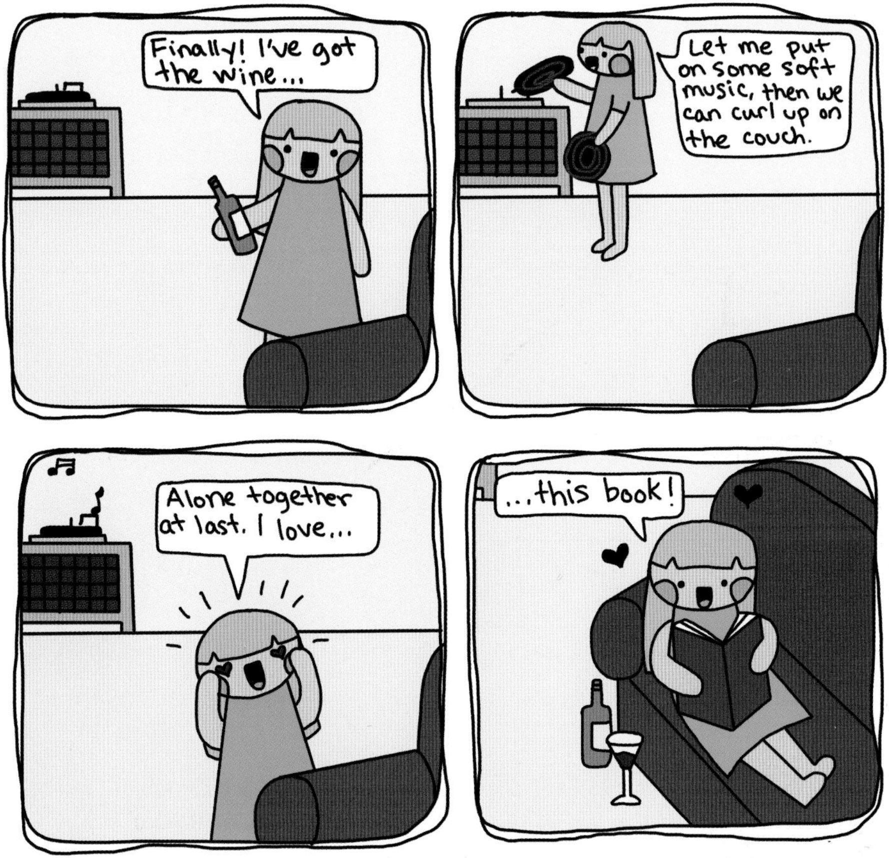
Finally! I've got the wine...
Let me put on some soft music, then we can curl up on the couch.
Alone together at last. I love...
...this book!

9 TEES EVERY INTROVERT NEEDS

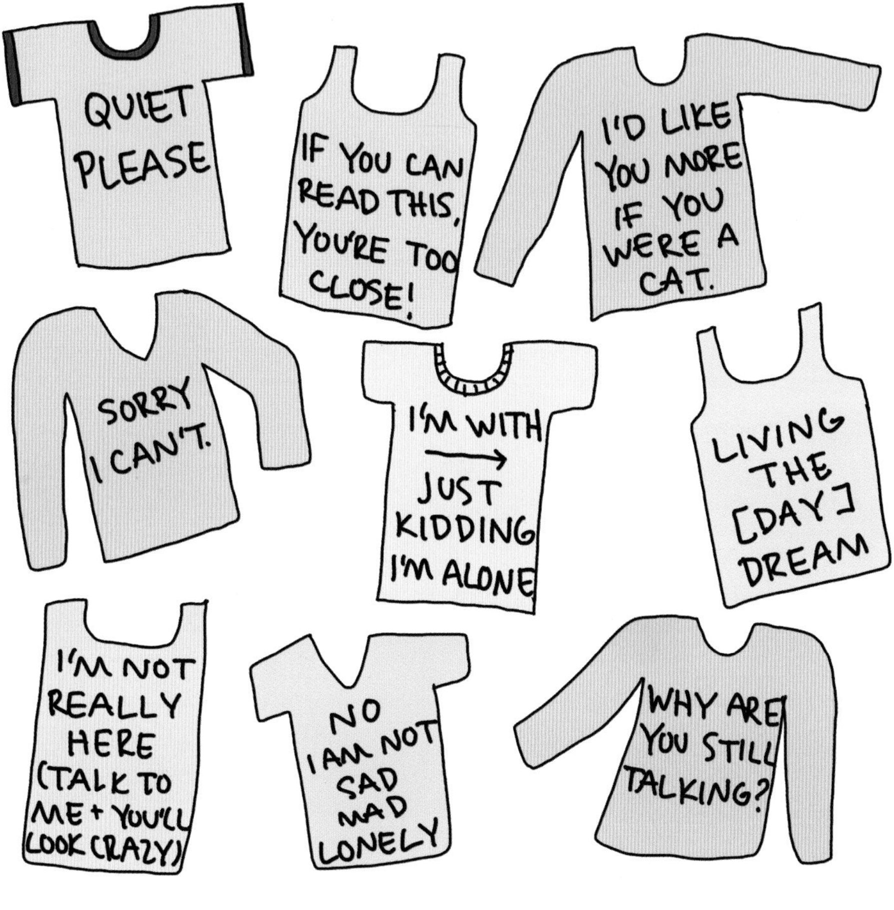
QUIET PLEASE
IF YOU CAN READ THIS, YOU'RE TOO CLOSE!
I'D LIKE YOU MORE IF YOU WERE A CAT.
SORRY I CAN'T.
I'M WITH → JUST KIDDING I'M ALONE
LIVING THE [DAY] DREAM
I'M NOT REALLY HERE (TALK TO ME + YOU'LL LOOK CRAZY)
NO I AM NOT SAD MAD LONELY
WHY ARE YOU STILL TALKING?

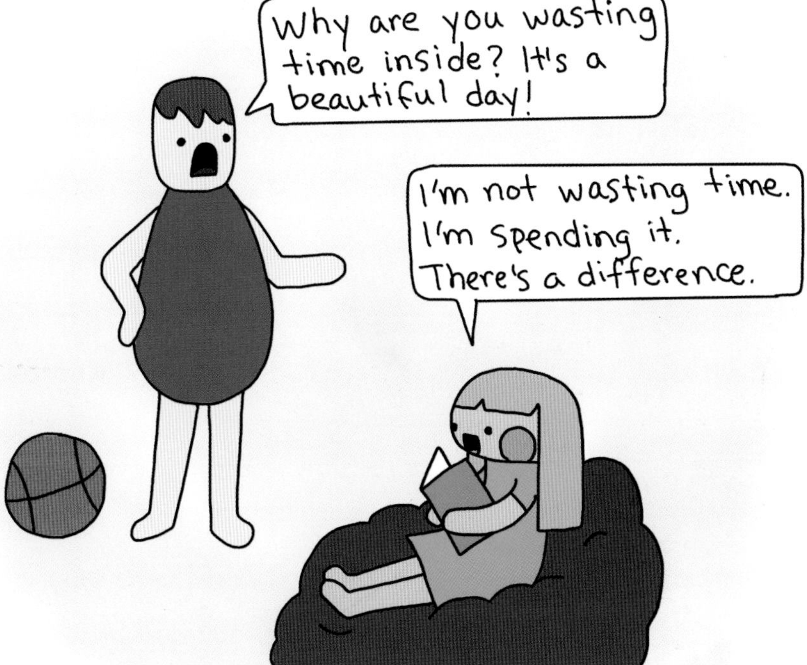
Why are you wasting time inside? It's a beautiful day!
I'm not wasting time. I'm spending it. There's a difference.

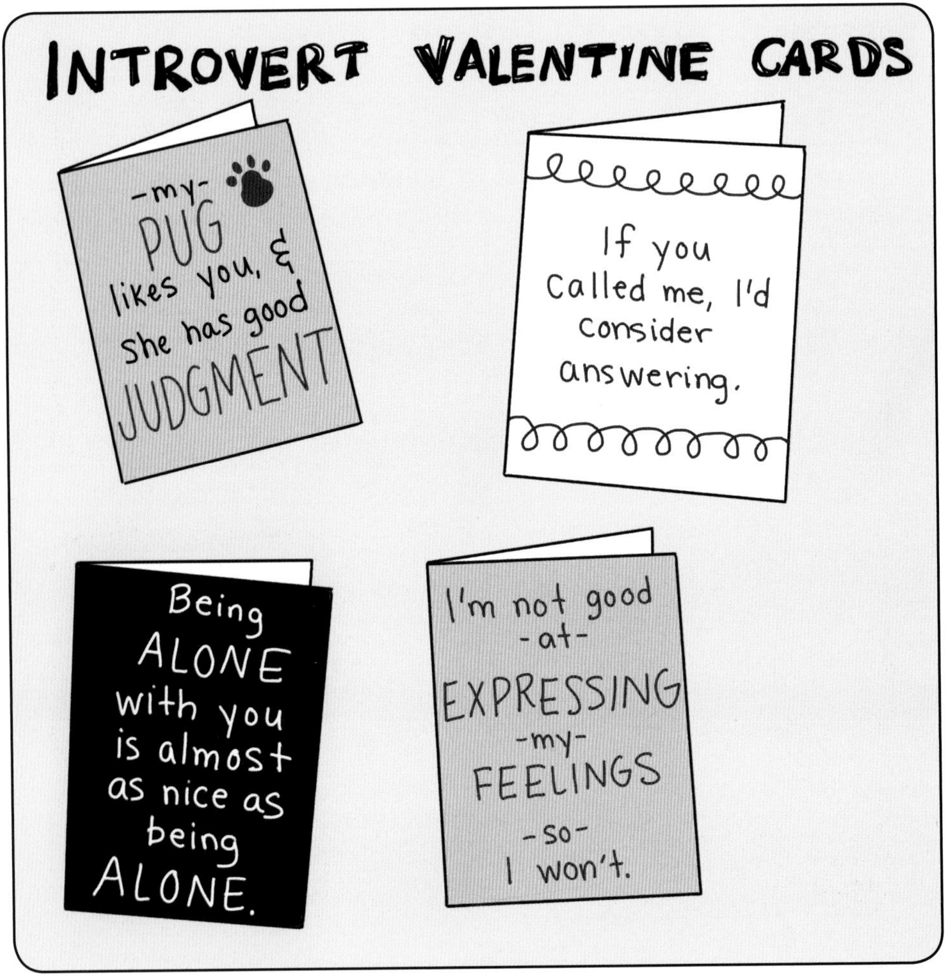
INTROVERT VALENTINE CARDS
-my- PUG likes you, & she has good JUDGMENT
If you called me, I'd consider answering.
Being ALONE with you is almost as nice as being ALONE.
I'm not good -at- EXPRESSING -my- FEELINGS -so- I won't.

INTROVERT CONVERSATIONS

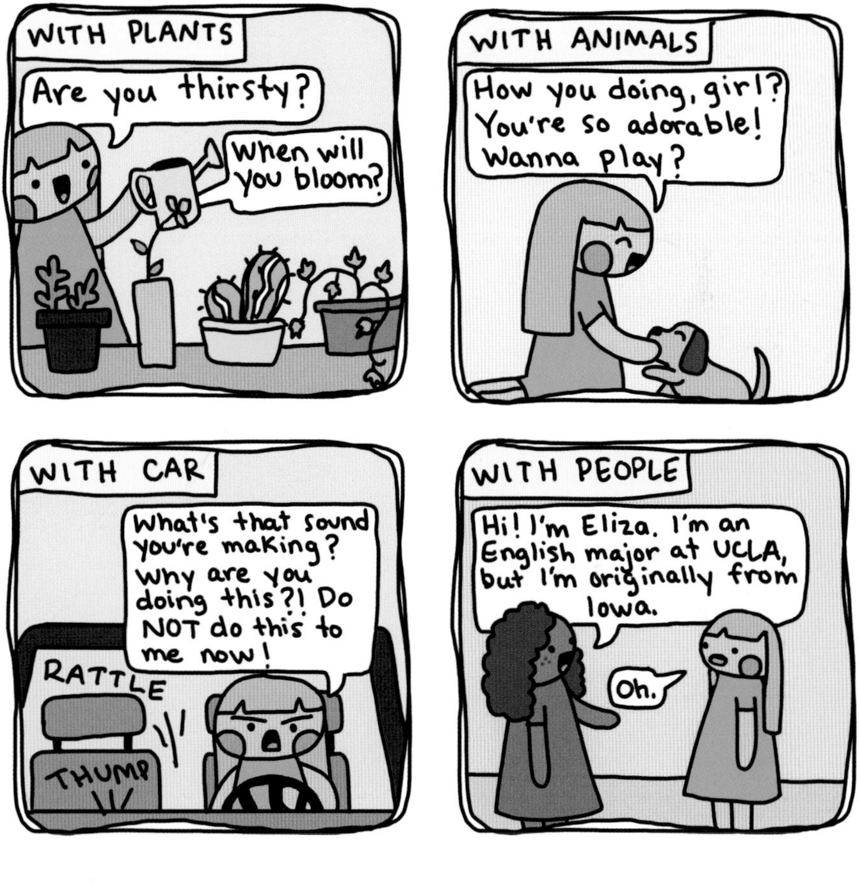
WITH PLANTS
Are you thirsty?
When will you bloom?
WITH ANIMALS
How you doing, girl!? You're so adorable! Wanna play?
WITH CAR
What's that sound you're making? Why are you doing this?! Do NOT do this to me now!
RATTLE
THUMP
WITH PEOPLE
Hi! I'm Eliza. I'm an English major at UCLA, but I'm originally from Iowa.
Oh.

THANKSGIVING SURVIVAL TIPS

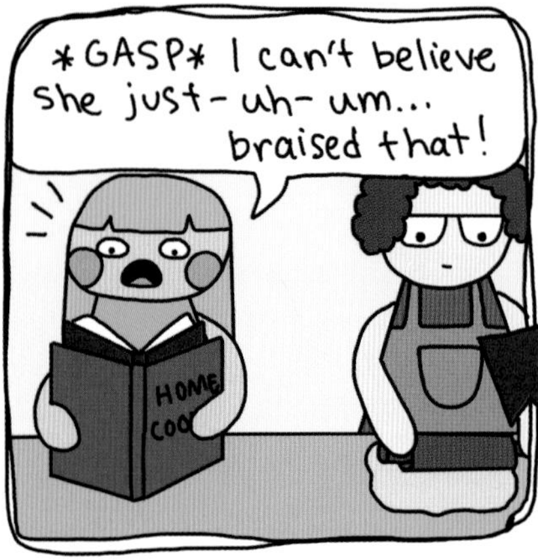
GASP I can't believe she just-uh-um... braised that!
HOME COO

Slide your novel inside a cookbook to appear engaged in the festivities

Shuffle place cards so you can sit at the kids' table.

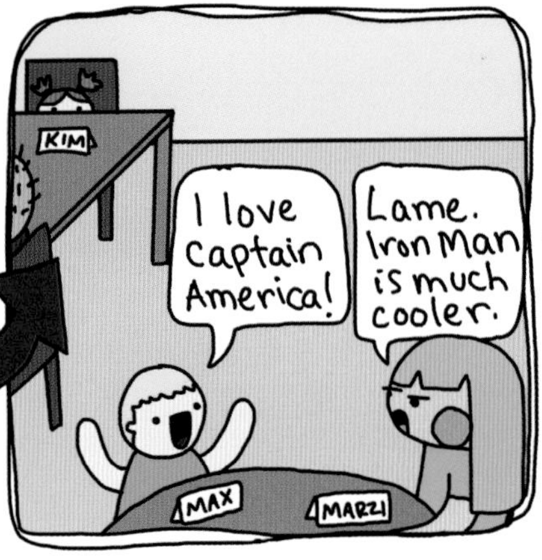
KIM
I love Captain America!
Lame. Iron Man is much cooler.
MAX
MARZI

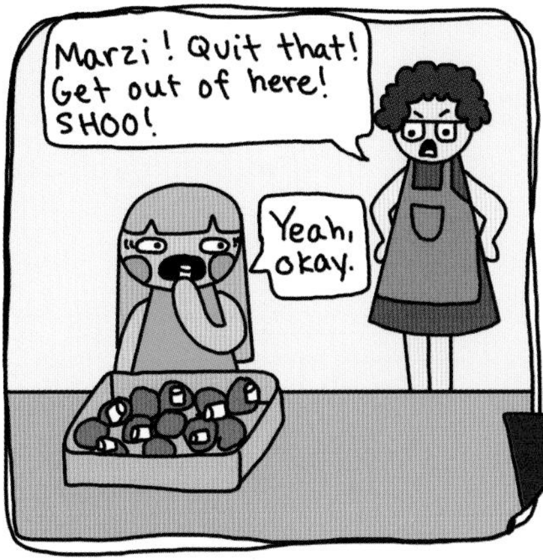
Marzi! Quit that! Get out of here! SHOO!
Yeah, okay.

You will be recruited for tasks in a crowded kitchen. Pick all of the marshmallows off the yams to get banned.

If it gets to be too much, escape to the bathroom. (TIP: Toilet paper pillow.)

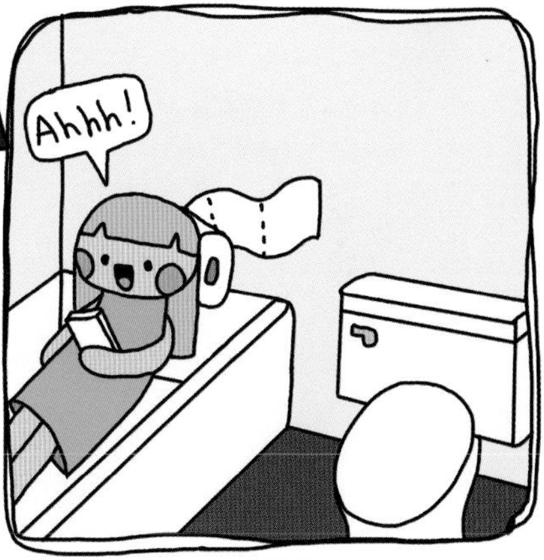
Ahhh!

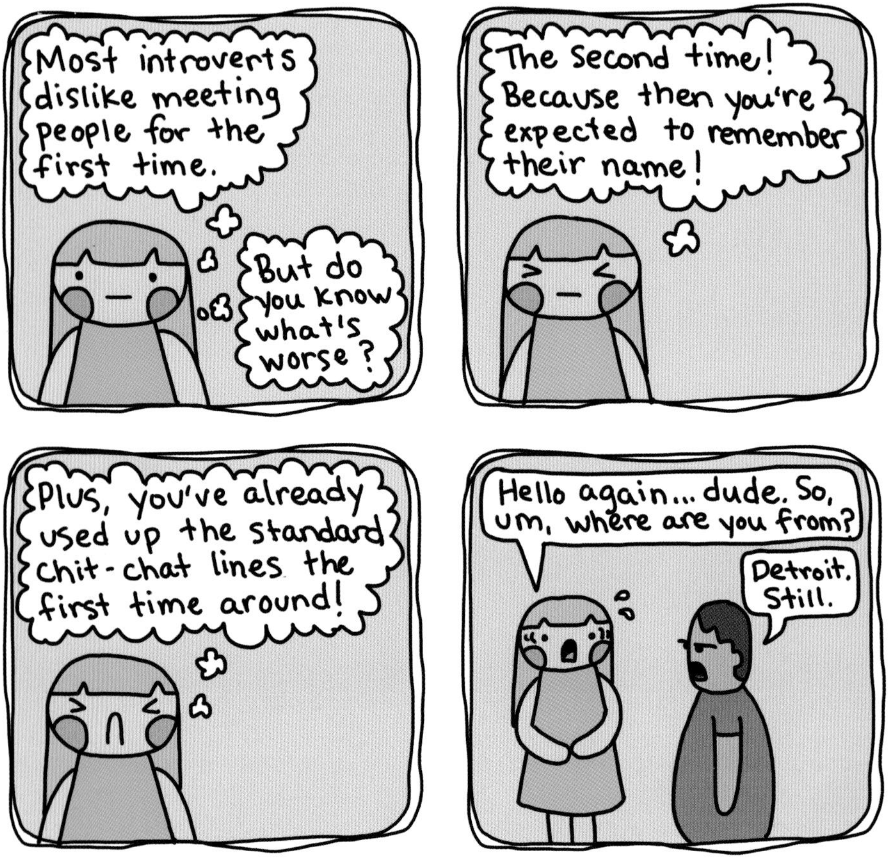
Most introverts dislike meeting people for the first time.
But do you know what's worse?
The second time! Because then you're expected to remember their name!
Plus, you've already used up the standard chit-chat lines the first time around!
Hello again... dude. So, um, where are you from?
Detroit. Still.

SHOULD YOU CALL ME?

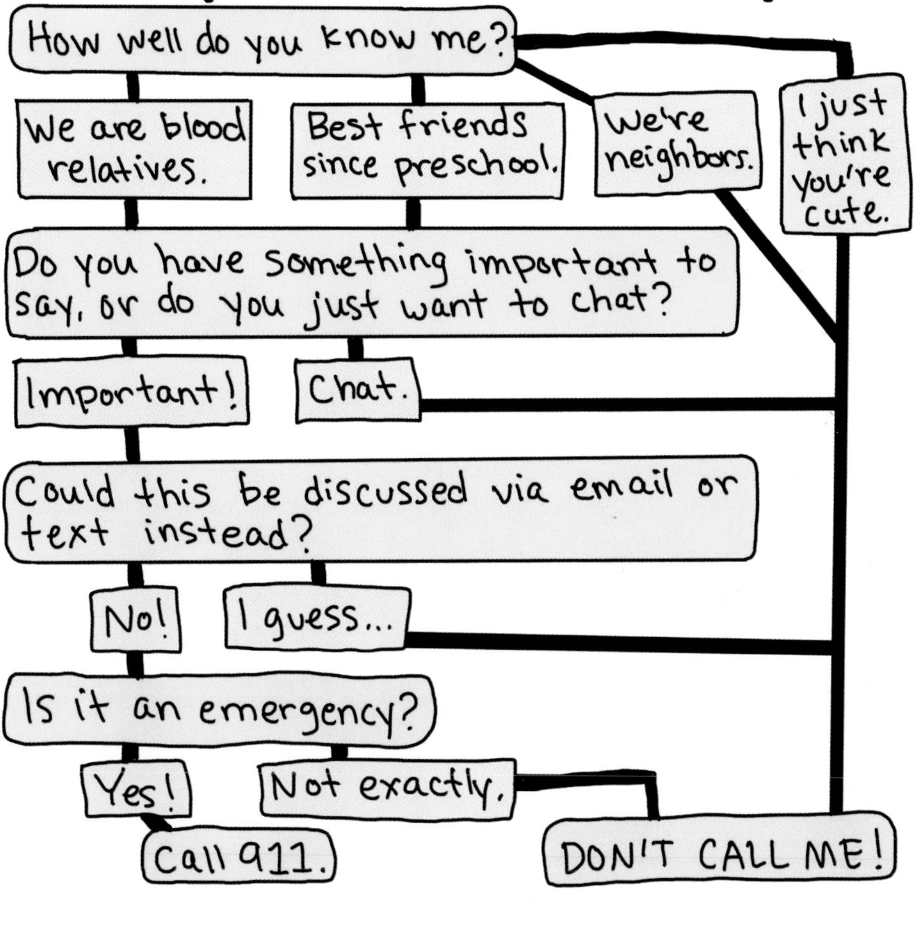
How well do you know me?
We are blood relatives.
Best friends since preschool.
We're neighbors.
I just think you're cute.
Do you have something important to say, or do you just want to chat?
Important!
Chat.
Could this be discussed via email or text instead?
No!
I guess...
Is it an emergency?
Yes!
Not exactly.
Call 911.
DON'T CALL ME!

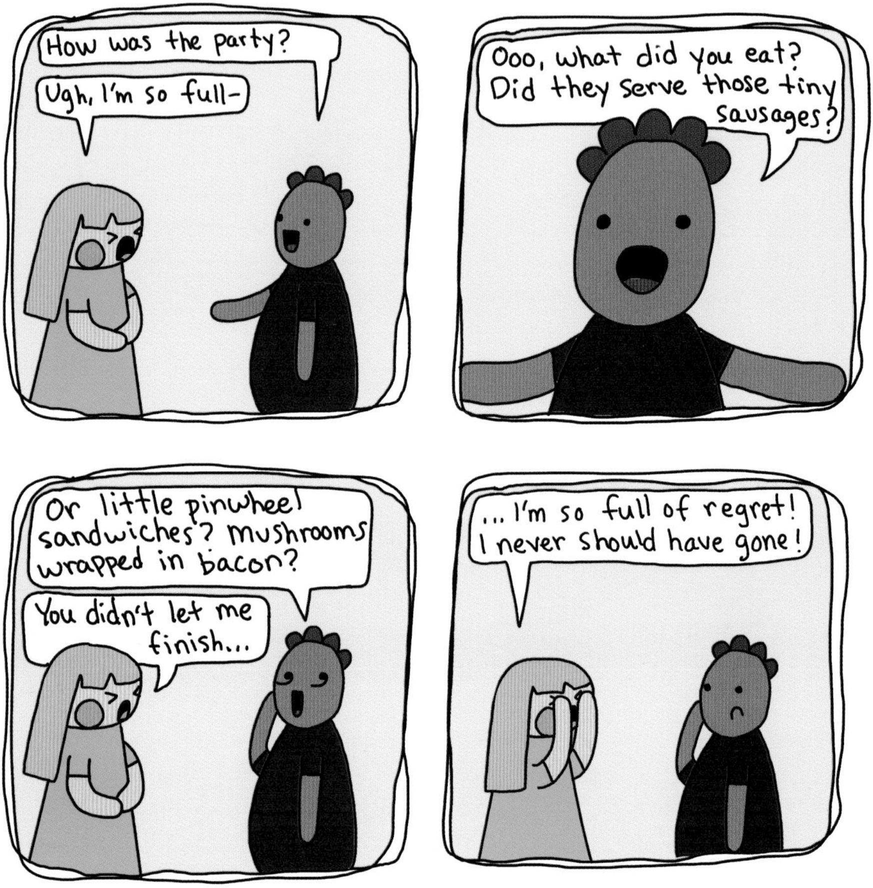
How was the party?
Ugh, I'm so full-
Ooo, what did you eat? Did they serve those tiny sausages?
Or little pinwheel sandwiches? Mushrooms wrapped in bacon?
You didn't let me finish...
... I'm so full of regret! I never should have gone!

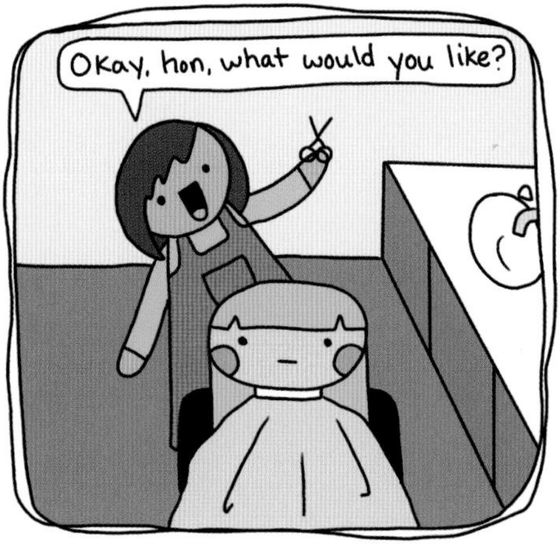
Okay, hon, what would you like?

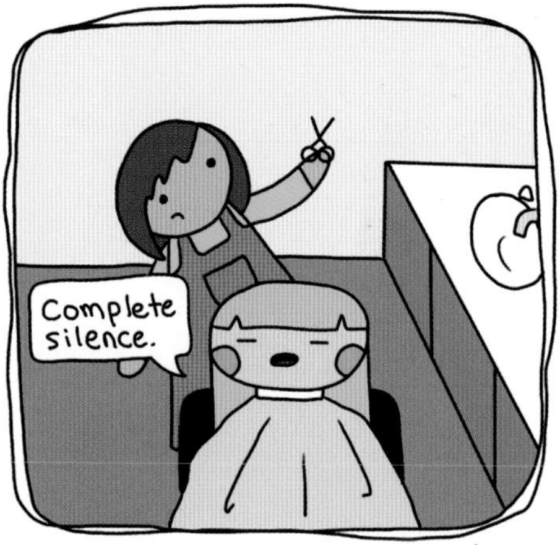
Complete silence.

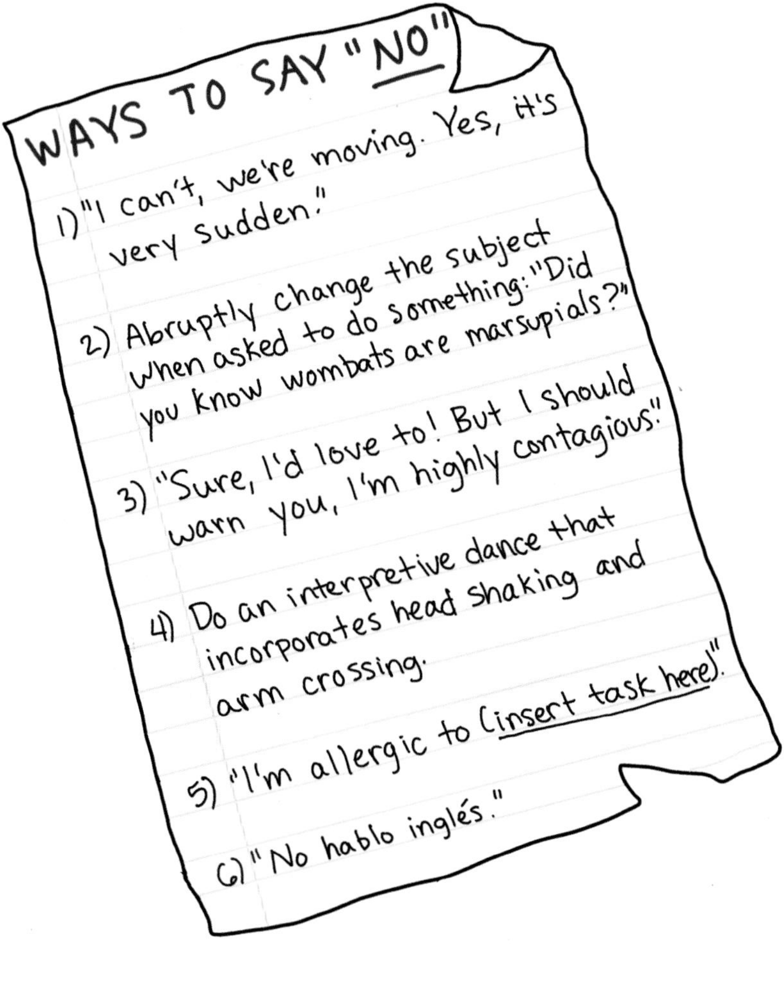
WAYS TO SAY "NO"
1) "I can't, we're moving. Yes, it's very sudden."
2) Abruptly change the subject when asked to do something: "Did you know wombats are marsupials?"
3) "Sure, I'd love to! But I should warn you, I'm highly contagious."
4) Do an interpretive dance that incorporates head shaking and arm crossing.
5) "I'm allergic to (insert task here)."
6) "No hablo inglés."

PEOPLE I INSTANTLY DISLIKE

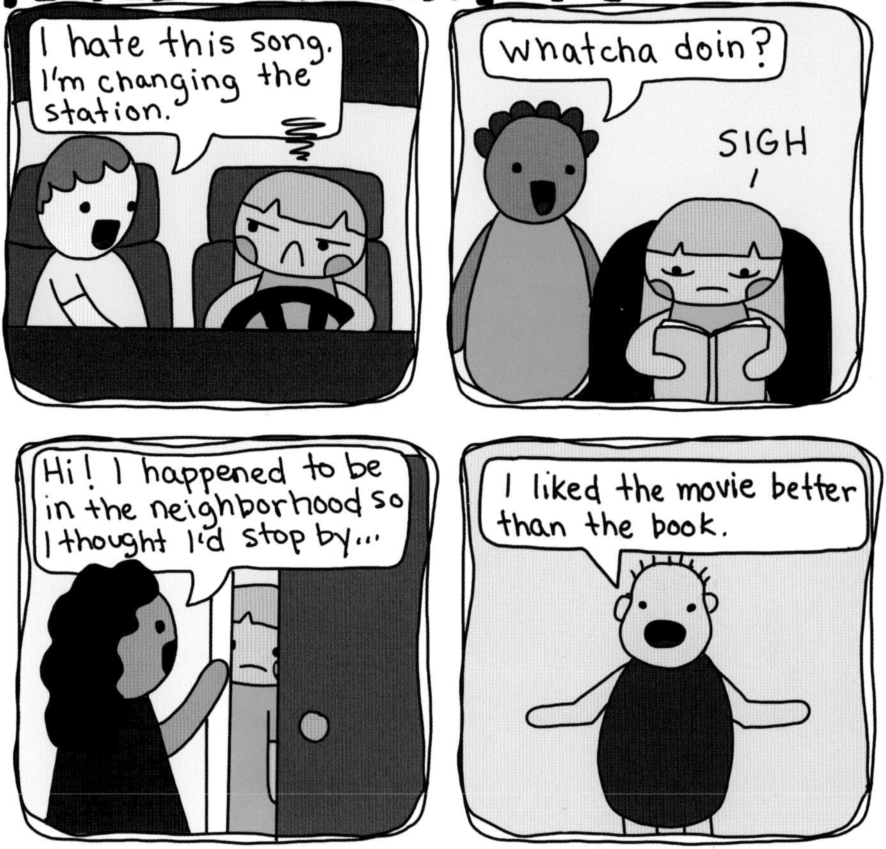
I hate this song. I'm changing the station.
Whatcha doin?
SIGH
Hi! I happened to be in the neighborhood so I thought I'd stop by...
I liked the movie better than the book.

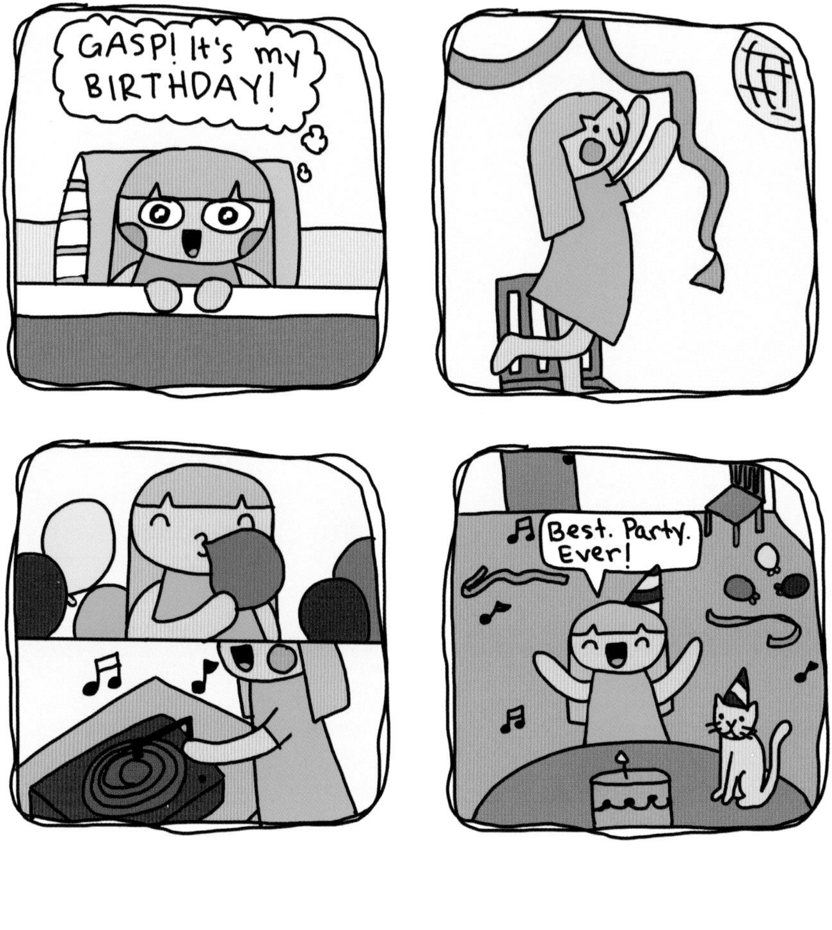
GASP! It's my BIRTHDAY!
Best. Party. Ever!

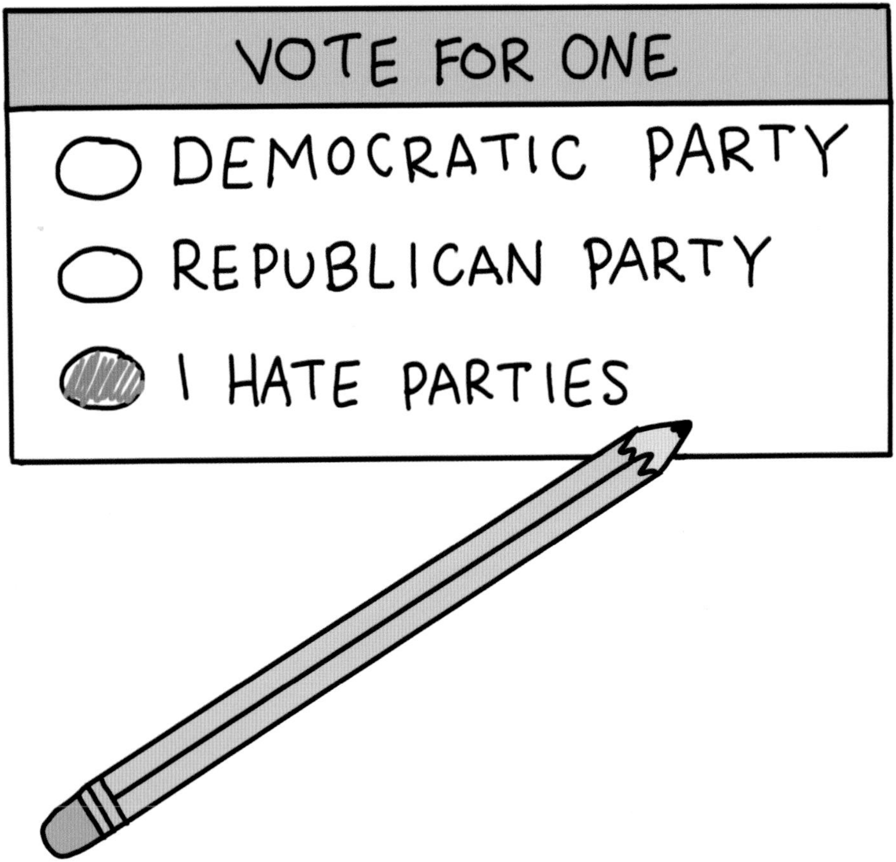
VOTE FOR ONE
DEMOCRATIC PARTY
REPUBLICAN PARTY
I HATE PARTIES

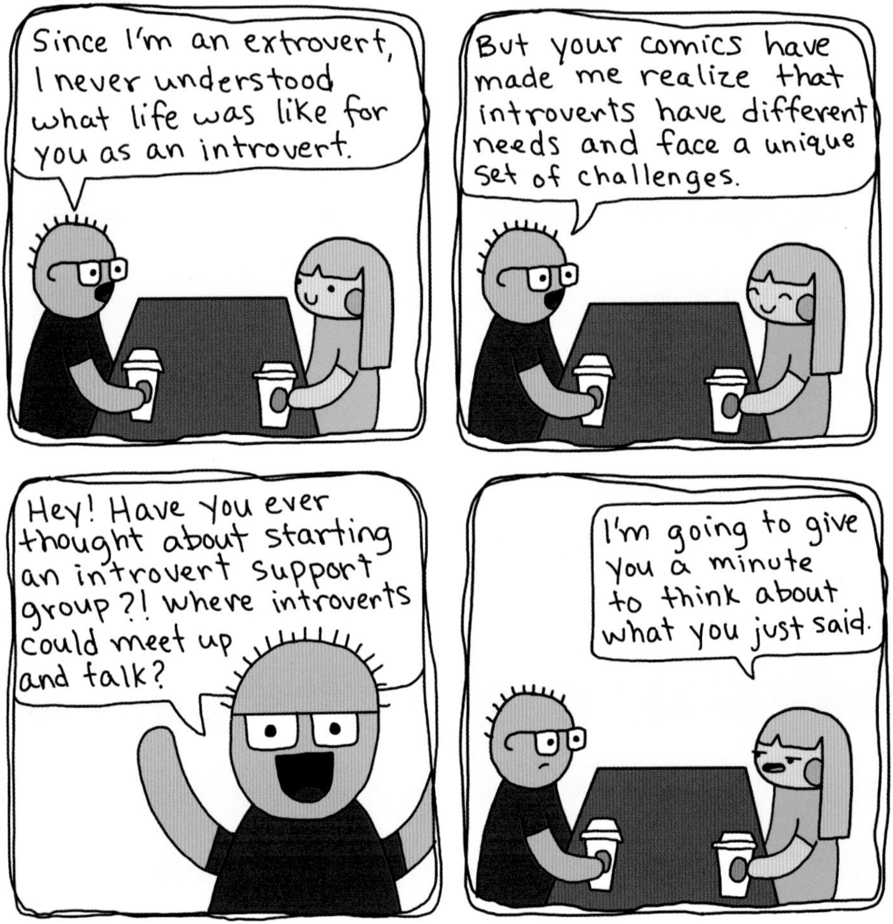
Since I'm an extrovert, I never understood what life was like for you as an introvert.
But your comics have made me realize that introverts have different needs and face a unique set of challenges.
Hey! Have you ever thought about starting an introvert support group?! Where introverts could meet up and talk?
I'm going to give you a minute to think about what you just said.

RELATABLE ANIMALS

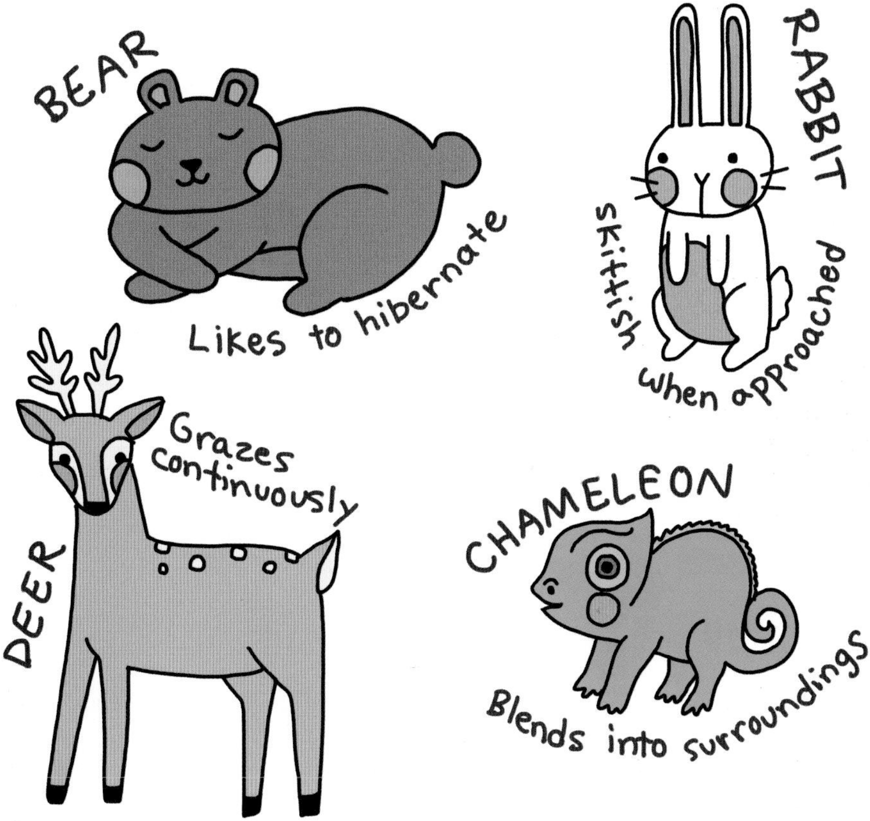
BEAR
Likes to hibernate
RABBIT
skittish when approached
DEER
Grazes continuously
CHAMELEON
Blends into surroundings

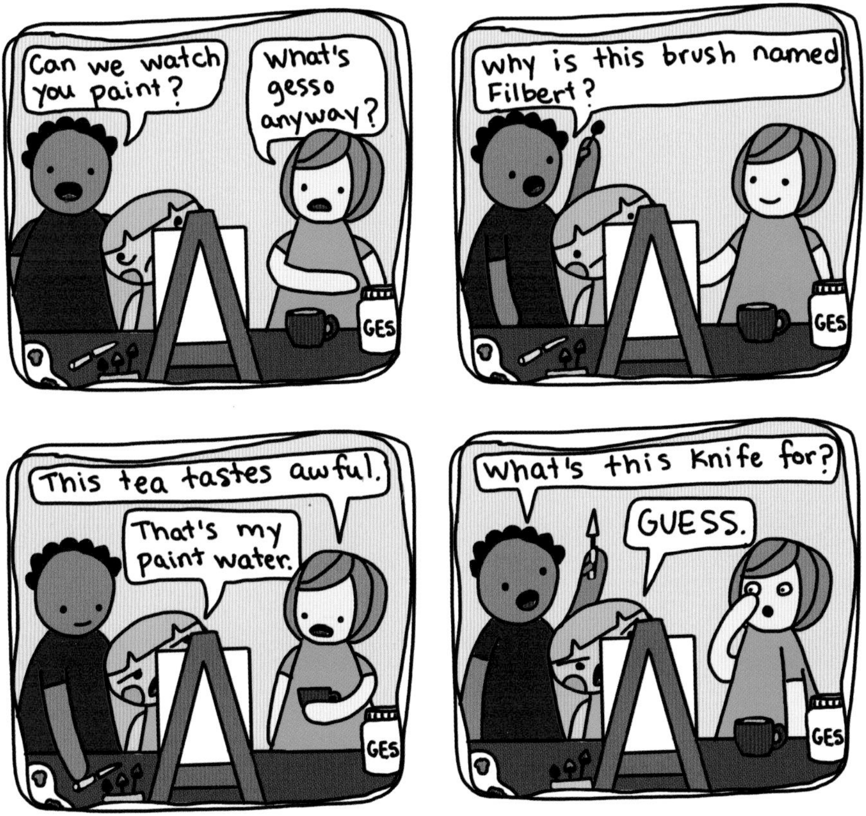
Can we watch you paint?
What's gesso anyway?
GES
Why is this brush named Filbert?
GES
This tea tastes awful.
That's my paint water.
GES
What's this knife for?
GUESS.
GES

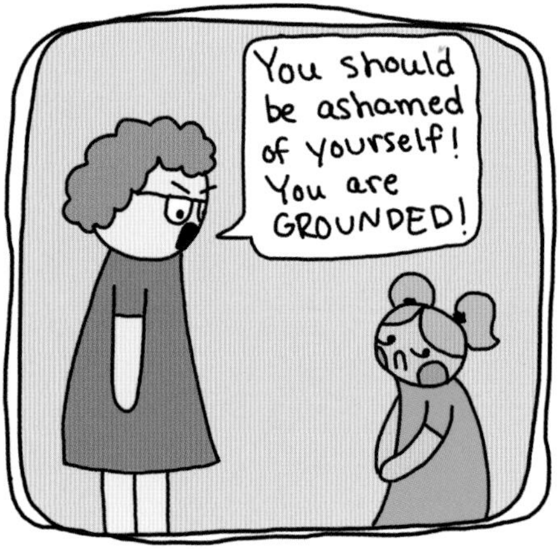
You should be ashamed of yourself! You are GROUNDED!

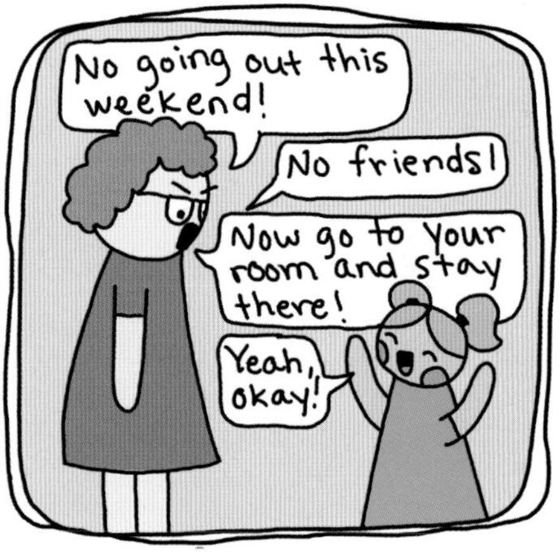
No going out this weekend!
No friends!
Now go to your room and stay there!
Yeah, okay!

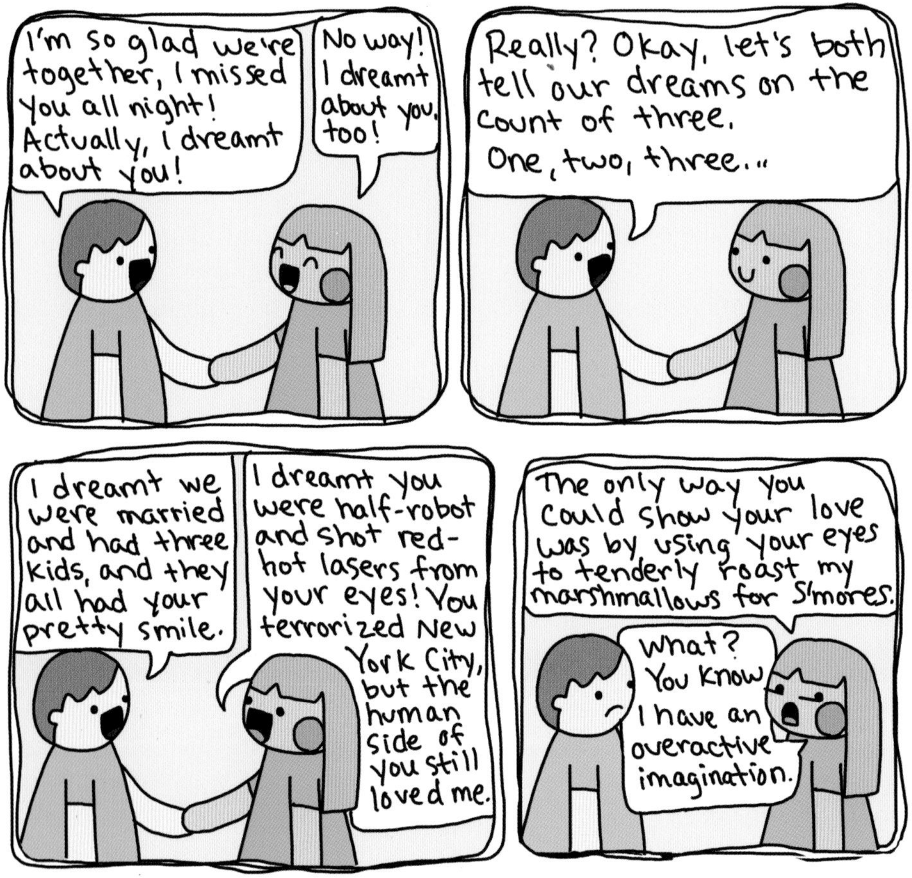
I'm so glad we're together, I missed you all night! Actually, I dreamt about you!
No way! I dreamt about you, too!
Really? Okay, let's both tell our dreams on the count of three. One, two, three...
I dreamt we were married and had three kids, and they all had your pretty smile.
I dreamt you were half-robot and shot red-hot lasers from your eyes! You terrorized New York City, but the human side of you still loved me.
The only way you could show your love was by using your eyes to tenderly roast my marshmallows for S'mores.
What? You know I have an overactive imagination.

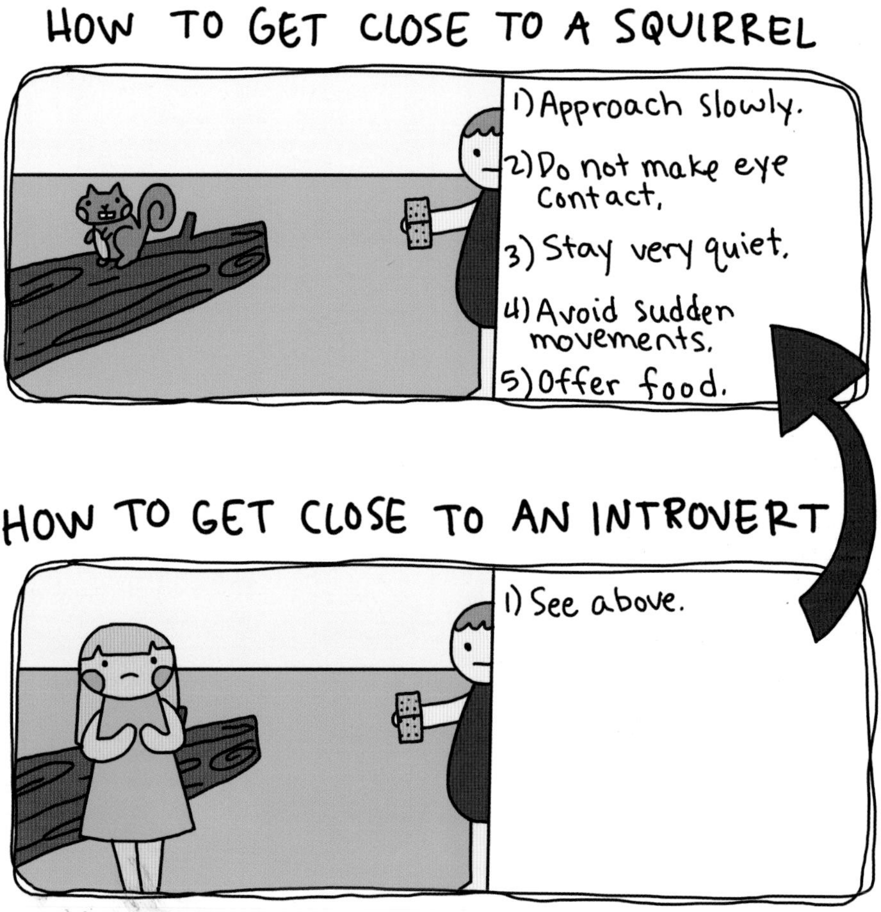
HOW TO GET CLOSE TO A SQUIRREL
1) Approach slowly.
2) Do not make eye contact.
3) Stay very quiet.
4) Avoid sudden movements.
5) Offer food.
HOW TO GET CLOSE TO AN INTROVERT
1) See above.

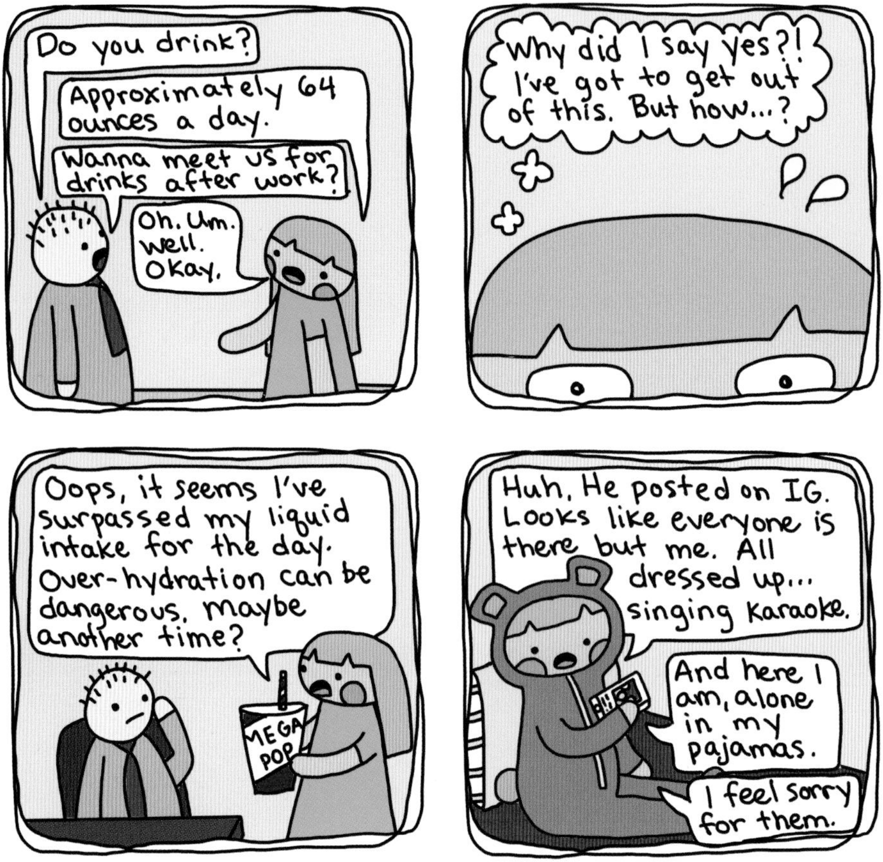
Do you drink?
Approximately 64 ounces a day.
Wanna meet us for drinks after work?
Oh. Um. Well. Okay.
Why did I say yes?! I've got to get out of this. But how...?
Oops, it seems I've surpassed my liquid intake for the day. Over-hydration can be dangerous. Maybe another time?
MEGA POP
Huh. He posted on IG. Looks like everyone is there but me. All dressed up... singing karaoke.
And here I am, alone in my pajamas.
I feel sorry for them.

THE SURPRISE VISIT

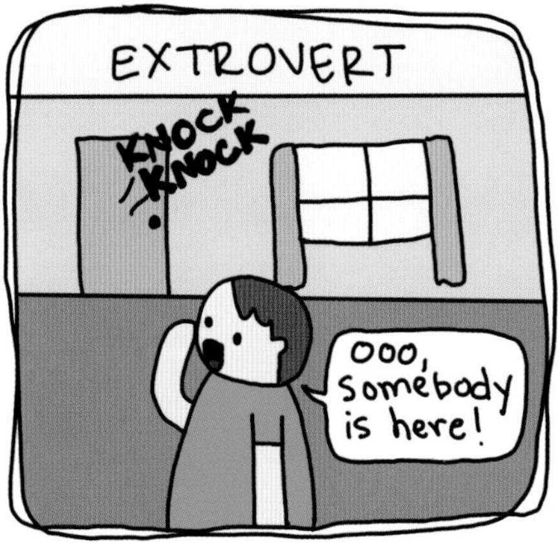
EXTROVERT
KNOCK KNOCK
ooo, somebody is here!

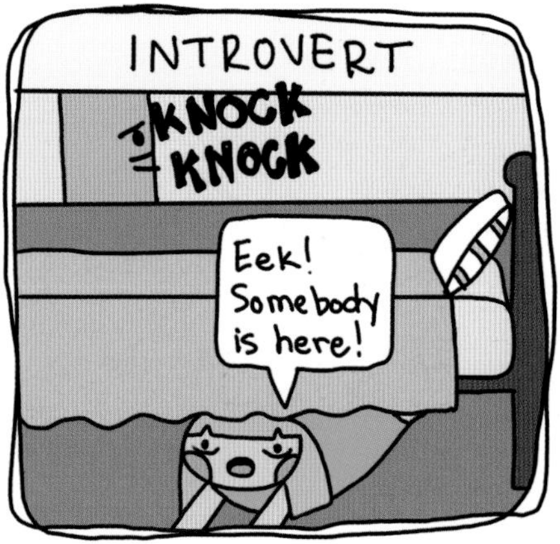
INTROVERT
KNOCK KNOCK
Eek! Somebody is here!

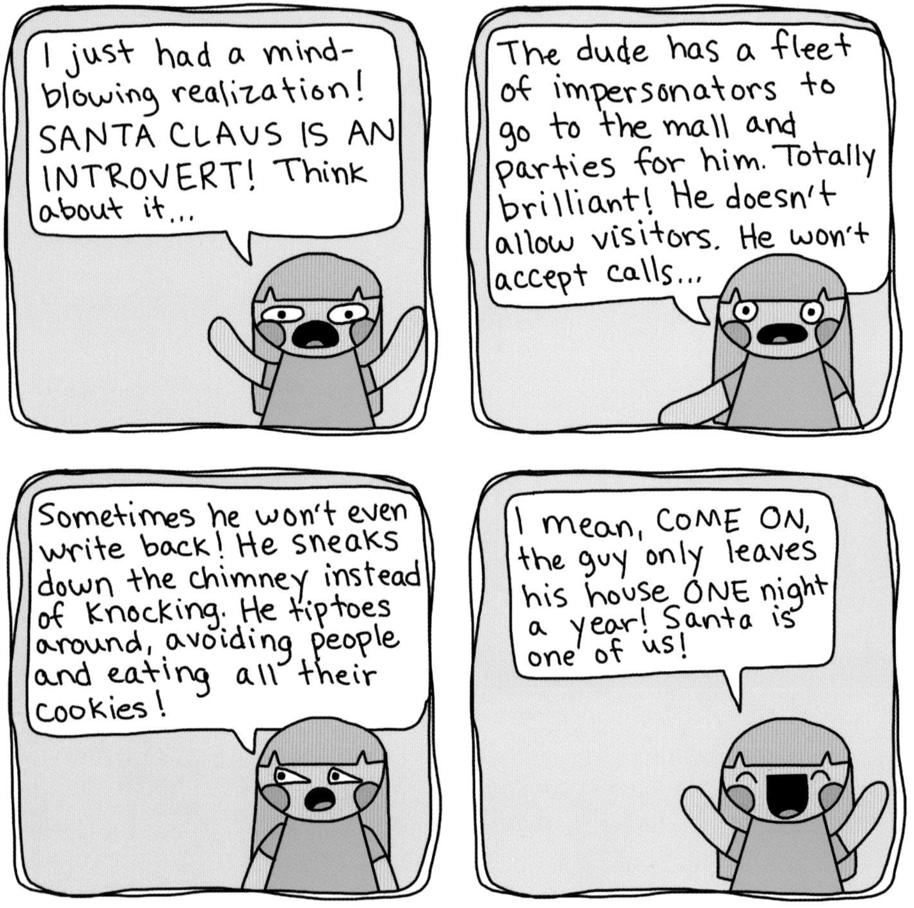
I just had a mind-blowing realization! SANTA CLAUS IS AN INTROVERT! Think about it...
The dude has a fleet of impersonators to go to the mall and parties for him. Totally brilliant! He doesn't allow visitors. He won't accept calls...
Sometimes he won't even write back! He sneaks down the chimney instead of knocking. He tiptoes around, avoiding people and eating all their cookies!
I mean, COME ON, the guy only leaves his house ONE night a year! Santa is one of us!

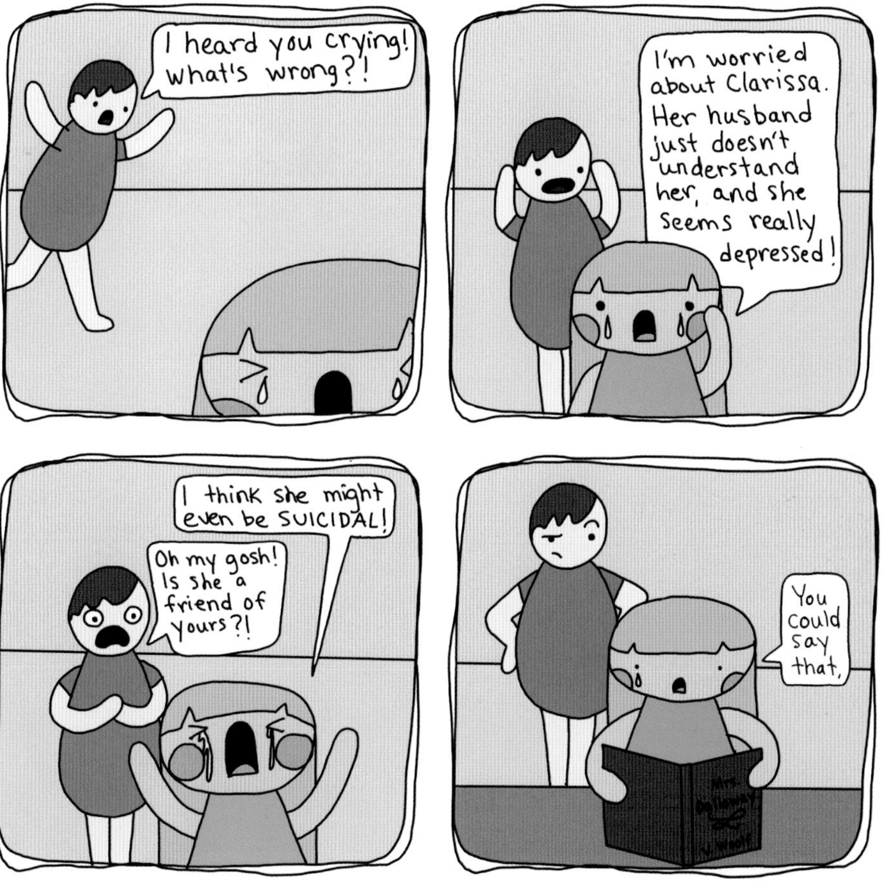

I heard you crying! what's wrong?!
I'm worried about Clarissa. Her husband just doesn't understand her, and she seems really depressed!
I think she might even be SUICIDAL!
Oh my gosh! Is she a friend of yours?!
You could say that.
Mrs. Dalloway
V. Woolf

PARTY SURVIVAL TIPS:

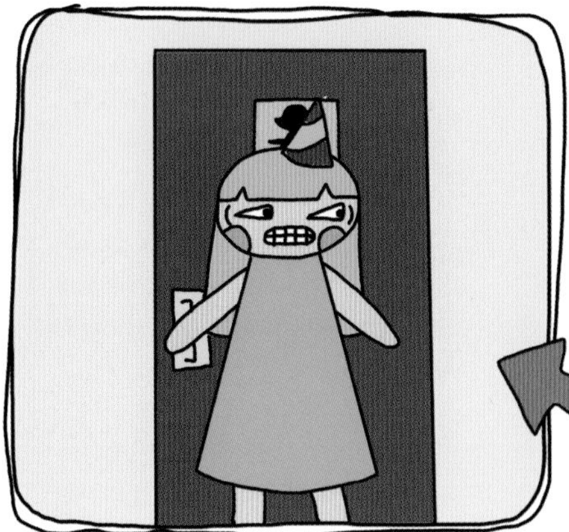

Immediately upon arrival, identify all exits as well as bathrooms. Position yourself accordingly.

Canvass the area for pets to play with. In a pinch, small children will suffice.

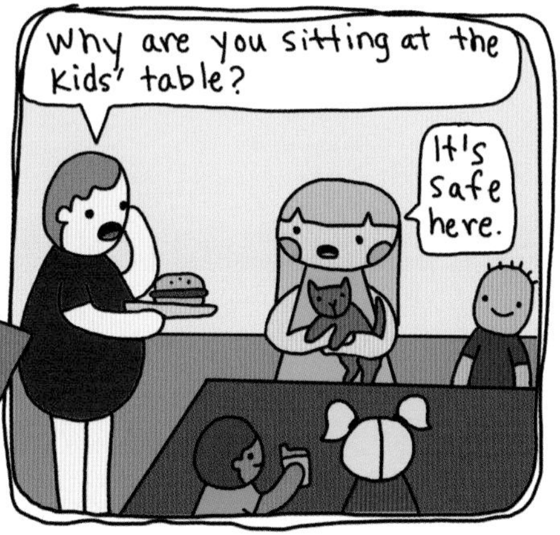

Why are you sitting at the kids' table?
It's safe here.

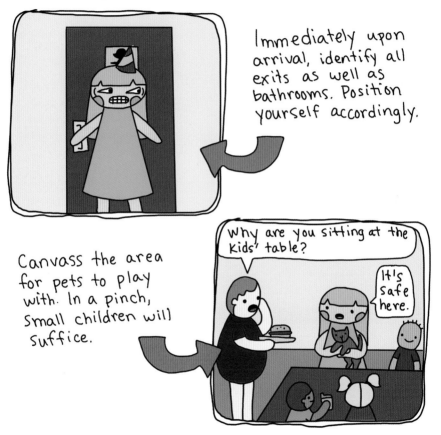

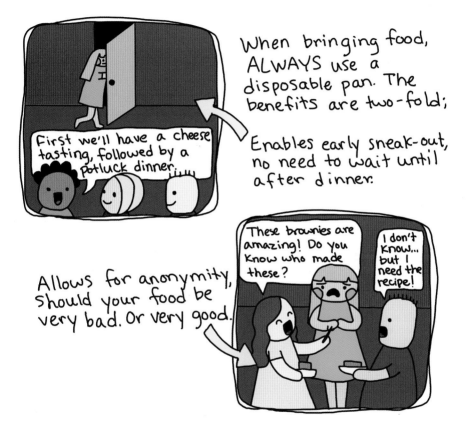

When bringing food, ALWAYS use a disposable pan. The benefits are two-fold;

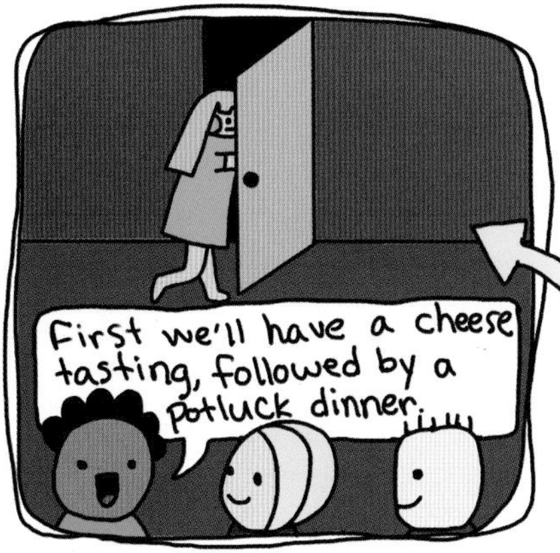
First we'll have a cheese tasting, followed by a potluck dinner.

Enables early sneak-out, no need to wait until after dinner.

Allows for anonymity, should your food be very bad. Or very good.

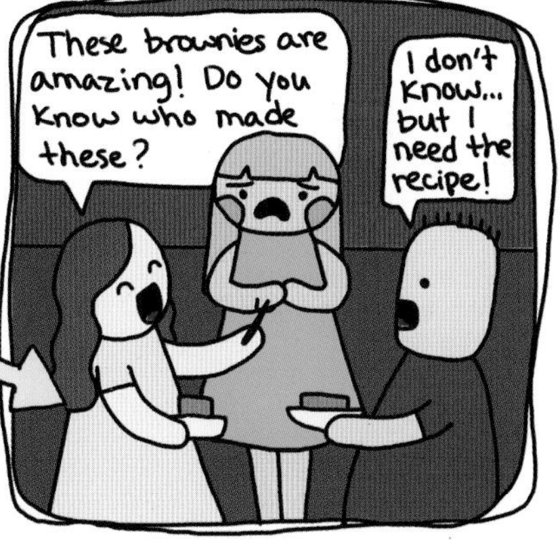
These brownies are amazing! Do you know who made these?
I don't know... but I need the recipe!

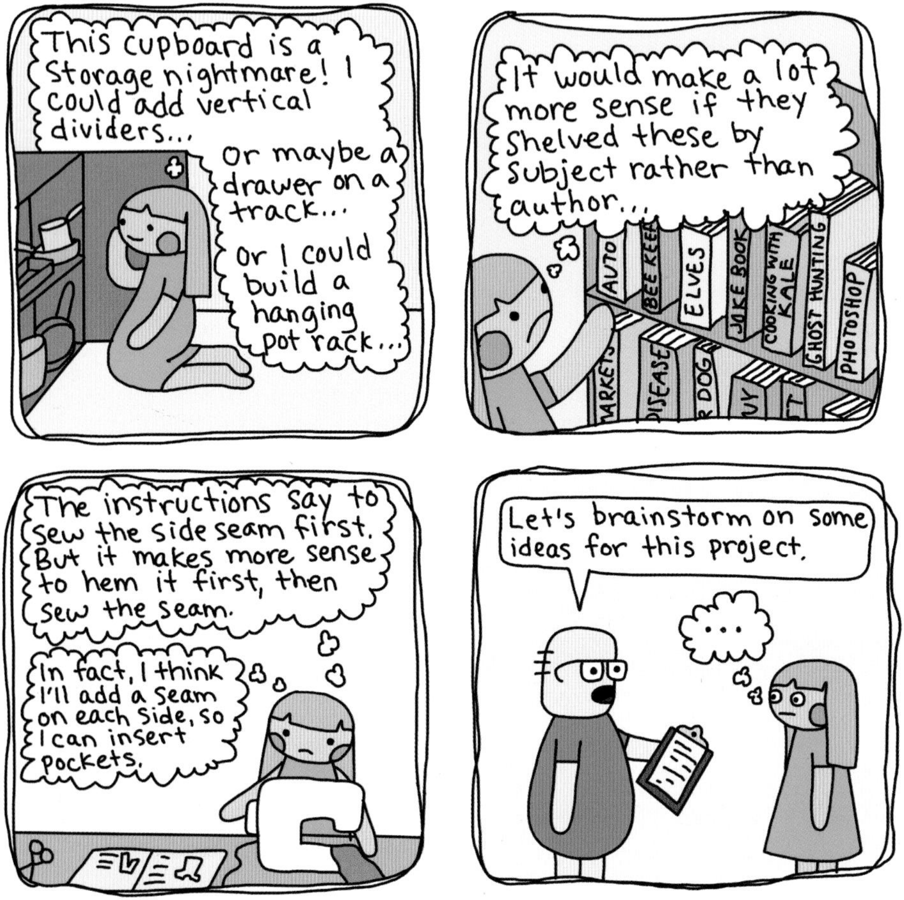
This cupboard is a storage nightmare! I could add vertical dividers...
Or maybe a drawer on a track...
Or I could build a hanging pot rack...
It would make a lot more sense if they shelved these by subject rather than author...
AUTO
ELVES
JOKE BOOK
COOKING WITH KALE
GHOST HUNTING
PHOTOSHOP
The instructions say to sew the side seam first. But it makes more sense to hem it first, then sew the seam.
In fact, I think I'll add a seam on each side, so I can insert pockets.
Let's brainstorm on some ideas for this project.
...

MARZI TRIES SPEED DATING

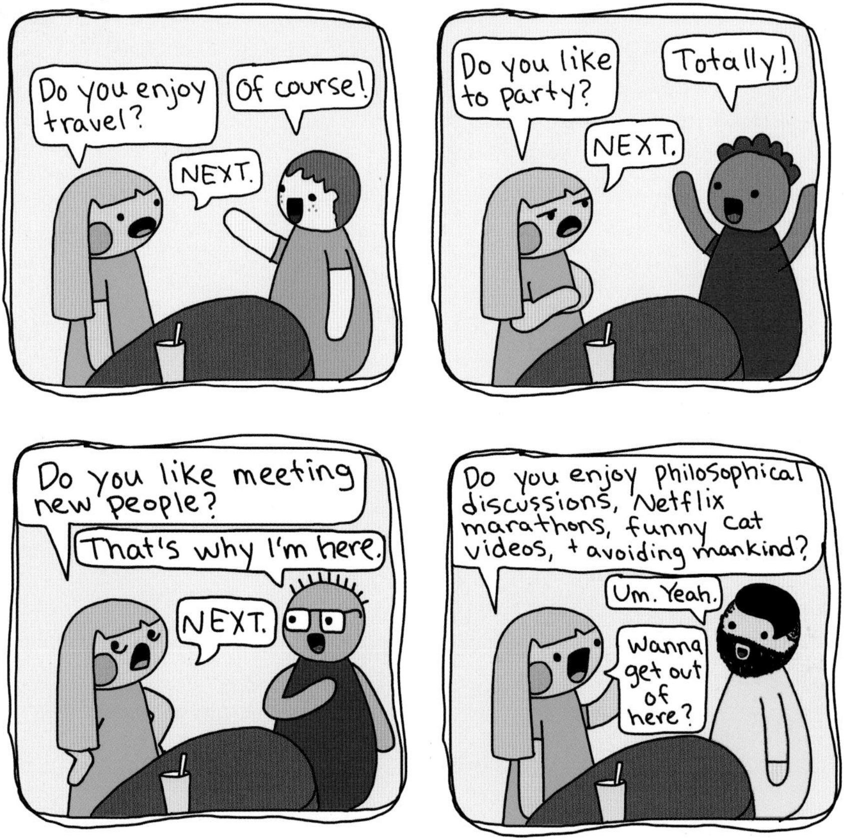
Do you enjoy travel?
Of course!
NEXT.
Do you like to party?
Totally!
NEXT.
Do you like meeting new people?
That's why I'm here.
NEXT.
Do you enjoy philosophical discussions, Netflix marathons, funny cat videos, + avoiding mankind?
Um. Yeah.
Wanna get out of here?

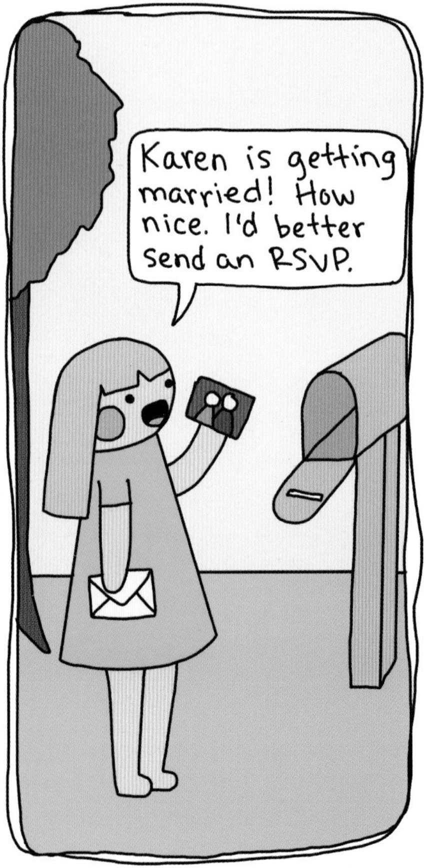
Karen is getting married! How nice. I'd better send an RSVP.

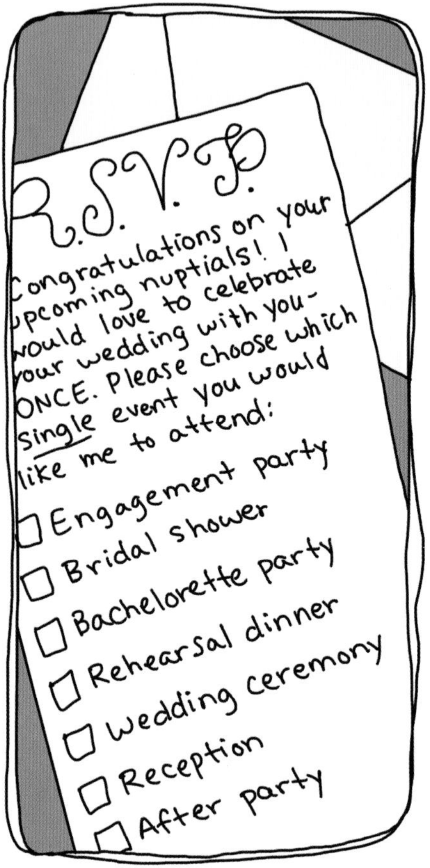
R.S.V.P.
Congratulations on your upcoming nuptials! I would love to celebrate your wedding with you-ONCE. Please choose which single event you would like me to attend:
Engagement party
Bridal shower
Bachelorette party
Rehearsal dinner
Wedding ceremony
Reception
After party

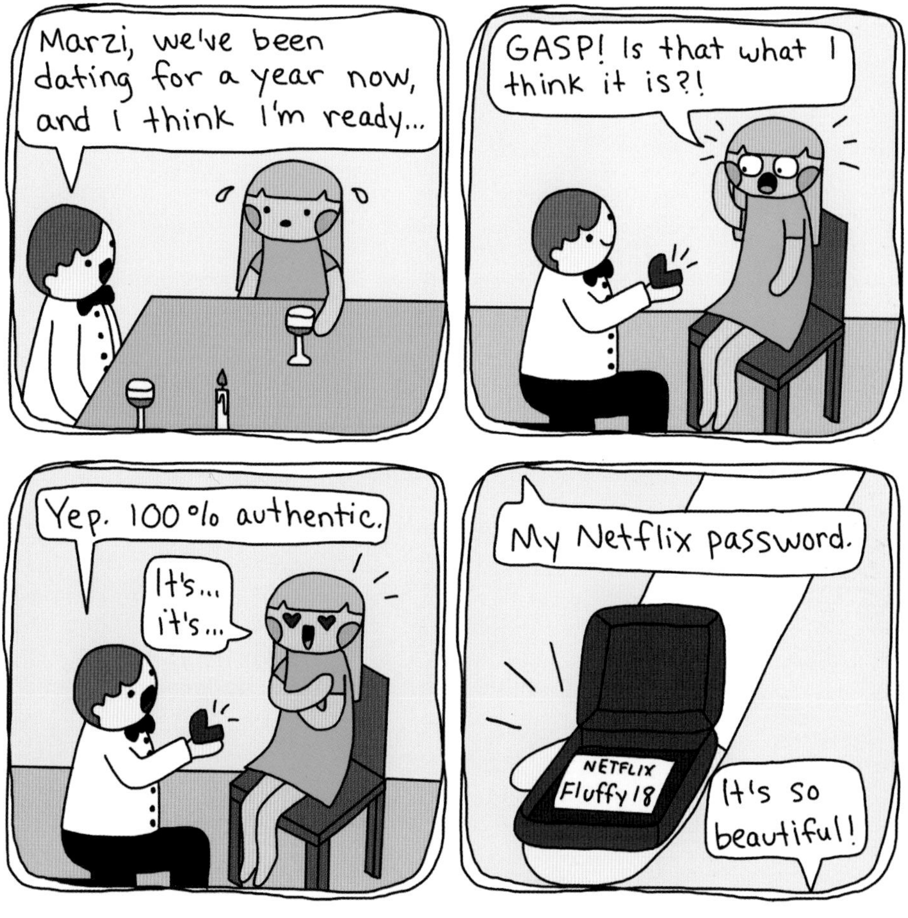
Marzi, we've been dating for a year now, and I think I'm ready...
GASP! Is that what I think it is?!
Yep. 100% authentic.
It's... it's...
My Netflix password.
NETFLIX
Fluffy18
It's so beautiful!

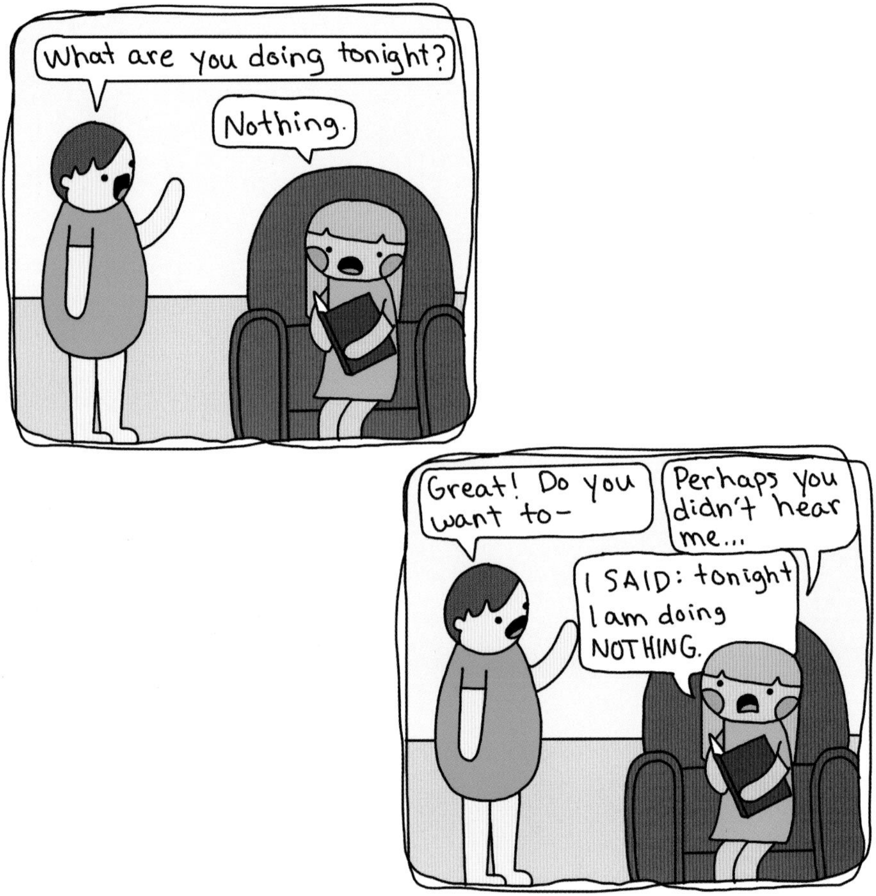
What are you doing tonight?
Nothing.
Great! Do you want to-
Perhaps you didn't hear me...
I SAID: tonight I am doing NOTHING.

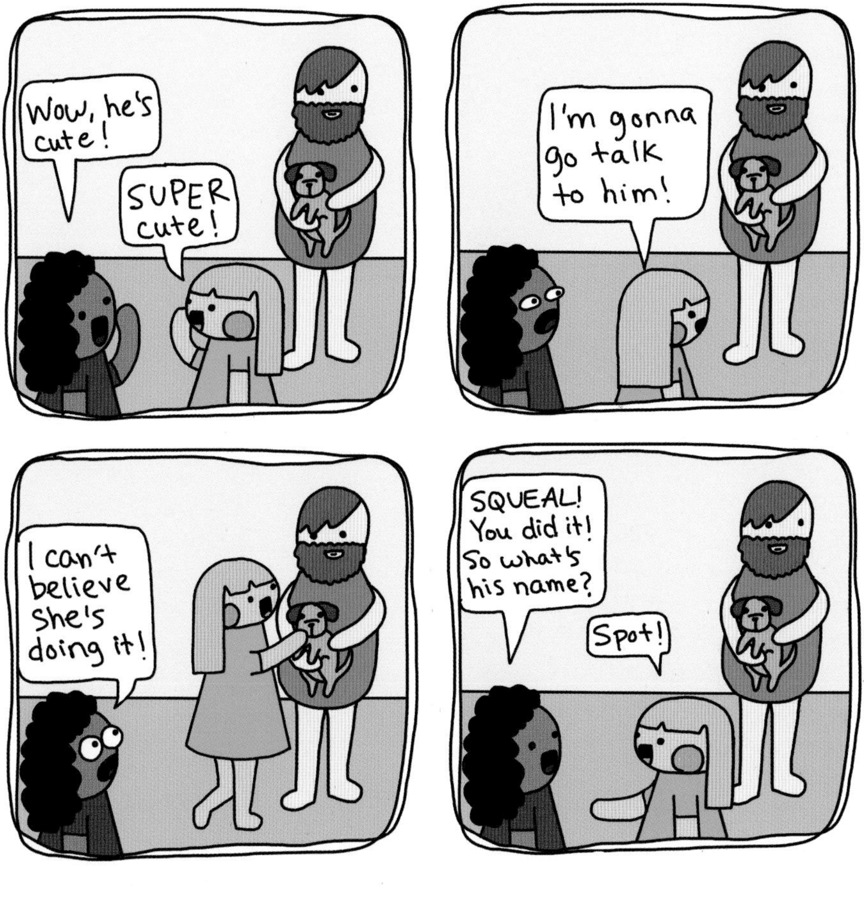
Wow, he's cute!
SUPER cute!
I'm gonna go talk to him!
I can't believe she's doing it!
SQUEAL! You did it! So what's his name?
Spot!

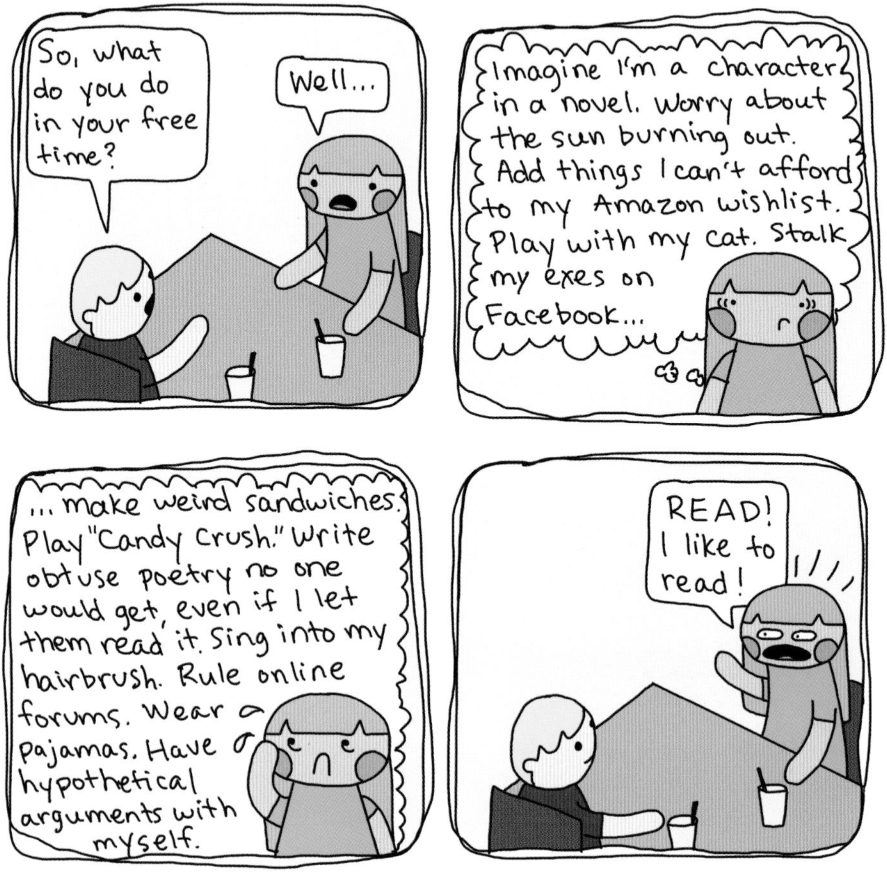
So, what do you do in your free time?
Well...
Imagine I'm a character in a novel. Worry about the sun burning out. Add things I can't afford to my Amazon wishlist. Play with my cat. Stalk my exes on Facebook...
... make weird sandwiches. Play "Candy Crush." Write obtuse poetry no one would get, even if I let them read it. Sing into my hairbrush. Rule online forums. Wear pajamas. Have hypothetical arguments with myself.
READ! I like to read!

PARENTING AN INTROVERTED CHILD

Tip: Surprise parties are a bad idea.

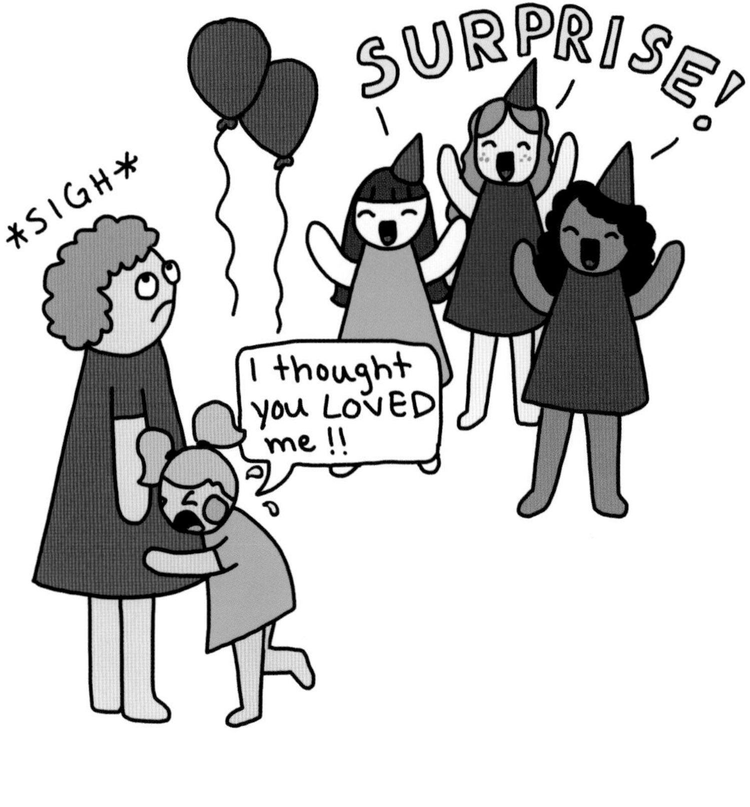
SURPRISE!
SIGH
I thought you LOVED me!!

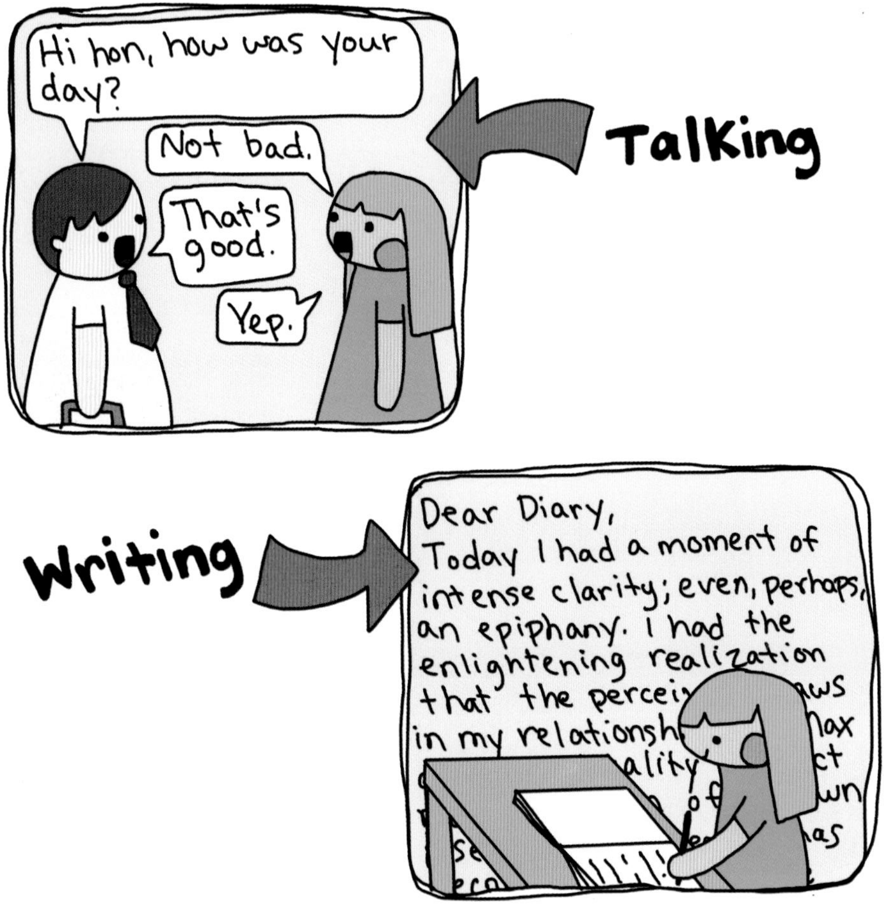
Hi hon, how was your day?
Not bad.
That's good.
Yep.
Talking
Writing
Dear Diary,
Today I had a moment of
intense clarity; even, perhaps,
an epiphany. I had the
enlightening realization

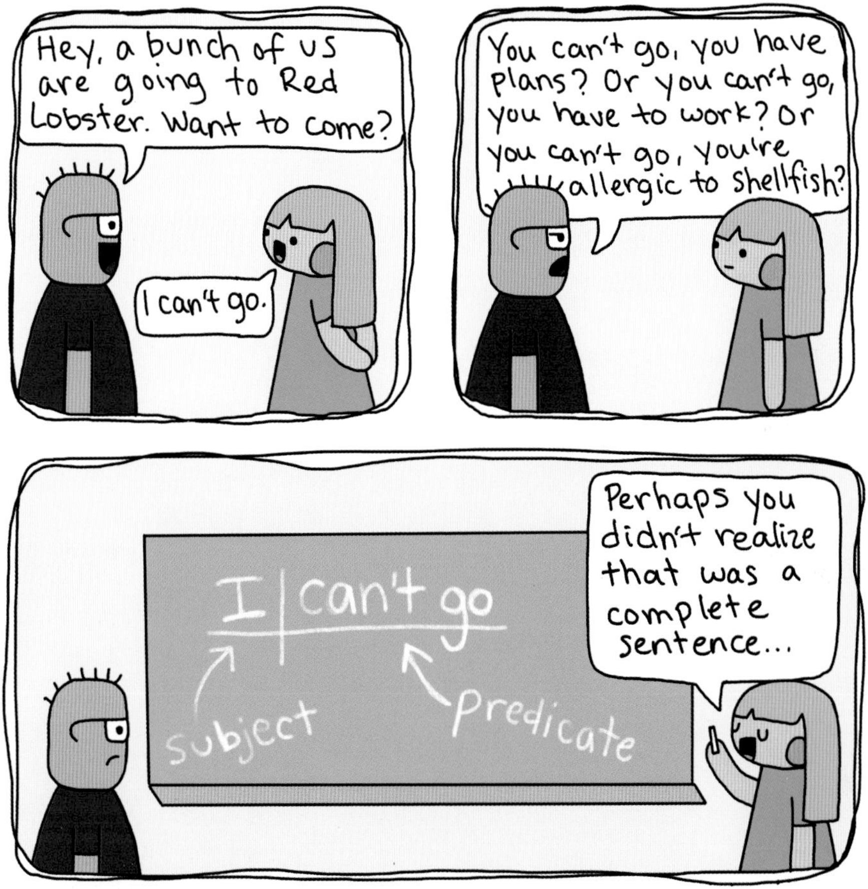
Hey, a bunch of us are going to Red Lobster. Want to come?
I can't go.
You can't go, you have plans? Or you can't go, you have to work? Or you can't go, you're allergic to shellfish?
I | can't go
subject
Predicate
Perhaps you didn't realize that was a complete sentence...

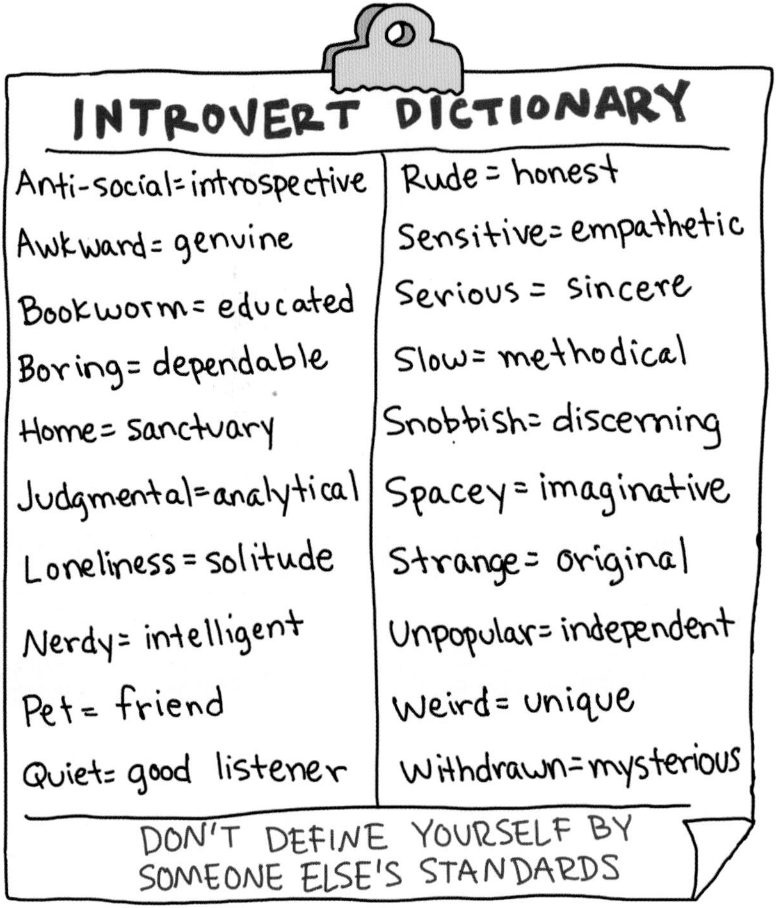
INTROVERT DICTIONARY
Anti-social = introspective
Awkward = genuine
Bookworm = educated
Boring = dependable
Home = sanctuary
Judgmental = analytical
Loneliness = solitude
Nerdy = intelligent
Pet = friend
Quiet = good listener
Rude = honest
Sensitive = empathetic
Serious = sincere
Slow = methodical
Snobbish = discerning
Spacey = imaginative
Strange = original
Unpopular = independent
Weird = unique
Withdrawn = mysterious
DON'T DEFINE YOURSELF BY SOMEONE ELSE'S STANDARDS

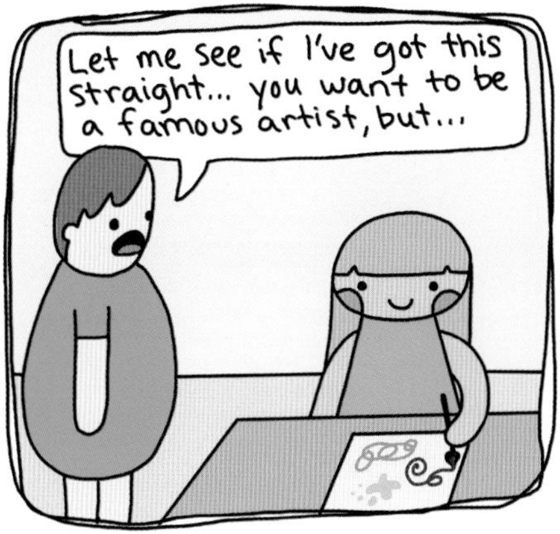
Let me see if I've got this straight... you want to be a famous artist, but...

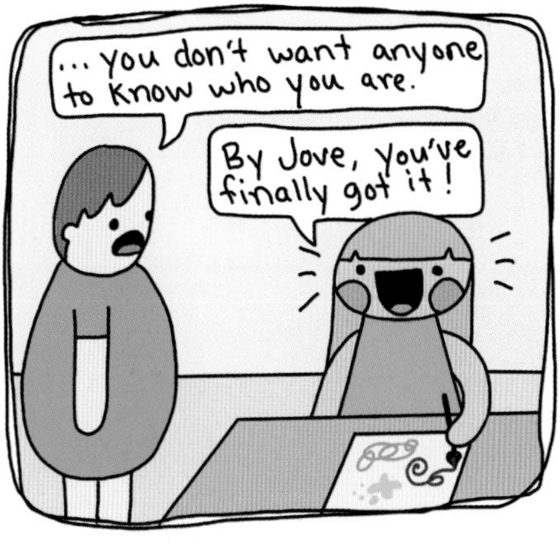
... you don't want anyone to know who you are.
By Jove, you've finally got it!

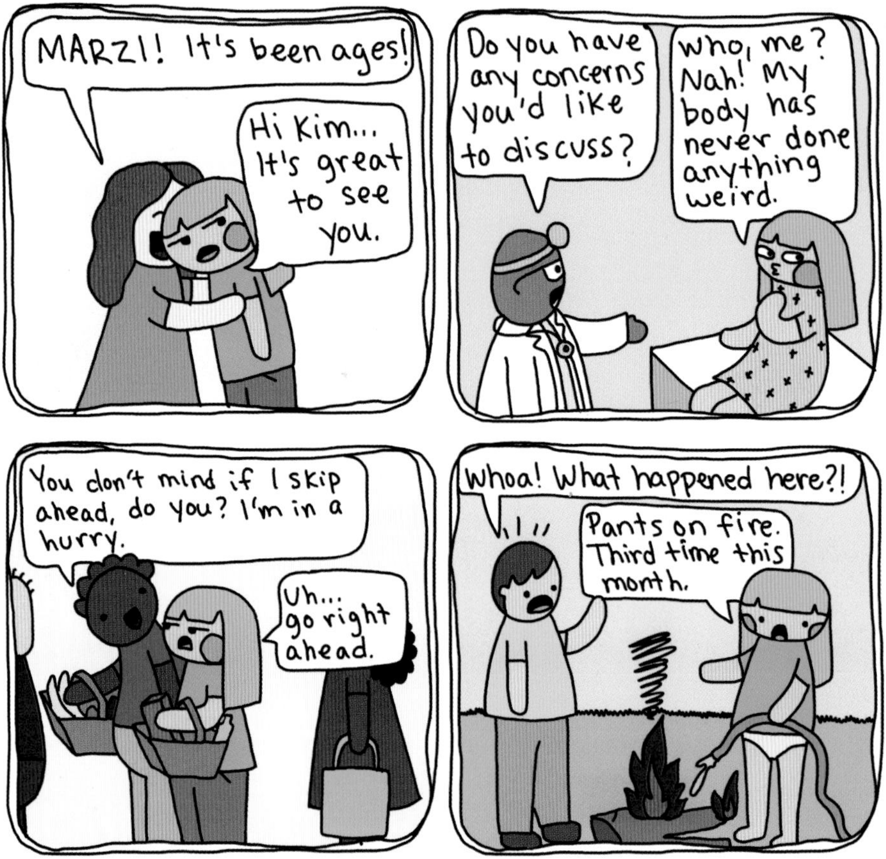
MARZI! It's been ages!
Hi Kim... It's great to see you.
Do you have any concerns you'd like to discuss?
Who, me? Nah! My body has never done anything weird.
You don't mind if I skip ahead, do you? I'm in a hurry.
Uh... go right ahead.
Whoa! What happened here?!
Pants on fire. Third time this month.

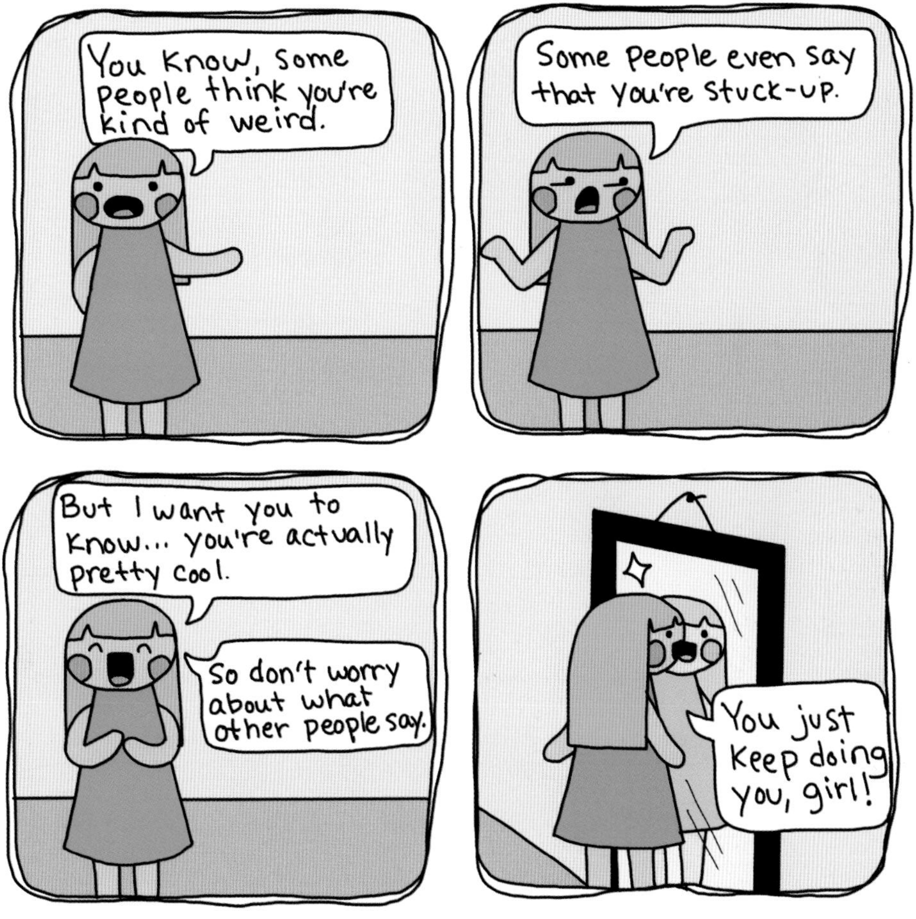

You know, some people think you're kind of weird.
Some people even say that you're stuck-up.
But I want you to know... you're actually pretty cool.
So don't worry about what other people say.
You just keep doing you, girl!

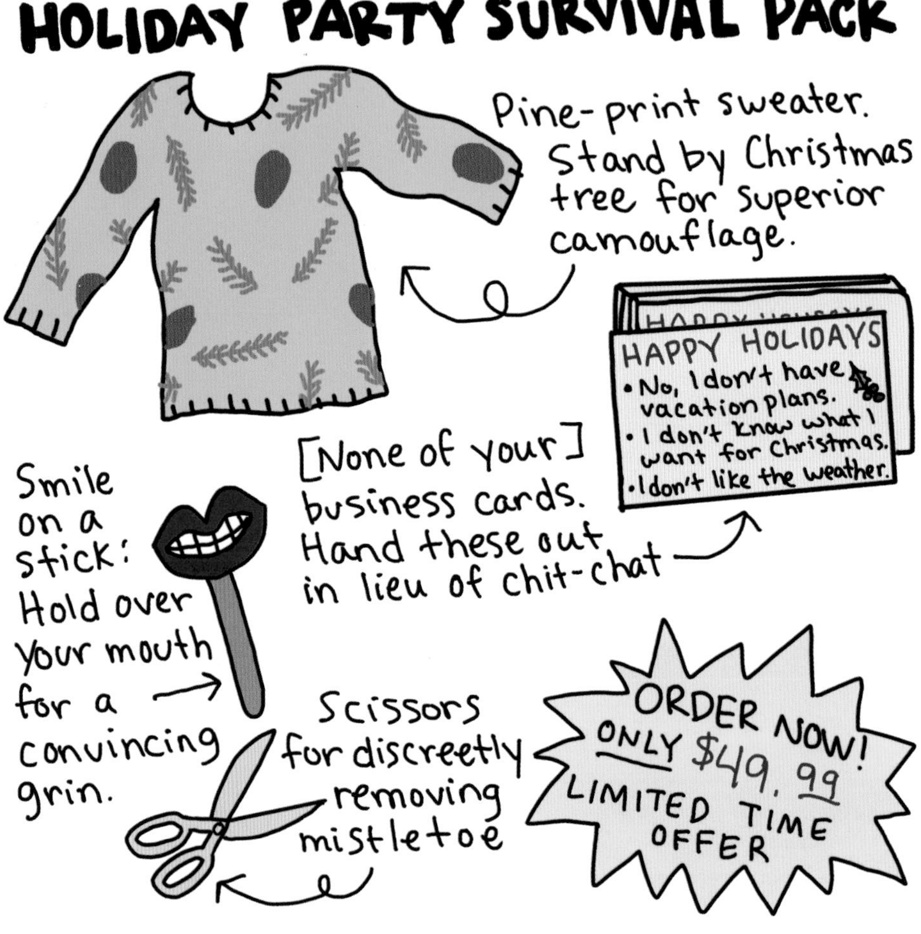
HOLIDAY PARTY SURVIVAL PACK
Pine-print sweater. Stand by Christmas tree for superior camouflage.
HAPPY HOLIDAYS
• No, I don't have vacation plans.
• I don't know what I want for Christmas.
• I don't like the weather.
[None of your] business cards. Hand these out in lieu of chit-chat
Smile on a stick: Hold over your mouth for a convincing grin.
Scissors for discreetly removing mistletoe
ORDER NOW!
ONLY $49.99
LIMITED TIME OFFER

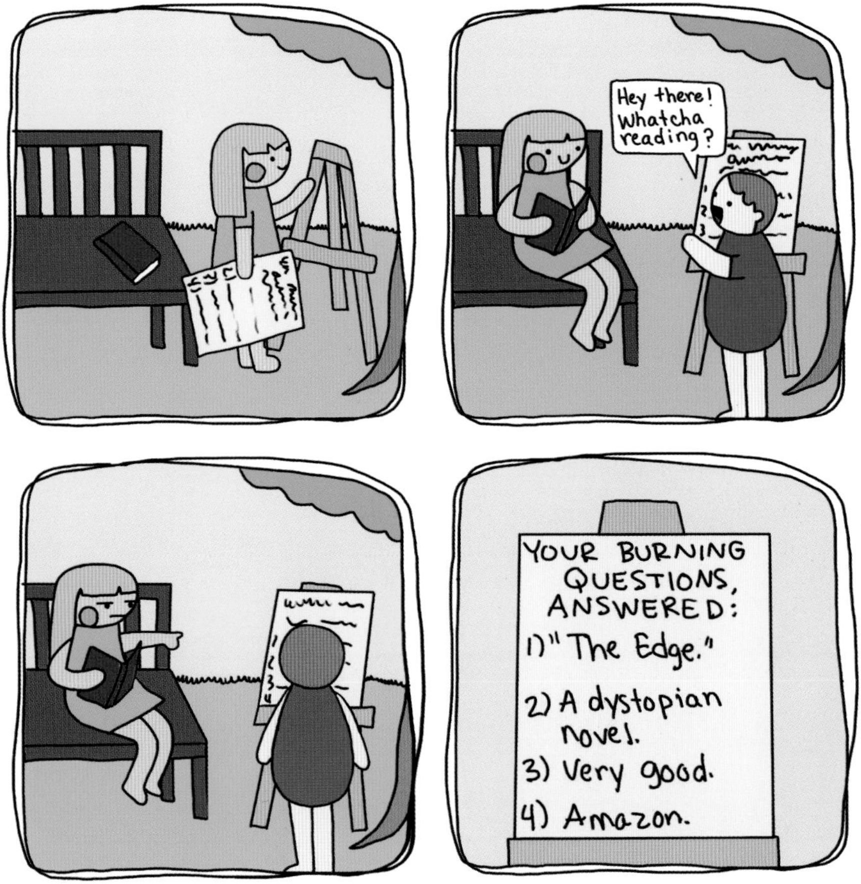
Hey there! Whatcha reading?
YOUR BURNING QUESTIONS, ANSWERED:
1) "The Edge."
2) A dystopian novel.
3) Very good.
4) Amazon.

HOW TO DISCOURAGE VISITORS

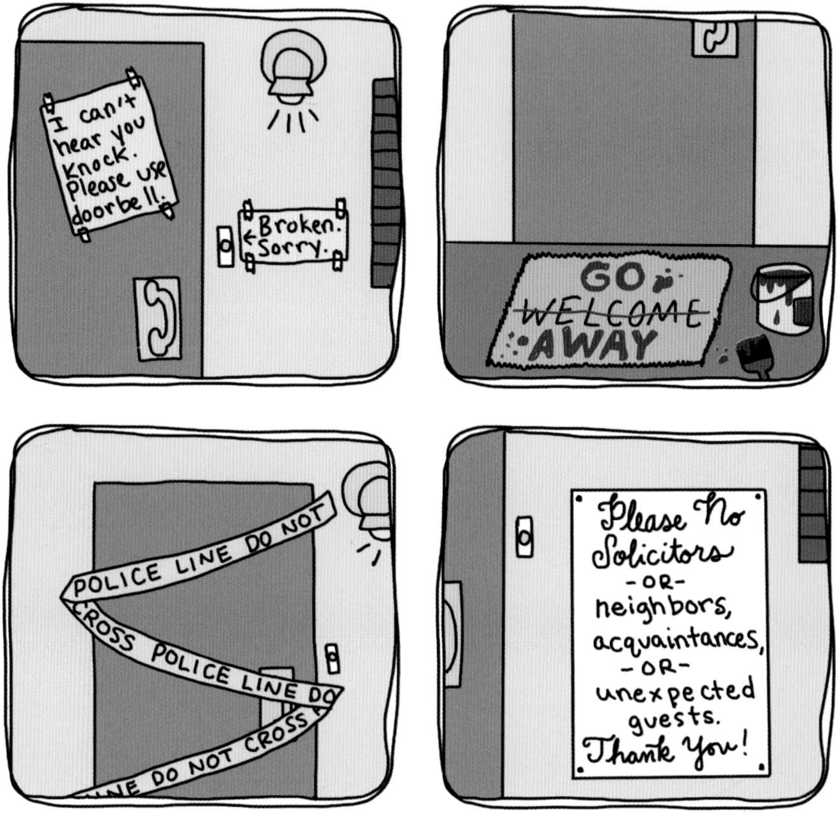
I can't hear you knock. Please use doorbell.
← Broken. Sorry.
GO ~~WELCOME~~ AWAY
POLICE LINE DO NOT
CROSS POLICE LINE DO
DO NOT CROSS
Please No Solicitors
-OR-
neighbors, acquaintances,
-OR-
unexpected guests.
Thank You!

THINGS THAT ARE PRACTICALLY USELESS

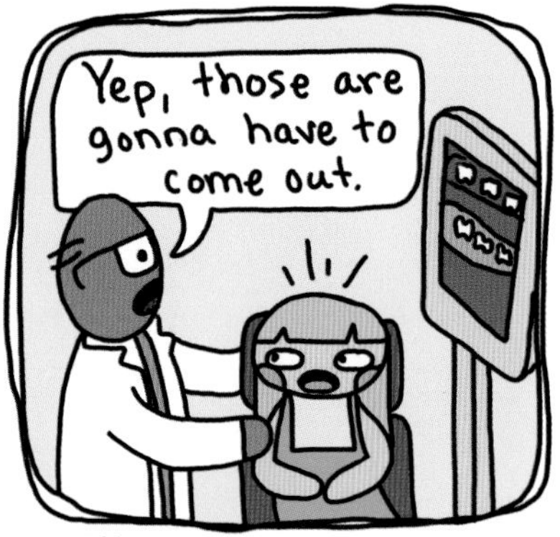
Yep, those are gonna have to come out.

Wisdom teeth

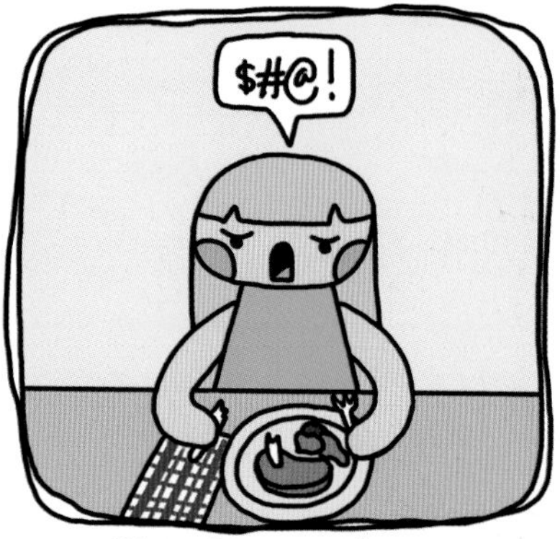
$#@!

Plastic knives

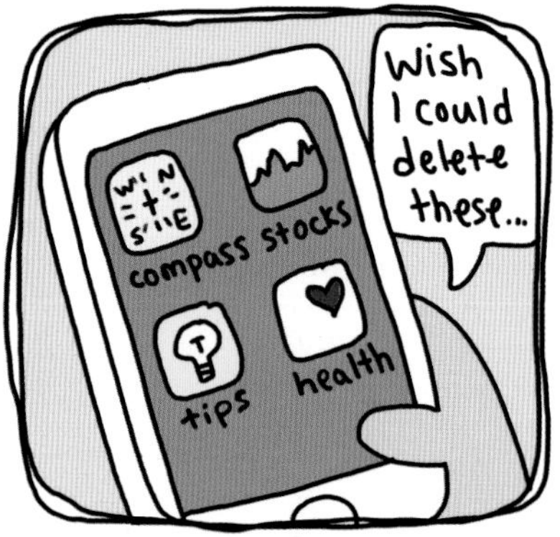
Wish I could delete these...
compass
stocks
tips
health

Pre-loaded apps

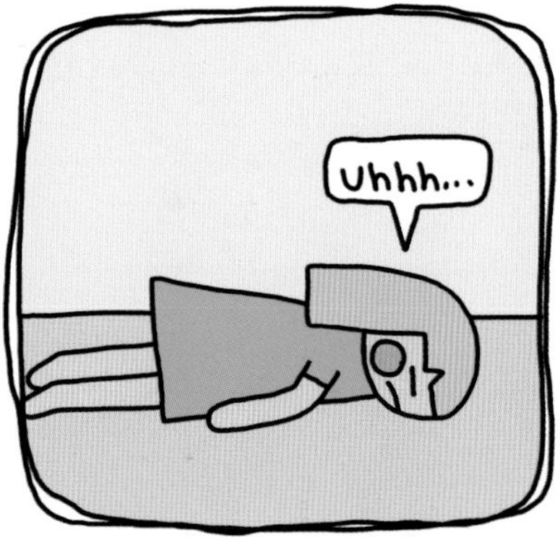
Uhhh...

Me on a Monday

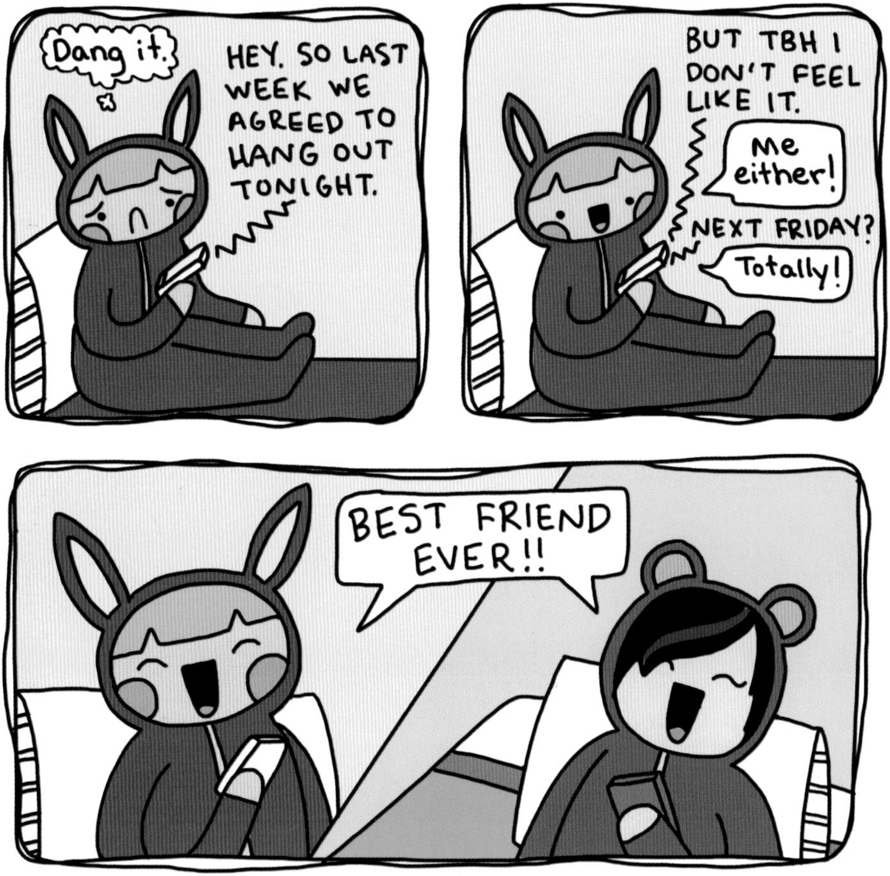
Dang it.
HEY. SO LAST WEEK WE AGREED TO HANG OUT TONIGHT.
BUT TBH I DON'T FEEL LIKE IT.
Me either!
NEXT FRIDAY?
Totally!
BEST FRIEND EVER!!

YOU MIGHT BE AN INTROVERT IF..

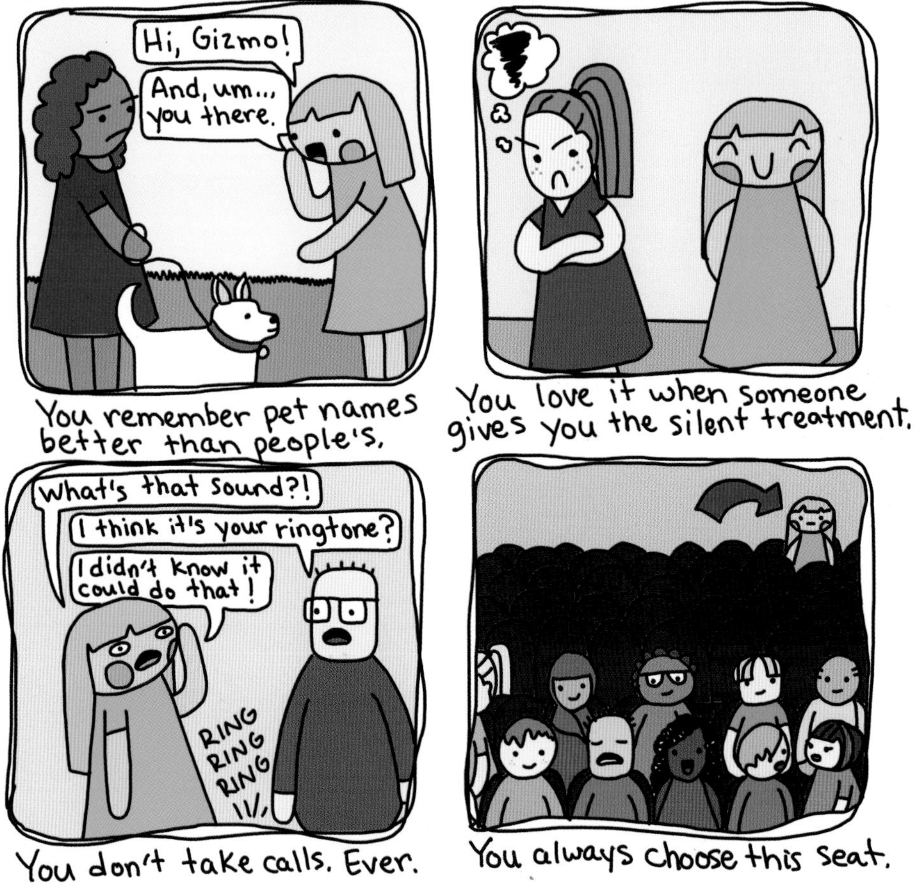
Hi, Gizmo!
And, um... you there.
You remember pet names better than people's.
You love it when someone gives you the silent treatment.
What's that sound?!
I think it's your ringtone?
I didn't know it could do that!
RING RING RING RING
You don't take calls. Ever.
You always choose this seat.

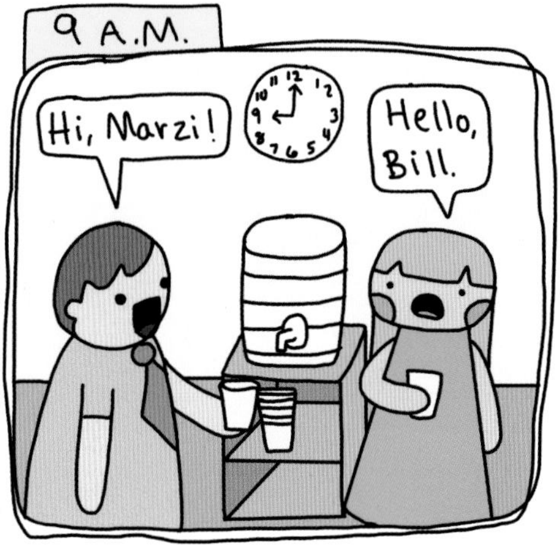
9 A.M.
Hi, Marzi!
Hello, Bill.

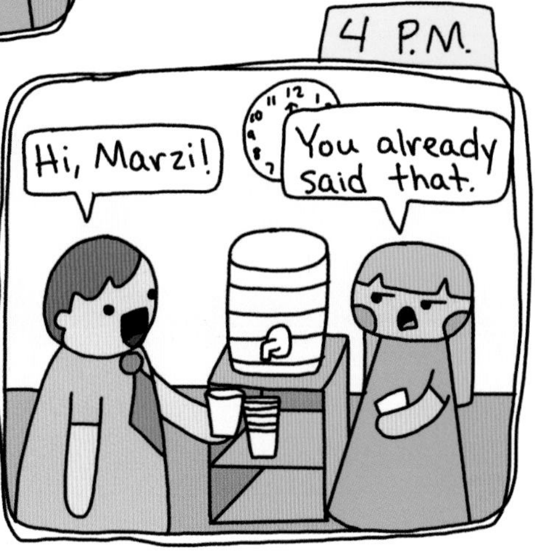
4 P.M.
Hi, Marzi!
You already said that.

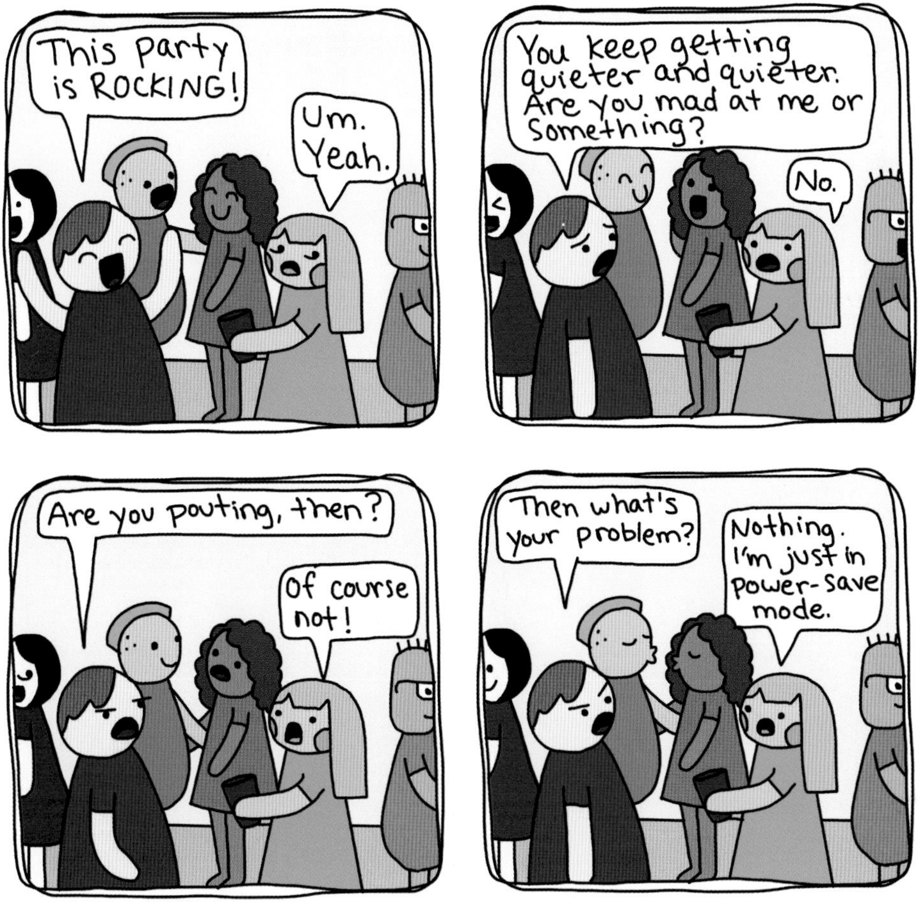
This party is ROCKING!
Um. Yeah.
You keep getting quieter and quieter. Are you mad at me or Something?
No.
Are you pouting, then?
Of course not!
Then what's your problem?
Nothing. I'm just in power-save mode.

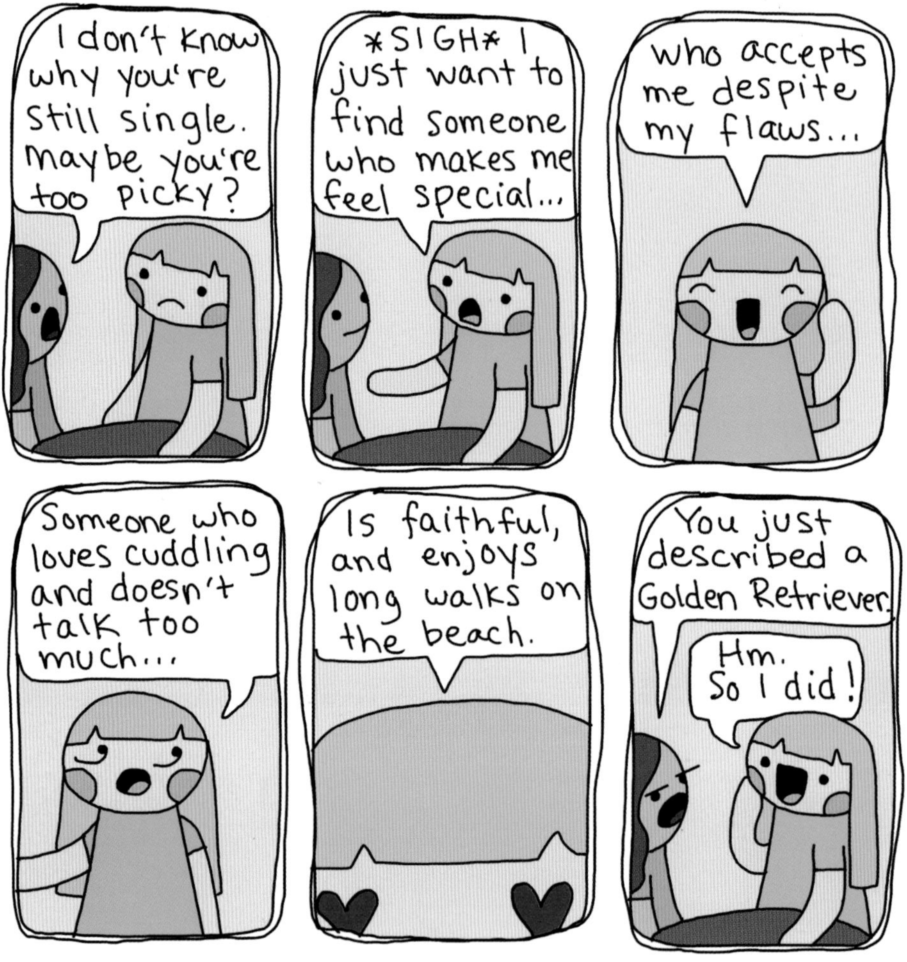
I don't know why you're still single. maybe you're too picky?
SIGH I just want to find someone who makes me feel special...
who accepts me despite my flaws...
Someone who loves cuddling and doesn't talk too much...
Is faithful, and enjoys long walks on the beach.
You just described a Golden Retriever.
Hm. So I did!

HOW TO AVOID AWKWARD HANDSHAKES

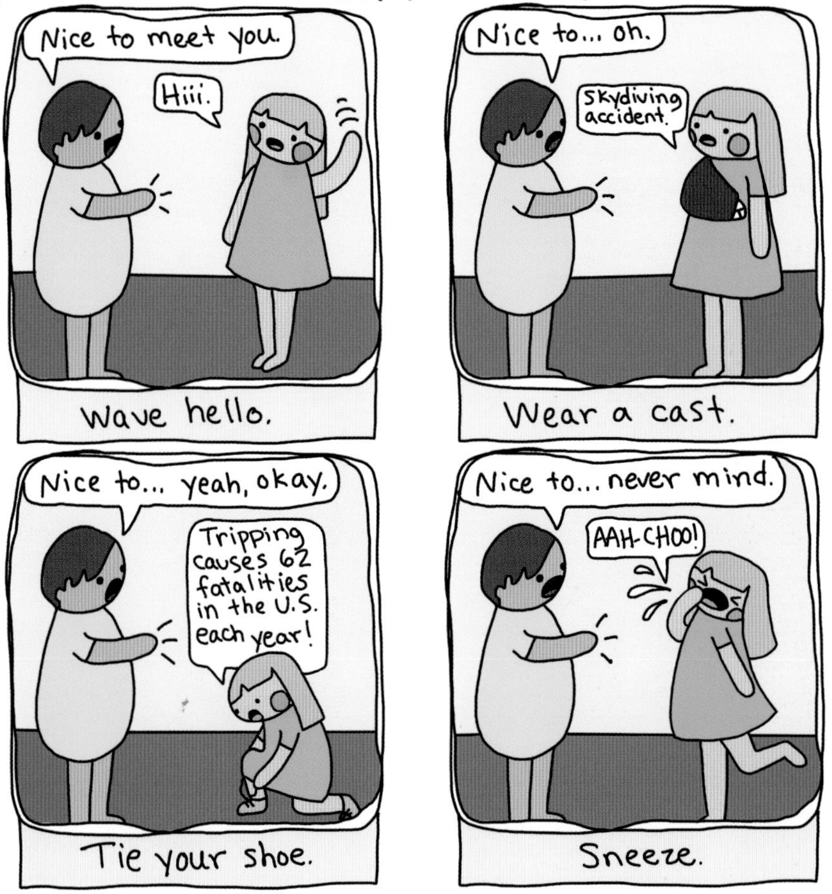
Nice to meet you.
Hiii.
Wave hello.
Nice to... oh.
Skydiving accident.
Wear a cast.
Nice to... yeah, okay.
Tripping causes 62 fatalities in the U.S. each year!
Tie your shoe.
Nice to... never mind.
AAH-CHOO!
Sneeze.

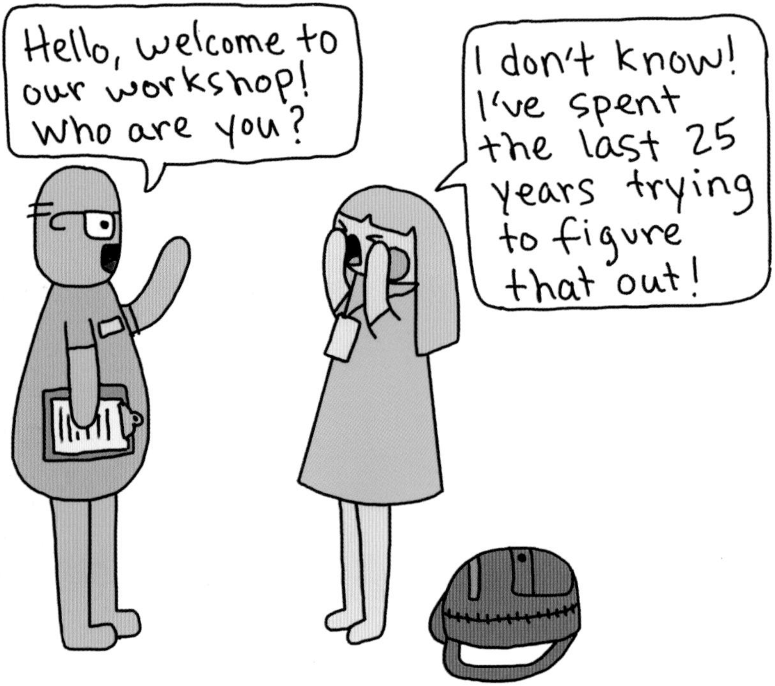
Hello, welcome to our workshop! Who are you?
I don't know! I've spent the last 25 years trying to figure that out!

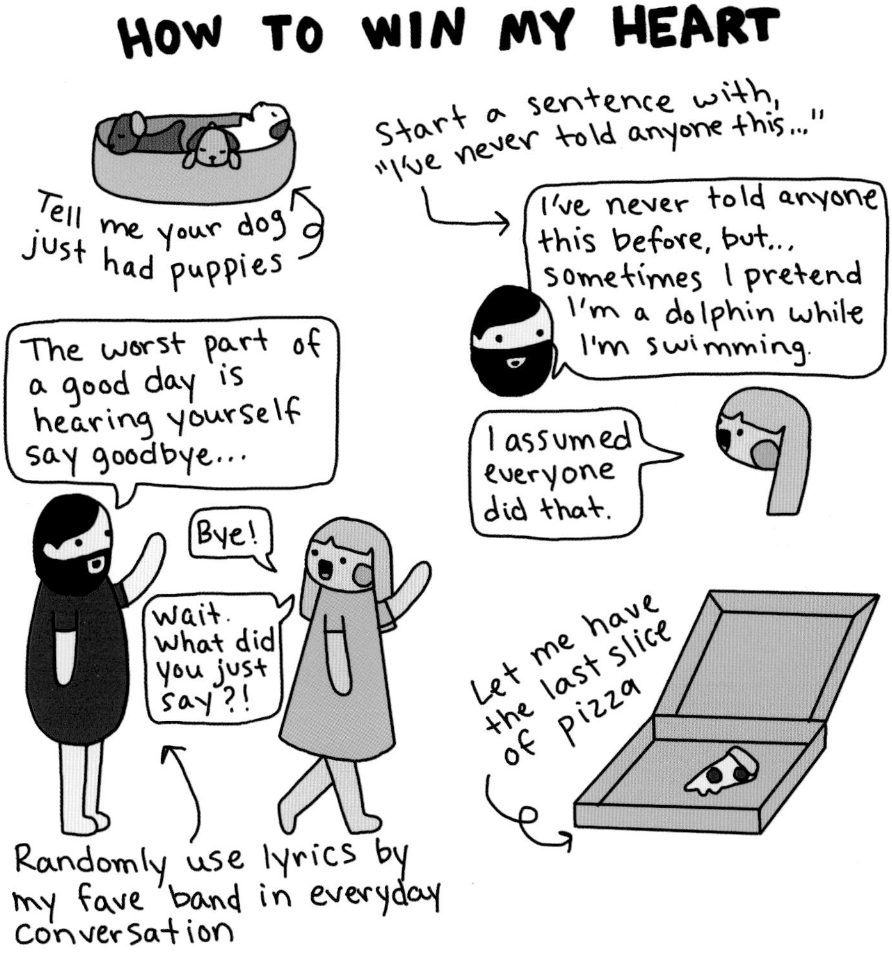
HOW TO WIN MY HEART
Tell me your dog just had puppies
Start a sentence with, "I've never told anyone this..."
I've never told anyone this before, but... sometimes I pretend I'm a dolphin while I'm swimming.
I assumed everyone did that.
The worst part of a good day is hearing yourself say goodbye...
Bye!
Wait. What did you just say?!
Randomly use lyrics by my fave band in everyday conversation
Let me have the last slice of pizza

HOW TO WIN AT INTROVERT GIFTING

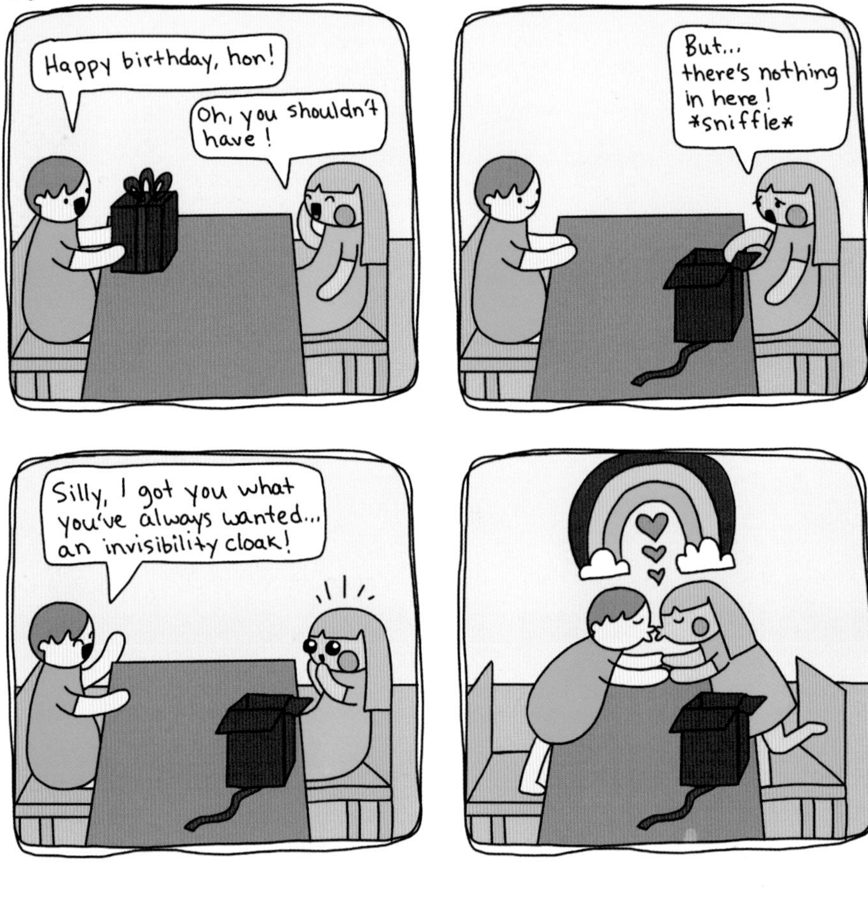
Happy birthday, hon!
Oh, you shouldn't have!
But... there's nothing in here! *sniffle*
Silly, I got you what you've always wanted... an invisibility cloak!

INTROVERT MAGIC 8 BALL

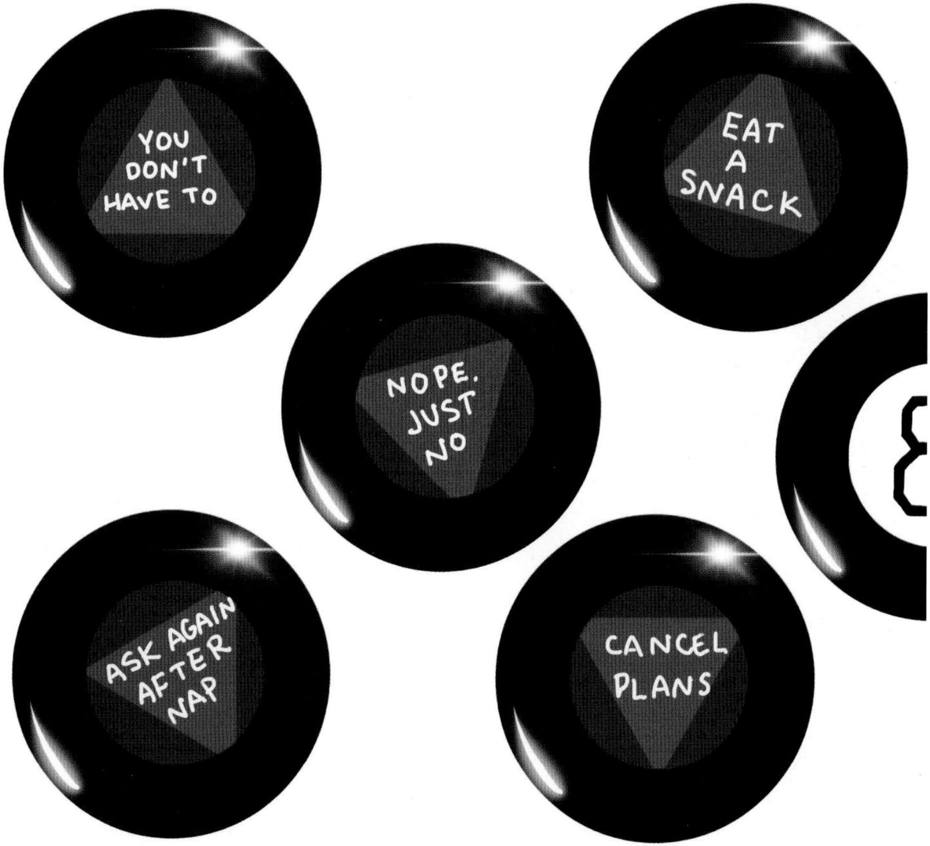
YOU DON'T HAVE TO
EAT A SNACK
NOPE. JUST NO
ASK AGAIN AFTER NAP
CANCEL PLANS

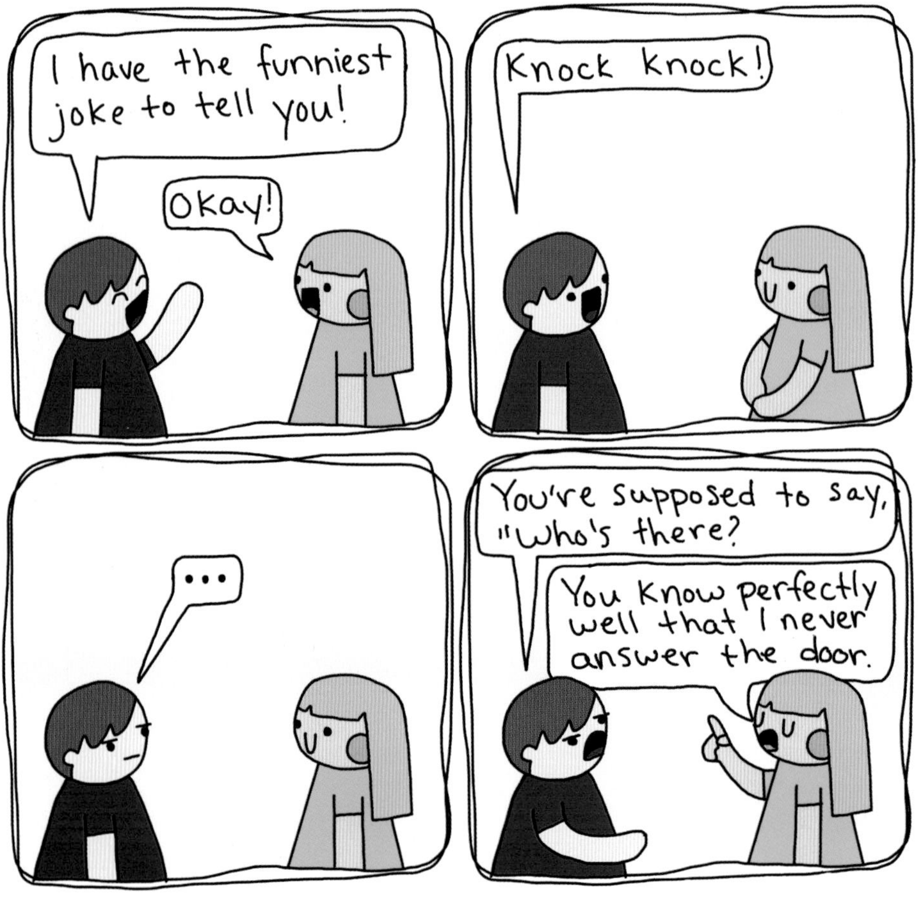
I have the funniest joke to tell you!
Okay!
Knock knock!
...
You're supposed to say, "who's there?
You know perfectly well that I never answer the door.

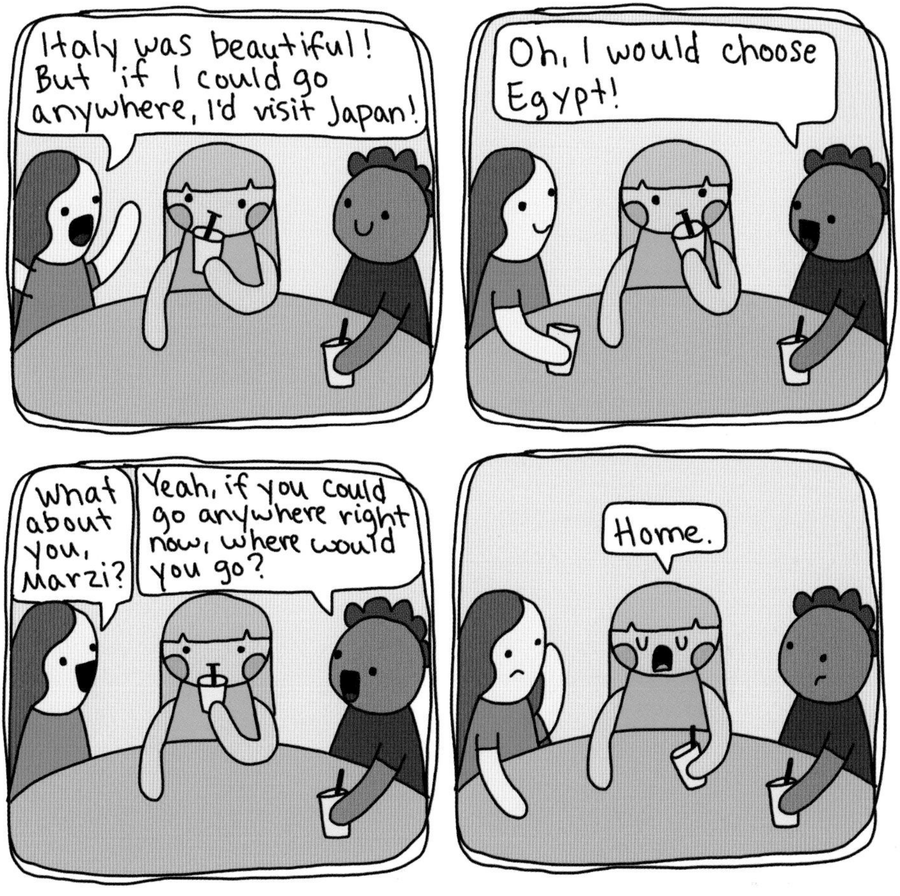
Italy was beautiful! But if I could go anywhere, I'd visit Japan!
Oh, I would choose Egypt!
What about you, Marzi?
Yeah, if you could go anywhere right now, where would you go?
Home.

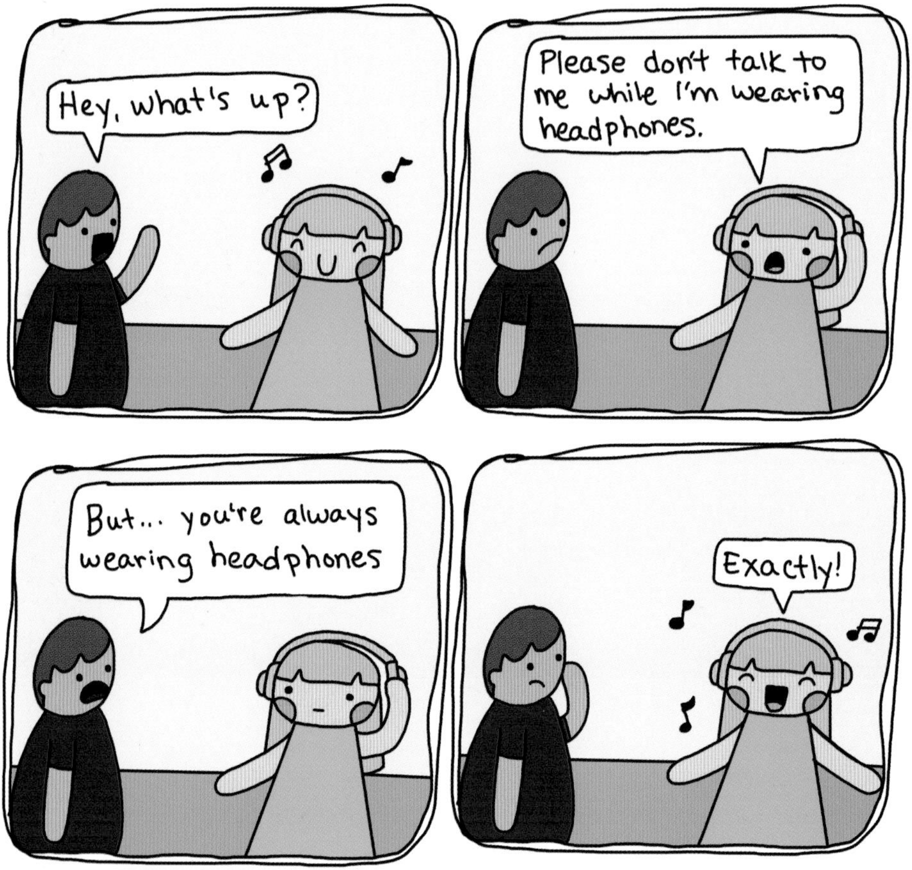
Hey, what's up?
Please don't talk to me while I'm wearing headphones.
But... you're always wearing headphones
Exactly!

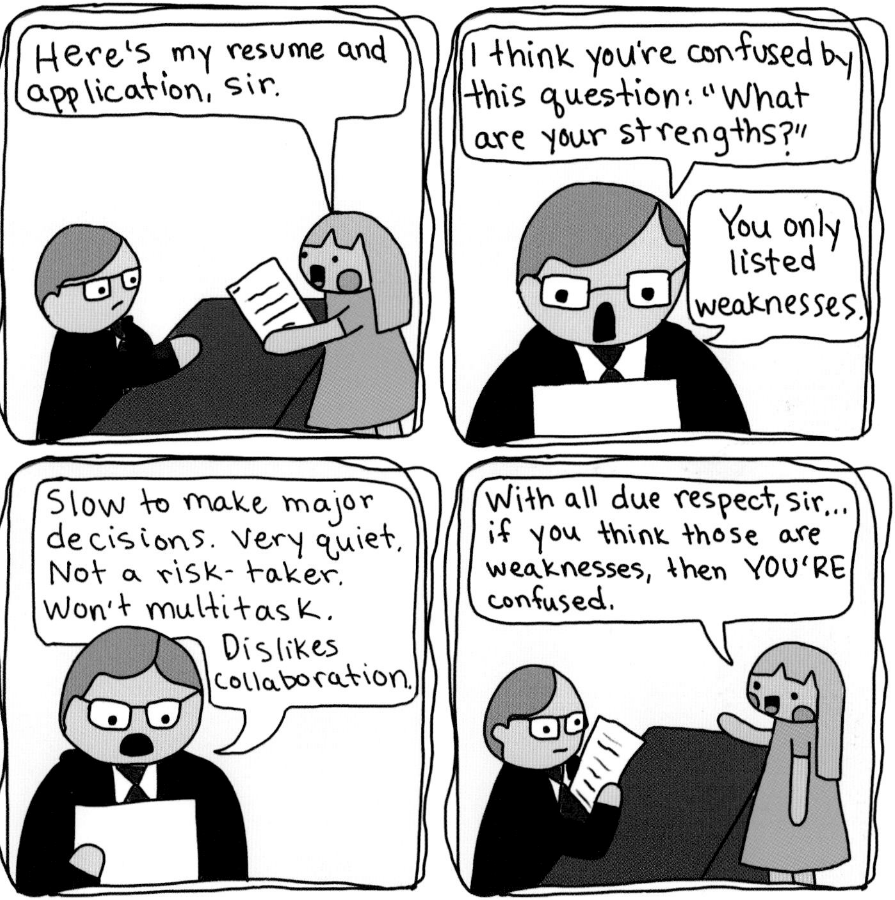
Here's my resume and application, sir.
I think you're confused by this question: "What are your strengths?"
You only listed weaknesses.
Slow to make major decisions. Very quiet. Not a risk-taker. Won't multitask.
Dislikes collaboration.
With all due respect, sir... if you think those are weaknesses, then YOU'RE confused.

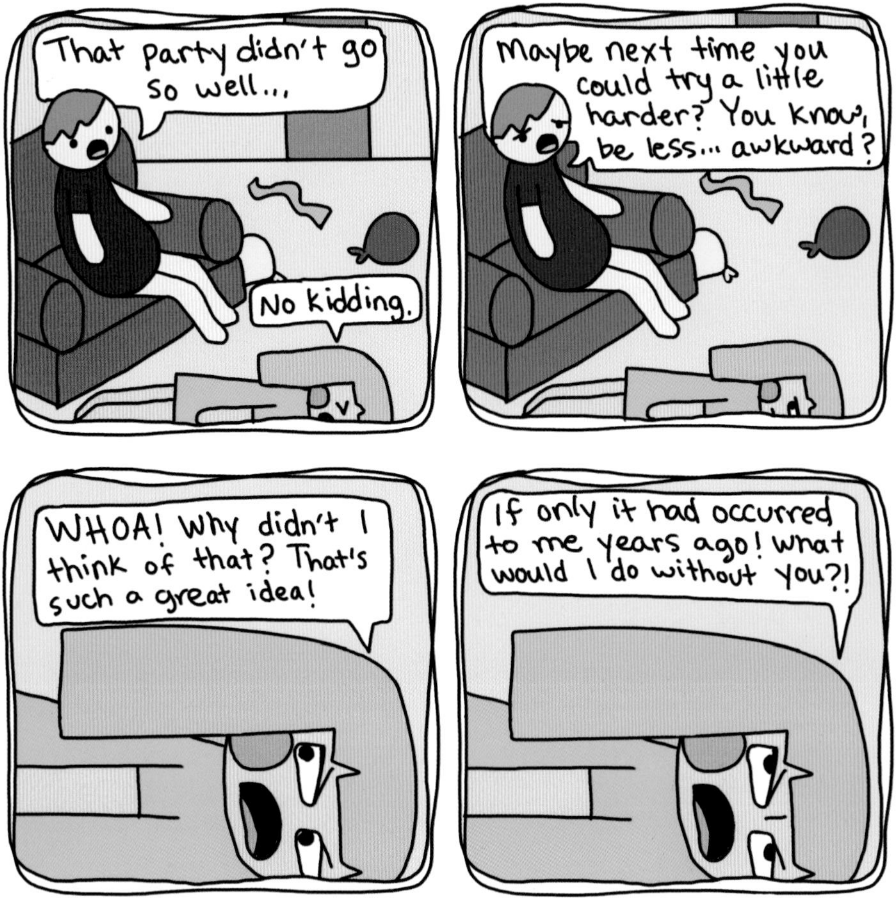
That party didn't go so well...
No kidding.
Maybe next time you could try a little harder? You know, be less... awkward?
WHOA! Why didn't I think of that? That's such a great idea!
If only it had occurred to me years ago! What would I do without you?!

BECAUSE THIS...

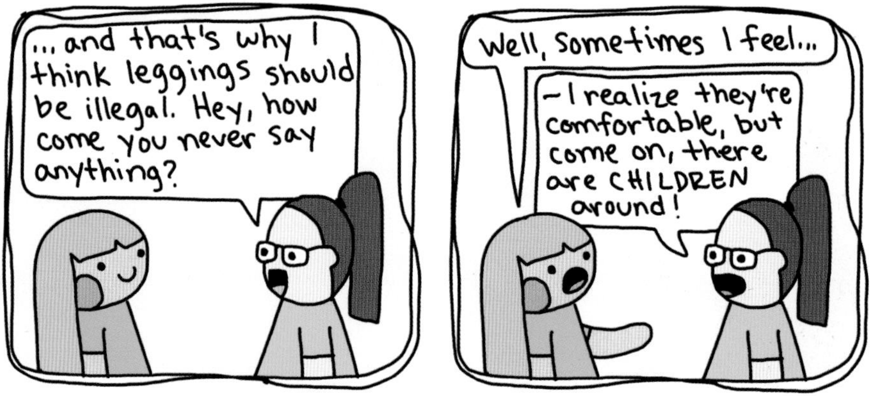
...and that's why I think leggings should be illegal. Hey, how come you never say anything?
Well, sometimes I feel...
-I realize they're comfortable, but come on, there are CHILDREN around!

... OR THIS

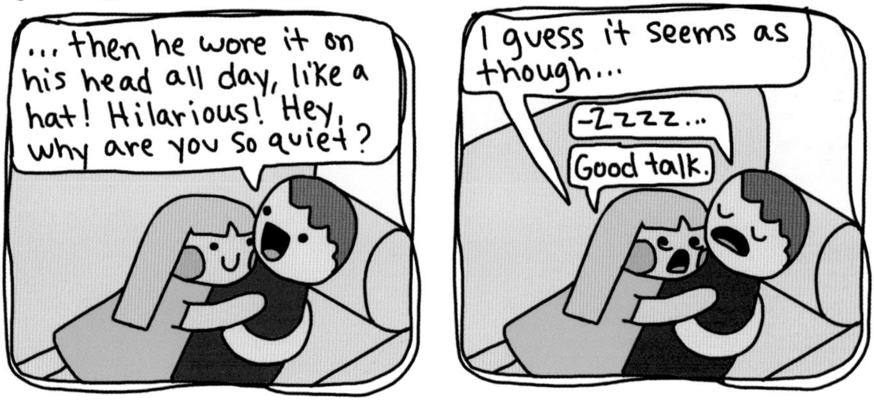
...then he wore it on his head all day, like a hat! Hilarious! Hey, why are you so quiet?
I guess it seems as though...
-Zzzz...
Good talk.

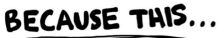

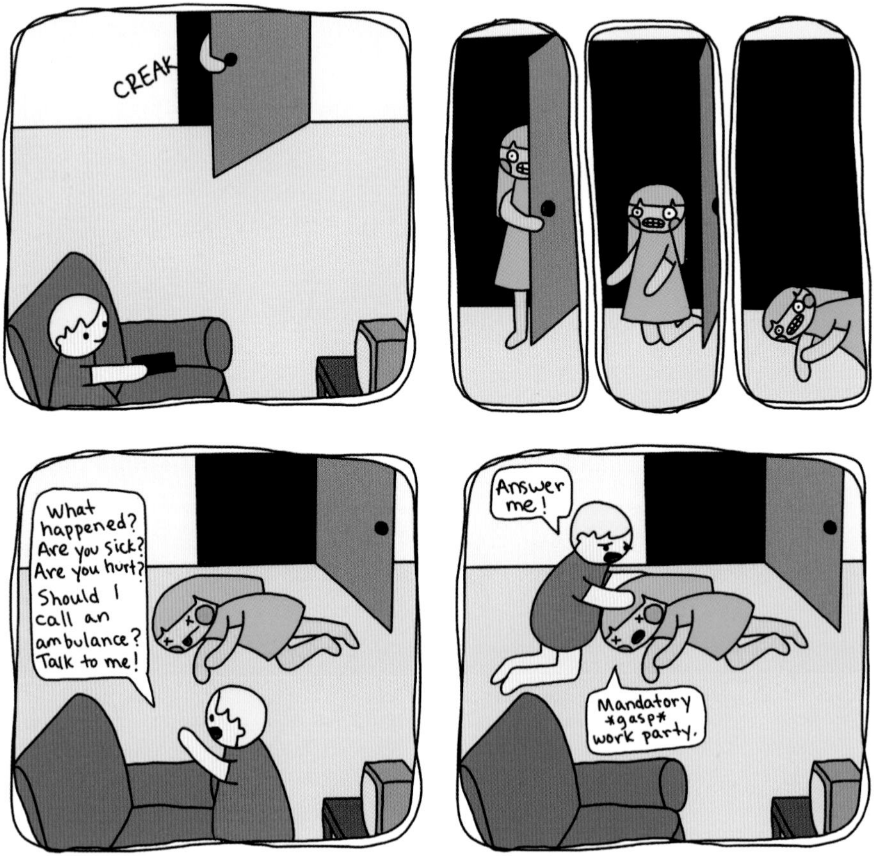
CREAK
What happened? Are you sick? Are you hurt? Should I call an ambulance? Talk to me!
Answer me!
Mandatory *gasp* work party.

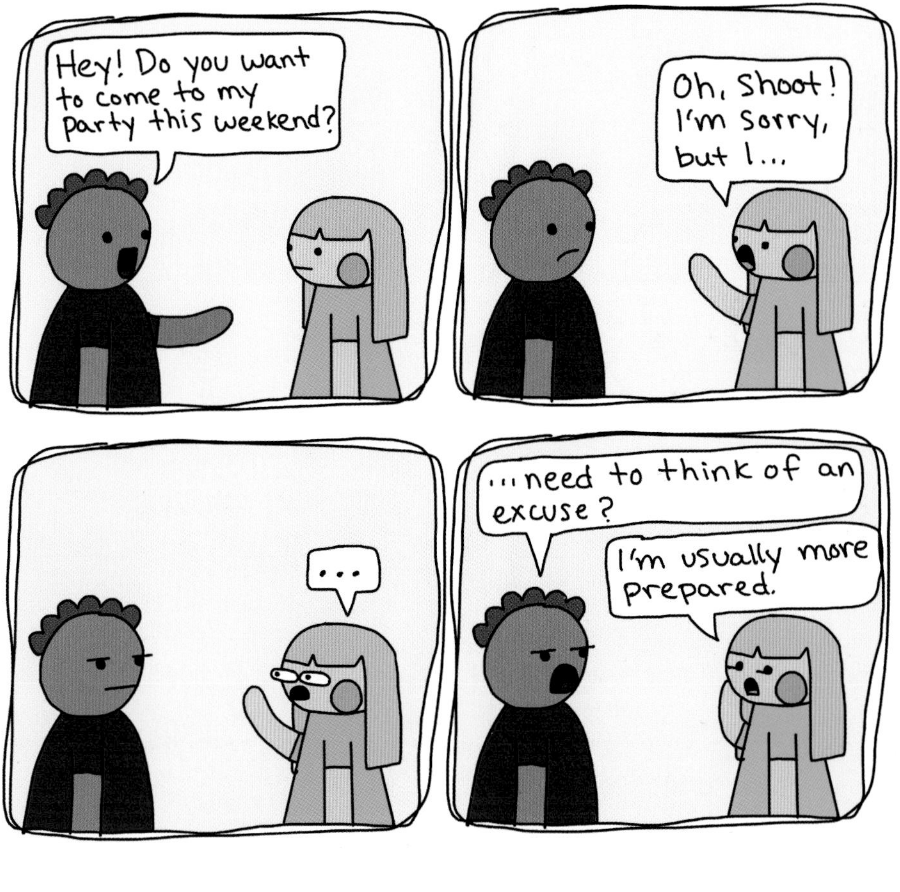
Hey! Do you want to come to my party this weekend?
Oh, Shoot! I'm sorry, but I...
...
...need to think of an excuse?
I'm usually more prepared.

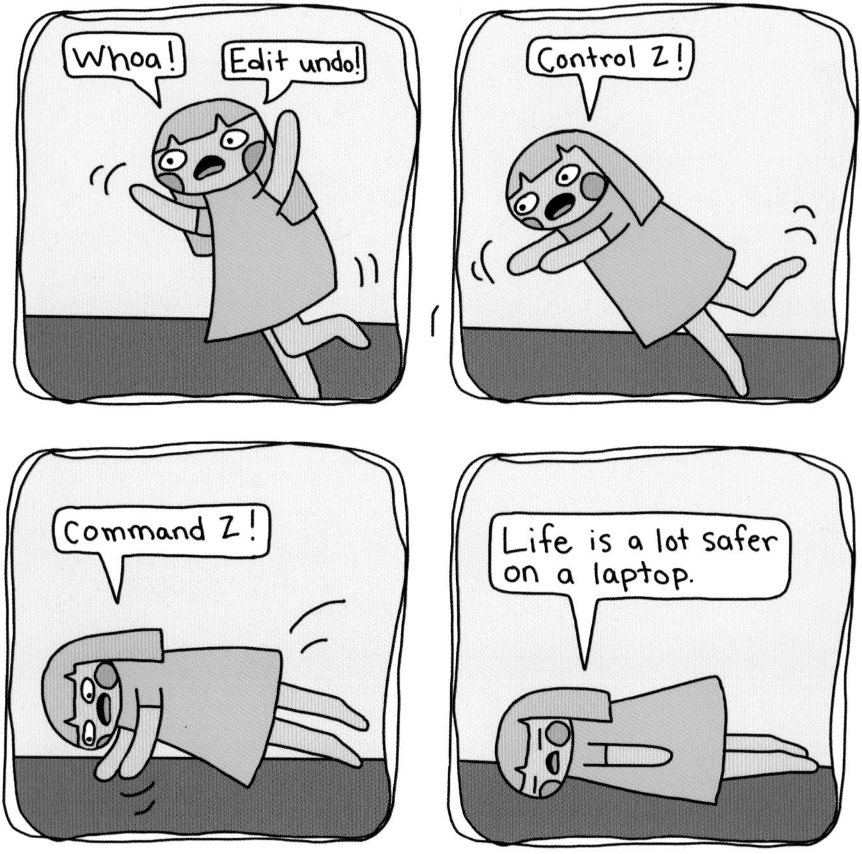
Whoa!
Edit undo!
Control Z!
Command Z!
Life is a lot safer on a laptop.

INTROVERT BINGO

I let that phone call go to voicemail.	I read 3+ books last month.	My house is my favorite place.	I actively avoided someone today.
I'm the king of good excuses.	I've had a crush on a fictional character.	I took a nap today.	I often think about thinking.
My best friend is literally an animal.	I'm better at writing than talking.	I'm adorably awkward.	I'm a good listener.
I'm much cooler on the internet.	I fangirl over artists + authors.	People make me tired.	I do most of my shopping online.

ABOUT THE AUTHOR

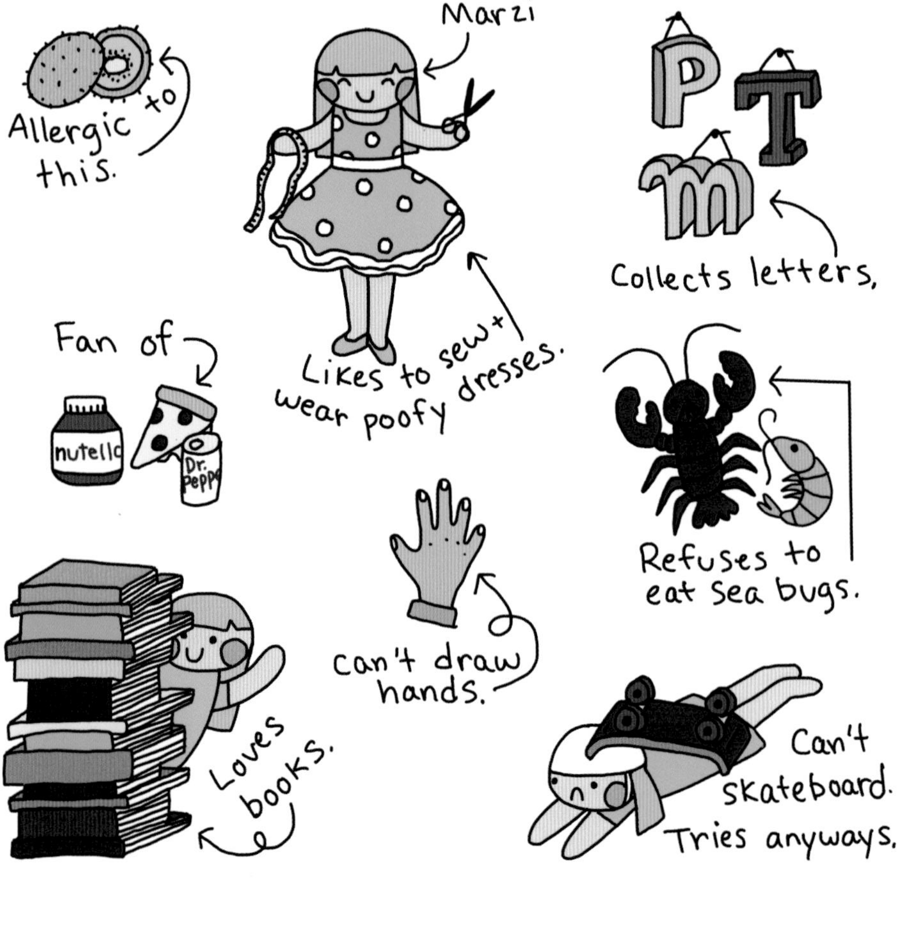
Marzi
Allergic to this.
Collects letters.
Fan of
nutella
Dr. Pepper
Likes to sew + wear poofy dresses.
Refuses to eat sea bugs.
Can't draw hands.
Loves books.
Can't skateboard. Tries anyways.